HABITAT Jaguars live in North, Central, and South America. Their habitats are swamplands, rainforests, dry grasslands, scrub, and deserts.

Atlantic Ocean

Pacific Ocean

Pacific Ocean

Indian Ocean

BODY COVERING Most jaguars have brownish-yellow fur with dark rosettes, or spots, that look like paws.

SELF-PROTECTION Jaguars are one of only four wild cats that roar. A jaguar roars to scare other animals away from its territory.

TEETH The strong jaws and sharp teeth of a jaguar allows it to bite into prey.

Science

Jaguar

Harcourt
SCHOOL PUBLISHERS

Orlando   Austin   New York   San Diego   Toronto   London

Visit *The Learning Site!*
www.harcourtschool.com

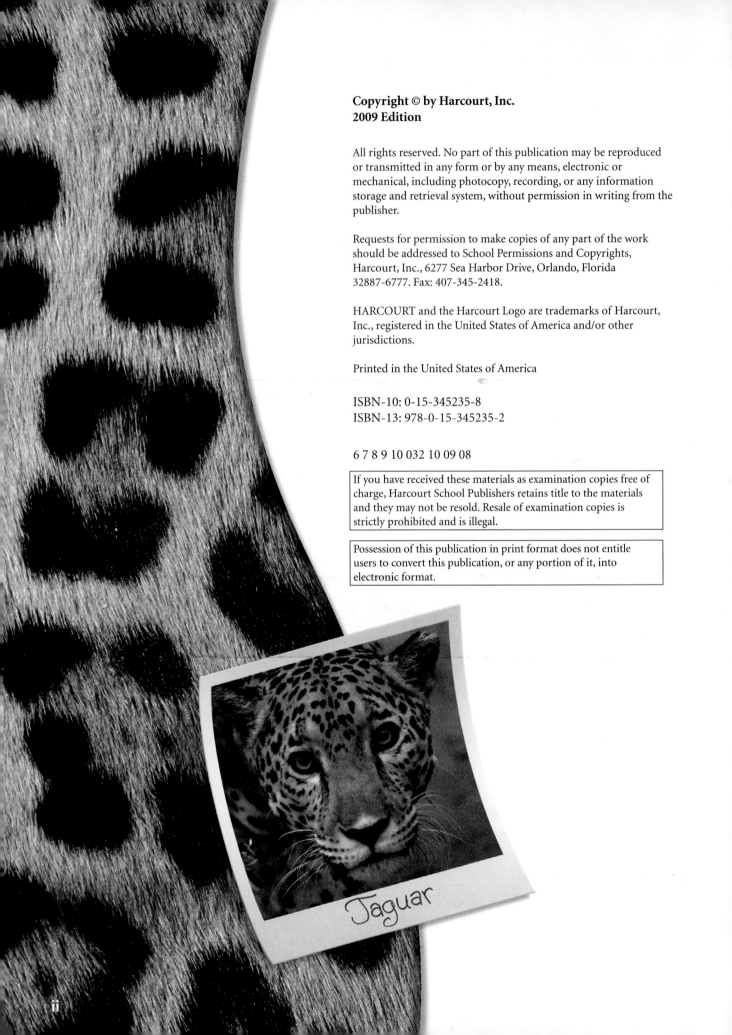

Jaguar

Consulting Authors

Michael J. Bell
Assistant Professor of Early Childhood Education
College of Education
West Chester University of Pennsylvania

Michael A. DiSpezio
Curriculum Architect
JASON Academy
Cape Cod, Massachusetts

Marjorie Frank
Former Adjunct, Science Education
Hunter College
New York, New York

Gerald H. Krockover
Professor of Earth and Atmospheric Science Education
Purdue University
West Lafayette, Indiana

Joyce C. McLeod
Adjunct Professor
Rollins College
Winter Park, Florida

Barbara ten Brink
Science Specialist
Austin Independent School District
Austin, Texas

Carol J. Valenta
Senior Vice President
St. Louis Science Center
St. Louis, Missouri

Barry A. Van Deman
President and CEO
Museum of Life and Science
Durham, North Carolina

Ohio Reviewers and Consultants

Linda Bierkortte
Teacher
Parkmoor Urban Academy
Columbus, Ohio

Napoleon Adebola Bryant, Jr.
Professor Emeritus of Education
Xavier University
Cincinnati, Ohio

Laurie Enia Godfrey
Director of Curriculum Development
Lorain City Schools
Lorain, Ohio

Christine Hamilton
Curriculum Specialist
Toledo Public Schools
Toledo, Ohio

Jerome Mescher
Science/Math Coordinator
Hilliard City Schools
Hilliard, Ohio

Cheryl Pilatowski
Science Support Teacher/Coordinator
Toledo Public Schools
Toledo, Ohio

Lisa Seiberling
Elementary Science Coordinator
Columbus Public Schools
Columbus, Ohio

Kathy Sparrow
Science Learning Specialist, K-12
Akron Public Schools
Akron, Ohio

Matthew Alan Teare
Science Resource Teacher
Miles Park Elementary School
Cleveland Municipal School District
Cleveland, Ohio

Shirley Welshans
Teacher
Parkmoor Urban Academy
Columbus, Ohio

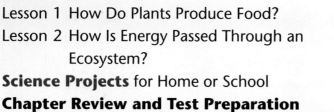

LIFE SCIENCES
UNIT B: 96

PHYSICAL SCIENCES

UNIT C: 192

OHIO EXPEDITIONS

Your Guide to Science in Ohio

Getting Ready for Science

Lesson 1 What Tools Do Scientists Use?

Lesson 2 What Inquiry Skills Do Scientists Use?

Lesson 3 What Is the Scientific Method?

Vocabulary

microscope
balance
investigation
inquiry
experiment
scientific method

What do YOU wonder?

This rocket won't travel into space, but it works in the same way as the rockets that carried people to the moon. How do rocket scientists try out their designs? What variables can they test to make a rocket fly farther and faster?

1

What Tools Do Scientists Use?

Fast Fact

That's a BIG Kite! One of the largest kites ever flown is the Megabite. It is 64 m (210 ft) long (including tails) and 22 m (72 ft) wide. That's only about 6 m (20 ft) shorter than a 747 jet airliner! Kite fliers around the world are always trying to set new records. How high can a kite go? How big or small can a kite be? Setting a record depends on accurate measurements. In the Investigate, you'll practice several different ways of measuring objects.

Measuring Up!

Materials
- balloon
- ruler
- tape measure
- hand lens
- string
- spring scale

Procedure

1. Observe the empty balloon with the hand lens. Copy the chart, and record your observations.

2. Measure the length and circumference of the balloon. Record your measurements.

3. Use the spring scale to measure the weight of the balloon. Record its weight.

4. Now blow up the balloon.

5. Match a length of string to the length of the balloon. Measure that string length with the ruler or tape measure. Record the length.

6. Measure the circumference of the balloon as in Step 5. Record your measurement.

7. Measure the weight of the balloon with the spring scale. Record your measurement.

Step 2

	Balloon	Balloon with Air
Hand lens		
Length		
Circumference		
Weight		

Draw Conclusions

1. How did the measurements change when you blew up the balloon? Why?

2. Do you think that your measurement of the length of the empty balloon or the blown-up balloon was more accurate? Why?

3. **Inquiry Skill** Work with another group to identify variables in your measurements. What variables caused different groups to get different measurements?

Investigate Further

How can you find the volume of a blown-up balloon? Plan and conduct a simple investigation to find out.

VOCABULARY
microscope p. 4
balance p. 7

SCIENCE CONCEPTS
▶ how tools are used to make better observations
▶ why a balance and a scale measure different things

READING FOCUS SKILL

MAIN IDEA AND DETAILS Look for details about how and when each tool is used.

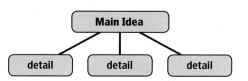

Using Science Inquiry Tools

People in many jobs must use tools. Cooks use pots and pans. Mechanics use screwdrivers and wrenches. Scientists use tools to measure and observe objects in nature.

Your Science Tool Kit includes a dropper to move liquids, as well as forceps to pick up solids. A hand lens and a magnifying box help you see details. You can measure temperature with the thermometer, length with the ruler or tape measure, and volume with the measuring cup. The spring scale measures weight.

MAIN IDEA AND DETAILS What are four tools you can use to measure objects?

◀ A thermometer measures the temperature of liquids and the air. It measures in degrees Celsius (°C).

A tape measure helps you measure the length of curved or irregular surfaces. ▶

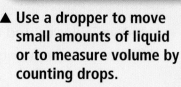

▲ Use a dropper to move small amounts of liquid or to measure volume by counting drops.

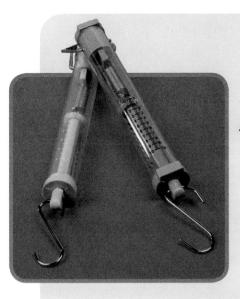

◀ A spring scale measures forces, such as weight or friction. It measures in units called newtons (N).

▲ A ruler measures the length and width of objects in centimeters (cm) and millimeters (mm).

▲ You can place an insect, pebble, or other small object in the magnifying box. Looking through the lid helps you see the object clearly.

▲ A measuring cup is used to measure the volume of liquids. It measures in liters (L) and milliliters (mL).

◀ Forceps help you pick up or hold small objects. They are handy for holding small objects under the hand lens.

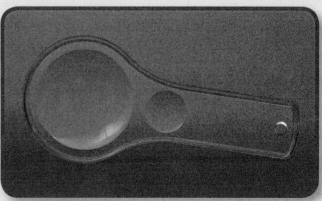

▲ A hand lens makes objects look larger and helps you see more detail.

Microscopes

Without a telescope, you can't identify what look like tiny objects in the sky. In the same way, you can't see tiny parts of an insect, colored particles in a rock, or cells in a leaf without a microscope. A **microscope** is a tool that makes small objects appear larger. It lets you see details you couldn't see with your eyes alone.

People have known for a long time that curved glass can *magnify,* or make things look larger. An early Roman scholar read books through a glass ball filled with water. People started making eyeglasses a thousand years ago. They called the curved glass a *lens* because it looked like a lentil—a bean!

An early scientist named Anton van Leeuwenhoek (LAY•vuhn•hook) used a lens to see creatures in a drop of pond water. He called them animalcules.

In the late 1500s, a Dutch eyeglass maker put a lens in each end of a hollow tube. Changing the length of the tube made tiny objects look three to nine times their actual size. This was probably the first "modern" microscope.

In the 1600s, Robert Hooke used a microscope to study thin slices of cork. To describe the tiny, boxlike structures he saw, he used the word *cell,* the name now used for the smallest unit of living things.

Today, microscopes can magnify objects thousands of times. So a tiny "animalcule" might look as large a whale!

▲ Van Leeuwenhoek was the first person to see microscopic organisms. He placed tiny samples on the tip of a needle and looked at them through a single lens.

Using a simple microscope, you can make things look up to 400 times their actual size! ▼

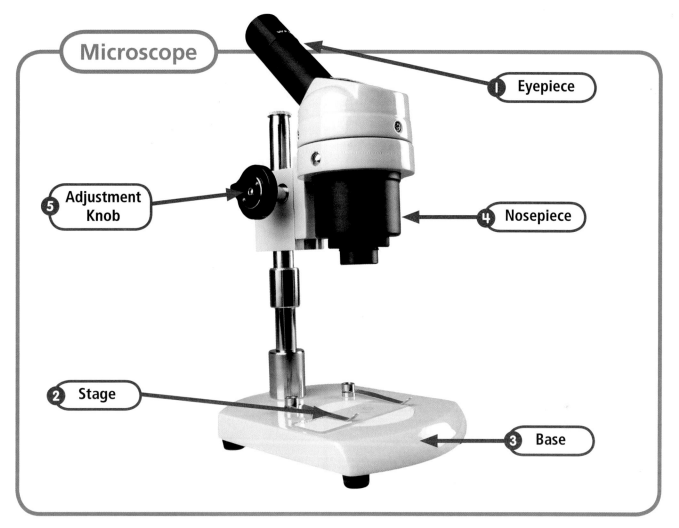

Microscope

1 Eyepiece

5 Adjustment Knob

4 Nosepiece

2 Stage

3 Base

Most classroom microscopes have several main parts:

1 The eyepiece contains one lens and is mounted at the end of a tube.

2 The stage holds the slide or object you are looking at.

3 The base supports the microscope. It usually holds a lamp or mirror that shines light through the object.

4 A nosepiece holds one or more lenses that can magnify an object up to 400 times.

5 Adjustment knobs help you focus the lenses.

MAIN IDEA AND DETAILS What are the main parts of a microscope?

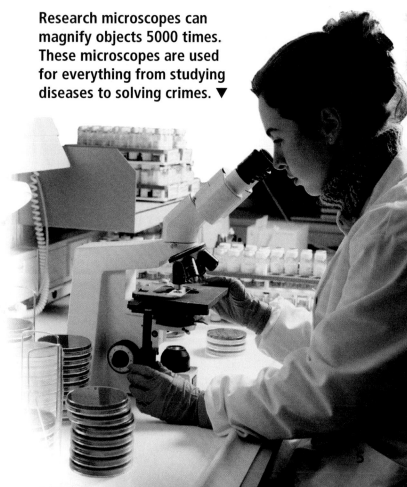

Research microscopes can magnify objects 5000 times. These microscopes are used for everything from studying diseases to solving crimes. ▼

Measuring Temperature

"Boy, it's hot today! It feels much hotter than yesterday." Without a thermometer, temperature isn't much more than how a person feels.

In 1592, an Italian scientist named Galileo found that a change in temperature made water rise and fall in a sealed tube. This device, a simple thermometer, helped Galileo study nature in a more precise way.

In the early 1700s, a German scientist named Fahrenheit sealed mercury in a thin glass tube. As it got warmer, the liquid metal took up more space. The mercury rose in the tube. As it cooled, the mercury took up less space. So the level of liquid in the tube fell. But how was this thermometer to be marked? What units were to be used?

Fahrenheit put the tube into freezing water and into boiling water and marked the mercury levels. Then he divided the difference between the levels into 180 equal units—called degrees.

In 1742, a Swedish scientist named Celsius made a thermometer with 100 degrees between the freezing and boiling points of water. The Celsius scale is used in most countries of the world. It is also the scale used by all scientists.

Thermometers can't measure extreme temperatures. For example, many metals get to several thousand degrees before they melt. Scientists have other temperature-sensing tools to measure very hot and very cold objects.

 MAIN IDEA AND DETAILS How does a thermometer work?

Measured on a Celsius thermometer, water boils at 100 degrees and freezes at 0 degrees. On a Fahrenheit thermometer, water boils at 212 degrees and freezes at 32 degrees.

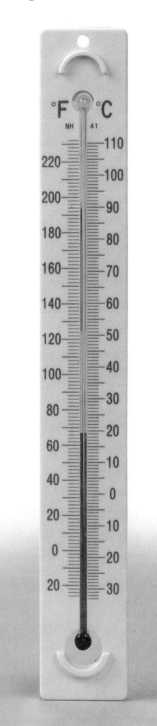

Balance or Spring Scale?

Suppose you're a merchant in Alaska in the early 1900s. A man wants food in exchange for some gold he got from the bottom of a river. But how much is the gold worth?

To find out, you use a tool that looks like a small seesaw. You place the gold at one end of a beam. Then you add objects of known mass at the other end until the beam is level. The objects balance! A **balance** is a tool that measures the amount of matter in an object—the object's *mass*.

The balance in your classroom measures mass by balancing an unknown object with one or more objects of known mass. Mass is measured in grams (g) or kilograms (kg).

When you want to measure an object's weight, you use a spring scale. You hang an object from a hook on the scale and let gravity pull it down. Gravity is a force that pulls on all objects on or near Earth. Weight is a measure of the force of gravity's pull. The unit for this measurement is the newton (N).

People often confuse mass and weight. But think what happens to the mass of an astronaut as he or she goes from Earth to the International Space Station. Nothing! The astronaut's mass stays the same, even though his or her weight goes down. The pull of gravity from Earth is countered by the space station's great speed in orbit.

MAIN IDEA AND DETAILS What does a balance measure? What does a spring scale measure?

▲ Find an object's mass, or amount of matter, by first placing the object on one pan. Then add a known mass to the other pan until the pointer stays in the middle.

▲ When you hang an object on the hook of the spring scale, you measure the force of gravity pulling on the object. This is the object's weight.

Insta-Lab

Do They Balance?

Place a blown-up balloon on one pan of a balance and an empty balloon on the other pan. Do they have the same mass? Why or why not?

Safety in the Lab

Working in the lab is fun. But you need to be careful to stay safe. Here are some general rules to follow:

- Study all the steps of an investigation so you know what to expect. If you have any questions, ask your teacher.
- Be sure you watch for safety icons and obey all caution statements.

Scientists in the lab wear safety goggles to protect their eyes. Smart students do the same thing! When you work with chemicals or water, a lab apron protects your clothes.

Be careful with sharp objects!

- Scissors, forceps, and even a sharp pencil should be handled with care.
- If you break something made of glass, tell your teacher.
- If you cut yourself, tell your teacher right away.

Be careful with electricity!

- Be especially careful with electrical appliances.
- Keep cords out of the way.
- Never pull a plug out of an outlet by the cord.
- Dry your hands before unplugging a cord.
- If you have long hair, pull it back out of the way. Roll or push up long sleeves to keep them away from your work.
- Never eat or drink anything during a science activity.
- Don't use lab equipment to drink from.
- Never work in the lab by yourself.
- Wash your hands with soap and water after cleaning up your work area.

 MAIN IDEA AND DETAILS What are four ways to keep safe in the lab?

1. MAIN IDEA AND DETAILS Draw and complete this graphic organizer.

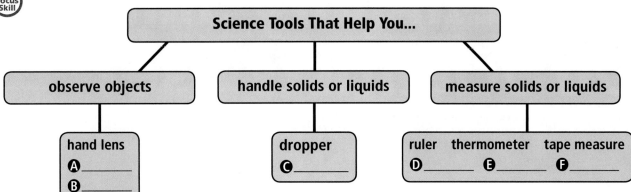

Science Tools That Help You...

observe objects | handle solids or liquids | measure solids or liquids

hand lens
Ⓐ_____
Ⓑ_____

dropper
Ⓒ_____

ruler   thermometer   tape measure
Ⓓ_____ Ⓔ_____ Ⓕ_____

2. SUMMARIZE Write two sentences that tell the most important information in this lesson.

3. DRAW CONCLUSIONS Why are different tools used to measure mass and weight?

4. VOCABULARY Write one sentence describing each vocabulary term.

Test Prep

5. Critical Thinking You are doing an investigation and accidentally spill water on the floor. How could this be a safety problem?

6. Why is using a thermometer or measuring cup more scientific than estimating temperature or volume?

   A. It is easier.

   B. It is more accurate.

   C. It looks more scientific.

   D. It uses up more class time.

Links

Writing

Narrative Writing

Use reference materials to learn about the life of Anton van Leeuwenhoek. Write a **story** that includes what he is famous for and what kinds of things he observed using his microscope.

Math (9÷3)

Choose Measuring Devices

A bottle is half full of water. Describe three things you could measure about the water, and name the tools to use for the measurements.

Health

Measuring for Health

Which science tools are also used by doctors, nurses, lab workers in hospitals, or others involved in health care? Describe how they are used.

 For more links and activities, go to **www.hspscience.com**

What Inquiry Skills Do Scientists Use?

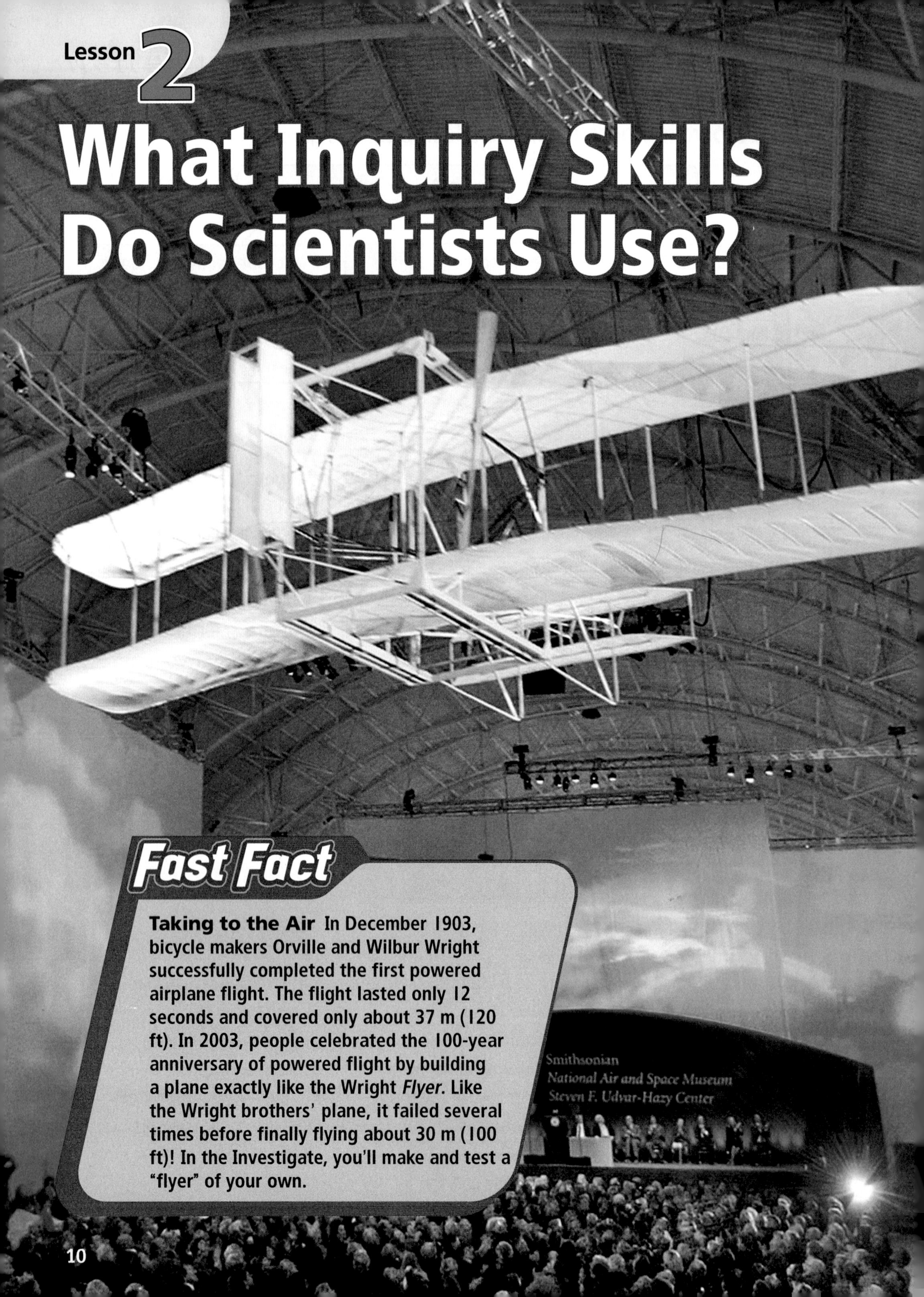

Fast Fact

Taking to the Air In December 1903, bicycle makers Orville and Wilbur Wright successfully completed the first powered airplane flight. The flight lasted only 12 seconds and covered only about 37 m (120 ft). In 2003, people celebrated the 100-year anniversary of powered flight by building a plane exactly like the Wright *Flyer*. Like the Wright brothers' plane, it failed several times before finally flying about 30 m (100 ft)! In the Investigate, you'll make and test a "flyer" of your own.

Smithsonian
National Air and Space Museum
Steven F. Udvar-Hazy Center

Design an Airplane

Materials • thick paper • stopwatch • ruler or tape measure
• tape

Procedure

1. Design a paper airplane. Then fold a sheet of thick paper to make the plane.

2. Measure a distance of 10 m in an open area. Mark one end of the distance as a starting line, and place a stick or stone every half meter from the starting line.

3. Test-fly your plane. Have a partner start the stopwatch as you're releasing the plane and stop it when the plane lands. Record the flight time in a table like the one shown.

4. Measure the distance the plane flew. Record the distance in the table.

5. Repeat Steps 3 and 4 for a second and a third trial.

6. Make a second airplane, with wings half as wide as your first plane.

7. Test-fly your second plane three times. Record all your measurements in the table.

Step 1

Data Table			
Trial		Airplane 1	Airplane 2
1	time		
	distance		
2	time		
	distance		
3	time		
	distance		

Draw Conclusions

1. How did changing the width of the wings affect the way your plane flew?

2. **Inquiry Skill** Why did some students' planes fly farther or longer than those of others? Write a hypothesis to explain your thinking.

Investigate Further

On one of your planes, add a paper-clip weight. Then fly the plane. What happens to the distance and time it flies? Infer the weight's effect on the plane.

Reading in Science

VOCABULARY
investigation p. 12
inquiry p. 12
experiment p. 15

SCIENCE CONCEPTS
▶ how inquiry skills help you gather information
▶ how an investigation differs from an experiment

(Focus Skill) READING FOCUS SKILL

MAIN IDEA AND DETAILS Look for information on when to use different inquiry skills.

Main Idea
detail detail detail

What Is Inquiry?

Suppose you wanted to learn about the way parachutes work. How would you begin? You might read a book about parachutes. Or you might investigate the subject on your own. An **investigation** is a procedure that is carried out to gather data about an object or event. An investigation can be as simple as measuring an object or observing a response to a stimulus. In this lesson, you investigated the way in which wing size affected flight.

So how can you begin your investigation about parachutes? Scientists usually begin an investigation by asking questions. Then they use inquiry skills to answer their questions. **Inquiry** is an organized way to gather information and answer questions. What questions do you have about parachutes?

Inquiry Skills

Observe—Use your senses to gather information about objects and events.

Measure—Compare the length, mass, volume, or some other property of an object to a standard unit, such as a meter, gram, or liter.

Gather, Record, and Display Data—Gather data by making observations and measurements. Record your observations and measurements in an organized way. Display your data so that others can understand and interpret it.

Use Numbers—Collect, display, and interpret data as numbers.

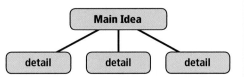

How does a parachute enable a person to jump from an airplane without getting hurt? ▶

How can you get answers to your questions? First, you might observe how parachutes are made. Look for diagrams in books or on the Internet. Go to a local airport, and ask to see some parachutes. Then gather, record, and display the data you collected. Measure and use numbers to express the data if possible.

You might wonder how a round parachute compares to a parachute like the one pictured on the previous page. What do they have in common? How are they different? What other shapes can a parachute have?

Once you compare different shapes, you can classify them. Some parachutes are used for doing tricks. Others are used to gently land heavy objects, such as space capsules. Some help sky divers land on a small target.

Now you've gathered a lot of data. The next step is to interpret the data. For example, how does the size or shape of the parachute relate to its use? Is there any pattern in the data? What shape of parachute appears easiest to control?

Data and observations can be used in many ways. It all depends on what questions you want to answer. You can use the data and logical reasoning to draw conclusions about things you haven't directly observed. For example, you might notice that narrow parachutes are used for tricks. From that, you can infer that this shape is easier to control. Or you might predict which parachute might win a sky-diving contest.

 MAIN IDEA AND DETAILS What are inquiry skills used for?

Inquiry Skills

Compare—Identify ways in which things or events are alike or different.

Classify—Group or organize objects or events into categories based on specific characteristics.

Interpret Data—Use data to look for patterns, to predict what will happen, or to suggest an answer to a question.

Infer—Use logical reasoning to come to a conclusion based on data and observations.

Predict—Use observations and data to form an idea of what will happen under certain conditions.

How does the size or shape of a parachute affect the way it works? ▶

Using Inquiry Skills

Suppose you were in a contest to find a way to drop a raw egg from a balcony without breaking the egg. What kind of parachute would you use?

First, you might plan and conduct a simple investigation. You might make parachutes of different shapes and sizes. You could tie weights on them, drop them, and see how they behave. How long do they stay in the air? How gently do they land? You could make observations and take measurements.

This experiment tested hypotheses about the type of parachute that would prevent a dropped egg from breaking! What variables were involved? ▼

Control Variables—Identify and control the factors that can affect the outcome of an experiment.

Draw Conclusions—Use data and experimental results to decide if your hypothesis is supported.

Communicate—Share results and information visually, orally, or electronically.

With that information, you could hypothesize. What design has the best chance to protect the egg? You may think that a large, round parachute is the best design. You could experiment to test your hypothesis. An **experiment** is a procedure you carry out under controlled conditions to test a hypothesis.

An experiment has more steps than a simple investigation. You have to decide what you will test. Then you have to be sure you control variables.

What are variables, and how can they be controlled? A variable is a factor, such as size, that can have more than one condition, such as large and small. You wouldn't test both the size and shape of parachutes at the same time. Why not? You wouldn't know whether the size or the shape caused the results. Suppose you compared a small, square parachute and a large, round one. How would you know if the size or the shape made a difference?

To test your hypothesis that large, round parachutes are best, you could first test round parachutes of different sizes. Everything except parachute size would be the same. You'd use the same egg size for each drop. You'd drop the eggs from the same height. And you'd drop each one several times to check the results. Then you'd do the whole thing again, using parachutes with different shapes instead of sizes! As before, you'd control all other variables.

During the experiment, you'd be careful to write down exactly what you did and how you did it. You'd record all observations and measurements.

The final step in an experiment is to draw conclusions. Did your experiment support your hypothesis? Was a large, round parachute the best way to protect the egg? What did the experiment show?

Finally, you'd write up your experiment to communicate your results to others. You might include tables for your data or draw diagrams of your parachute design.

 MAIN IDEA AND DETAILS Why do you have to control variables in an experiment?

Insta-Lab

What Causes Lift?

Cut a strip of newspaper or notebook paper about 2–3 cm wide and 10 cm long. Hold the end of the strip in your hand, and blow gently over the top of it. What happens? How might the result relate to airplane wings?

Models, Time, and Space

Have you ever watched a leaf fall from a tree? You might think of a falling leaf as a model for a parachute. It could give you ideas for a parachute design. Or you might make a model and test it before making an actual parachute. That can be very practical. Companies that build rockets, for example, save a lot of time and money by making and testing models before building the real things.

How will your parachute interact with what is attached to it? Thinking about time and space relationships is an important inquiry skill. For example, how do you make sure the parachute in a model rocket pops out at the right time? There's a lot to think about! Inquiry skills are ways to make sure your thinking and tests really work.

 MAIN IDEA AND DETAILS How do models help an investigation?

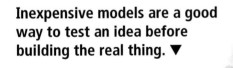

Inexpensive models are a good way to test an idea before building the real thing. ▼

1. MAIN IDEA AND DETAILS Draw and complete this graphic organizer.

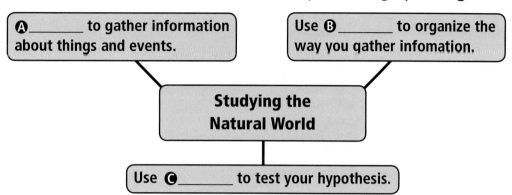

Ⓐ_____ to gather information about things and events.

Use Ⓑ_____ to organize the way you gather infomation.

Studying the Natural World

Use Ⓒ_____ to test your hypothesis.

2. SUMMARIZE Use your completed graphic organizer to write a lesson summary.

3. DRAW CONCLUSIONS If you wanted to learn more about birds, would you be more likely just to make observations first or to experiment first?

4. VOCABULARY Use the vocabulary terms in a paragraph describing how scientists study the natural world.

Test Prep

5. Critical Thinking Alberto shines red light on one group of plants and blue light on another. He measures the height of the plants each day. What hypothesis is he testing?

6. A factor that can affect the outcome of an experiment is called a

A. hypothesis.
B. prediction.
C. variable.
D. model.

Links

Writing

Narrative Writing
What inquiry skills do you use in everyday life? Write a screenplay about a day in your life. **Describe** how you use inquiry skills.

Math

Displaying Data
Make three different charts, tables, or graphs that show how many of your classmates were born in each month of the year.

Social Studies

Making Inferences
Use reference materials to find out how archaeologists make inferences. What information do they use to infer what life was like hundreds of years ago?

For more links and activities, go to www.hspscience.com

What Is the Scientific Method?

Fast Fact

Reaching for the Stars In October 2004, *SpaceShipOne* traveled nearly 112 km (70 mi) above the surface of Earth. The ship reached a speed of Mach 3—three times the speed of sound. However, *SpaceShipOne* wasn't built or launched by a government or a major aerospace company. It was the first successful launch of a private spaceship! In the Investigate, you too will build your own rocket.

Build a Rocket!

Materials
- string, 5 m
- goggles
- drinking straw
- 2 chairs
- balloon
- tape
- timer/stopwatch
- tape measure

Procedure

1. CAUTION: **Wear safety goggles.** Thread one end of the string through the straw.

2. Place the chairs about 4 m apart, and tie one end of the string to each chair.

3. Blow up the balloon, and pinch it closed.

4. Have a partner tape the balloon to the straw, with the balloon's opening near one chair.

5. Release the balloon. Use the stopwatch to time how long the balloon keeps going.

6. Measure and record the distance the balloon traveled. Also record its travel time.

7. Repeat Steps 3–6 with more air in the balloon. Then repeat Steps 3–6 with less air in the balloon than on the first trial.

Step 2

Draw Conclusions

1. Why did the balloon move when you released it?

2. How did the amount of air in the balloon affect the travel time and distance?

3. **Inquiry Skill** Would changing the shape of the balloon affect the distance it travels? Predict what would happen if you used a large, round balloon and a long, skinny balloon with the same amount of air.

Step 4

Investigate Further

Plan an investigation **to find out how the angle of the string affects the travel time and distance. How do you think the results will change when the angle is varied?**

Reading in Science

VOCABULARY
scientific method p. 20

SCIENCE CONCEPTS
▶ what steps are in the scientific method
▶ how scientists use the scientific method

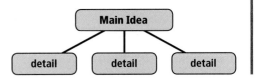 **READING FOCUS SKILL**

MAIN IDEA AND DETAILS Look for information on the steps of the scientific method.

The Scientific Method

In the Investigate, you predicted what would happen if you changed the shape of the balloon. How can you tell if your prediction is right? You could just play around with some balloons and see what happens. But a true experiment involves a series of steps that scientists use. The steps are called the **scientific method**.

Scientists use the scientific method to plan and carry out experiments. Some of the steps are the same as inquiry skills. And some inquiry skills are used in planning experiments.

There are five steps in the scientific method:

1. Observe, and ask questions.
2. Form a hypothesis.
3. Plan an experiment.
4. Conduct an experiment.
5. Draw conclusions, and communicate the results.

1 Observe, and Ask Questions

- Use your senses to make observations.
- Record *one* question that you would like to answer.
- Write down what you already know about the topic of your question.
- Do research to find more information on your topic.

2 Form a Hypothesis

- Write a possible answer to your question. A possible answer to a question is a *hypothesis*. A hypothesis must be a statement that can be tested.
- Write your hypothesis in a complete sentence.

Suppose you follow the steps of the scientific method. You form a hypothesis, and your experiment supports it. But when you tell other people your results, they don't believe you!

This is when the scientific method works especially well. You recorded your procedures. You have all your observations and data. All that another person has to do is repeat exactly what you did. That's one way scientists can check each other's experiments. If another person doesn't get the same results, you can try to figure out why. You can ask, "Did I do something differently? Were there variables I didn't control?"

Scientists can use the scientific method to repeat the experiments of other scientists. This helps them make sure that their conclusions are correct.

 MAIN IDEA AND DETAILS What are the steps of the scientific method?

3 Plan an Experiment

- Decide how to conduct a fair test of your hypothesis by controlling variables. Variables are factors that can affect the outcome of the experiment.
- Write down the procedure you will follow to do your test.
- List the equipment you will need.
- Decide how you will gather and record data.

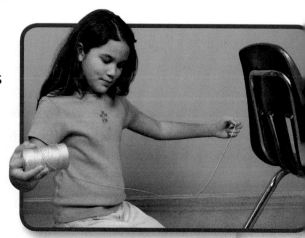

4 Conduct an Experiment

- Follow the procedure you wrote down.
- Observe and measure carefully.
- Record everything that happens, including what you observe and what you measure.
- Organize your data so it is easy to understand and interpret.

5 Draw Conclusions/Communicate Results

- Make charts, tables, or graphs to display your data.
- Analyze your observations and the data you collected.
- Write a conclusion. Describe the evidence you used to determine whether the experiment supported your hypothesis.
- Decide whether your hypothesis was supported or not.

Before and After

People don't always start with the scientific method. Suppose you have questions about something scientists have already studied. All you need to do is read about it. But when studying the natural world, you often find new problems that puzzle you. You think, "I wonder what would happen if. . . " That's when inquiry skills, investigations, and experiments come in handy.

What happens after you've done an experiment? Even if an experiment supports your hypothesis, you might have other questions—about the same topic—that can be tested. And if your hypothesis wasn't supported, you might want to form another hypothesis and test that.

Scientists never run out of questions. The natural world is filled with things that make people wonder. By asking questions and using the scientific method, scientists have learned a lot. They've learned how to send people to the moon. They've learned to cure many diseases. But there are still many things to be learned. Who knows? Maybe you're the one to make the next big discovery!

 MAIN IDEA AND DETAILS What do scientists do when experiments show their hypotheses to be incorrect?

▲ Computers can be used to research a problem, display data, and share the results of experiments with scientists all over the world.

Tables and charts make it easy for other people to understand and interpret your data. ▼

Insta-Lab

Make a Helicopter

Cut a piece of paper 3 cm wide and 13 cm long. Draw lines on the paper like those on the diagram above. Cut along all the solid lines. Fold one flap forward and one flap to the back. Fold the base up to add weight at the bottom. Drop your helicopter, and watch it fly. How does adding a paper clip to the bottom change the way the helicopter flies?

1. MAIN IDEA AND DETAILS Draw and complete this graphic organizer.

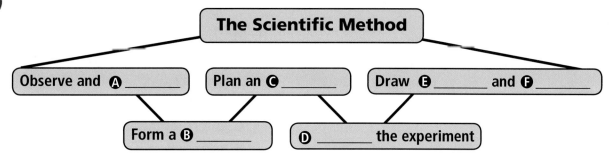

The Scientific Method

Observe and **A** _____

Plan an **C** _____

Draw **E** _____ and **F** _____

Form a **B** _____

D _____ the experiment

2. SUMMARIZE Use your graphic organizer to write a paragraph telling the steps of the scientific method.

3. DRAW CONCLUSIONS During which step of the scientific method would you identify variables and figure out how to control them?

4. VOCABULARY For each letter in *scientific method,* write a science-related word starting with the same letter. Skip repetitions of a letter.

Test Prep

5. Critical Thinking Karla heard that for making ice cubes, hot water is better than cold water because it freezes faster. How could she test that idea as a hypothesis?

6. What does an experiment test?
   A. a fact   **C.** a theory
   B. a hypothesis   **D.** a variable

Links

Writing

Expository Writing
Write a letter to a friend, **explaining** how he or she could use the scientific method to test a balloon rocket.

Math

Display Data
Make a table to display how long the balloon rockets flew in the Investigate. Then make a graph of the results.

Social Studies

Scientific Method
Use reference materials to compare how the Greeks studied science and what Francesco Redi added to their method. Write a story about what he showed.

 For more links and activities, go to **www.hspscience.com**

Review and Test Preparation

Vocabulary Review

Use the terms below to complete the sentences. The page numbers tell you where to look in the chapter if you need help.

microscope p. 4   **inquiry** p. 12
balance p. 7   **experiment** p. 15
investigation p. 12   **scientific method** p. 20

1. An organized way to gather information is called an _____.

2. A tool used to measure the mass of an object is a _____.

3. To test a hypothesis, you plan and conduct an _____.

4. A tool that makes objects appear larger is a _____.

5. A series of steps used by scientists to study the physical world is the _____.

6. When you gather information about an object or event, you do an _____.

Check Understanding

Write the letter of the best choice.

7. Which tool is used to measure volume in the metric system?
   A. balance   **C.** spring scale
   B. measuring cup   **D.** thermometer

8. **MAIN IDEA AND DETAILS** Which of the following steps to solve a problem is done first?
   F. test a hypothesis
   G. interpret data
   H. form a hypothesis
   J. observe and ask questions

9. Which inquiry skill can be used to save time and money before doing an experiment?
   A. form a hypothesis
   B. make and use models
   C. classify objects
   D. draw conclusions

The diagram shows four tools. Use the diagram to answer questions 10 and 11.

10. Which tool is used to measure the weight of an object?
    F. Tool Q   **H.** Tool S
    G. Tool R   **J.** Tool T

11. Which tool measures in grams?
    A. Tool Q   **C.** Tool S
    B. Tool R   **D.** Tool T

12. MAIN IDEA AND DETAILS Comparing, measuring, and predicting are examples of what process?

  F. communicating **H.** inquiry
  G. hypothesizing   **J.** investigating

13. When conducting an experiment, which is the best way to record data?

  A. Make a bar graph while taking the measurements.
  B. Write everything down after you are finished.
  C. Make a table to record your data as you collect it.
  D. Write things down on a sheet of paper and organize it later.

14. Juan is making and flying airplanes with different-shaped wings. What is he doing?

  F. experimenting **H.** investigating
  G. hypothesizing   **J.** communicating

15. Why do scientists do each part of their investigation several times?

  A. to be sure their data is accurate
  B. to make their experiment look more impressive
  C. to use up all of their materials
  D. because it's fun

16. If you wanted to see more detail on the surface of a rock, what tool would you use?

  F. dropper   **H.** microscope
  G. forceps   **J.** thermometer

Inquiry Skills

17. Andrea is testing balloon rockets by using balloons with different amounts of air. **Identify three variables** Andrea will need to control.

18. Which boat would you **predict** will finish second in the race?

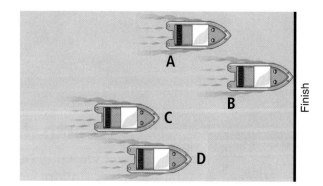

Critical Thinking

19. Why are safety goggles important when students are doing an investigation with scissors or glass?

20. The diagram shows an experiment. Different amounts of water were placed in 4 beakers. The beakers were heated at the same rate. The data shows how long it took each beaker to boil.

2.0 min.   4.0 min.   6.0 min.   7.9 min.

Part A What conclusion is supported by the experiment? Explain.

Part B What variables were controlled in the experiment?

UNIT A

Earth and Space Sciences

The Chapters and features in this unit address these Grade Level Indicators from the Ohio Academic Content Standards for Science.

Chapter 1 — Earth, Moon, and Beyond

ES-1 Describe how night and day are caused by Earth's rotation.

ES-2 Explain that Earth is one of several planets to orbit the sun, and that the moon orbits Earth.

ES-3 Describe the characteristics of Earth and its orbit about the sun.

ES-4 Explain that stars are like the sun, some being smaller and some larger, but so far away that they look like points of light.

Chapter 2 — Using Resources

ES-5 Explain how the supply of many non-renewable resources is limited and can be extended through reducing, reusing and recycling but cannot be extended indefinitely.

ES-6 Investigate ways Earth's renewable resources can be maintained.

Unit A Ohio Expeditions

The investigations and experiences in this unit also address many of the Grade Level Indicators for standards in Science and Technology, Scientific Inquiry, and Scientific Ways of Knowing.

TO:	mai-lin@hspscience.com
FROM:	traveler@hspscience2.com
RE:	Drake Planetarium

Dear Mai-Lin,
Today our class took a field trip to the Drake Planetarium, which is in Cincinnati. Do you know how far Saturn's orbit is from Earth's? It would take seven years to send a space probe there! We spent nearly an hour in the planetarium lab. We learned about different sizes of stars. Some are gigantic, but they are so far from Earth that we can barely see their light. I never knew we could know how hot a star is, how bright it is, and how far it is from Earth, all from its color.
Keep watching the sky!
LaToya

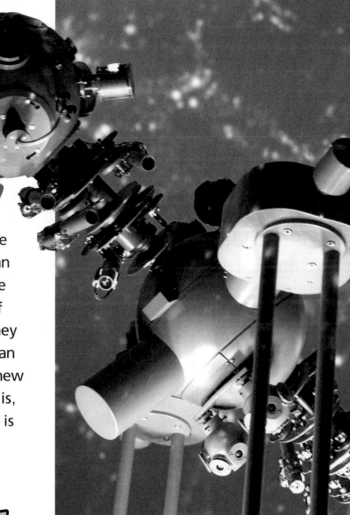

Experiment!

Studying the Universe

Scientists study the universe from Earth and from space. Studying the universe from space requires rockets that can launch heavy payloads. What rocket design will carry heavy payloads the farthest? Is one large rocket more powerful than several smaller rockets? Plan and conduct an experiment to find out.

1 Earth, Moon, and Beyond

Vocabulary

sun	star
rotate	solar system
axis	constellation
revolve	planet
orbit	universe
equator	galaxy
moon	
crater	
moon phase	
eclipse	
refraction	

What do YOU wonder?

The world's largest single-dish radio telescope is in Arecibo, Puerto Rico. Scientists use the telescope—whose dish is 305 m (1000 ft) wide— to study deep space. In what other ways do scientists study objects in space?

How Does Earth's Orbit Affect the Seasons?

Fast Fact

Sunrise from Space Astronauts in space may see 16 sunrises and 16 sunsets every day as they travel around Earth. In the Investigate, you'll learn about movements of Earth and the moon and why, here on Earth, we see only 1 sunrise and 1 sunset each day.

Moving Through Space

Materials • beach ball • baseball • table-tennis ball

Procedure

1. Work in a group of four. You will use a model to show the time/space relationships among Earth, the moon, and the sun. One person should hold the beach ball (the sun). Another should stand far away and hold the baseball (Earth). A third person should hold the table-tennis ball (the moon) near the baseball. The fourth person should record the movements.

2. For the model, Earth should move around the sun in a circle and spin at the same time. The real Earth spins about 365 times during each complete path around the sun.

3. While the model Earth moves, the model moon should move around Earth in a nearly circular path. The real moon spins once during each complete path around Earth. Earth spins about $29\frac{1}{2}$ times from one new moon to the next.

Step 1

Step 3

Draw Conclusions

1. One of the movements in the model represents a year. Which movement was that?

2. **Inquiry Skill** Use your understanding of time/space relationships to compare the moon's and Earth's movements. How are they alike? How are they different?

Investigate Further

Make a model **to show how you think the amount of sunlight reaching different parts of Earth changes during the year.**

VOCABULARY

sun p. 32
rotate p. 32
axis p. 32
revolve p. 34
orbit p. 34
equator p. 34

SCIENCE CONCEPTS

▶ how the movements of Earth and the sun result in day and night and the seasons

▶ why we have time zones

READING FOCUS SKILL

MAIN IDEA AND DETAILS Look for the details about Earth's movements.

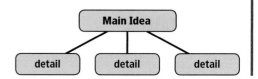

Day and Night

Every day the **sun**, the star at the center of our solar system, appears to rise in the east. It appears to reach its highest point around noon and to set in the west. After a period of darkness, this process repeats.

This cycle of day and night occurs because Earth **rotates**, or spins, on its axis. Earth's **axis** is an imaginary line that passes through the North and South Poles. When a place on Earth faces the sun, it is day in that place. When that place faces away from the sun, it is night.

Our system of time is based on Earth's 24-hour cycle of daylight and darkness. Because of Earth's rotation, sunrise and sunset occur at different times in different places. Long ago, people didn't need to know the exact time. And each place used local time—time based on sunrise and sunset in that place. This changed in the late 1800s. Trains were starting to travel long distances. If each train station had kept its own time, there would have been confusion. People needed to develop standard times.

The sun appears to rise and set. Of course, it doesn't actually do either one. Earth's rotation causes what appear to be a sunrise and a sunset. ▼

Time Zones

▲ It's 7 A.M. in Seattle, on the West Coast.

▲ Much of the United States is within four time zones. Time-zone lines aren't perfectly straight, partly because of state boundaries.

▲ In New York City, on the East Coast, it's 10 A.M.

In 1884, standard times were set up in 24 time zones around the world. Each time zone represents one of the hours in the day. All the places within a time zone use the same time. If you travel east from one time zone to the next, the time becomes one hour later. If you travel west from one time zone to the next, the time becomes one hour earlier. In the middle of the Pacific Ocean is the International Date Line. If you go west across that line, you travel into the next day. Crossing the line eastward, you travel into the previous day. For example, if it's 3 A.M. Tuesday and you go west across the International Date Line, the time becomes 2 A.M. Wednesday, not Tuesday.

The United States has seven time zones from Puerto Rico, in the east, to Hawai`i, in the west. If you're just about to have dinner at 6 P.M. in Florida and you call a friend in Oregon, it will be 3 P.M. there. Your friend may be just getting home from school.

MAIN IDEA AND DETAILS Explain why officials needed to set up time zones in the late 1800s.

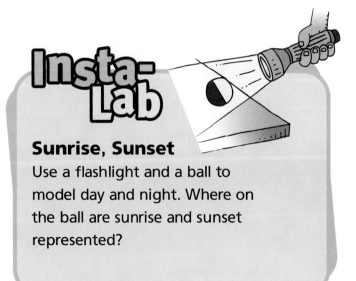

Sunrise, Sunset
Use a flashlight and a ball to model day and night. Where on the ball are sunrise and sunset represented?

Earth's Seasons

You probably know that most places on Earth have seasons. During the summer, there are more hours of daylight than hours of darkness. The temperature is usually higher, too. During the winter, there are fewer hours of daylight and the temperature is lower. These seasonal changes are a result of the tilt of Earth's axis.

In addition to rotating on its axis, Earth **revolves**, or travels in a path, around the sun. The path Earth takes as it revolves is its **orbit**. One orbit takes about 365 days, or one year.

Some people think we have seasons because Earth is closer to the sun in the summer than in the winter. This isn't so. (Earth is actually closer to the sun during our winter.) The shape of Earth's orbit is only slightly elliptical; that is, it's nearly circular. The tilt of Earth's axis is what produces seasons.

Earth's axis is not straight up and down in relation to its orbit. If it were, the angle of the sun's rays when they hit Earth would be the same all year long. There would be no seasons. But Earth's axis is tilted about 23.5°. During part of the year, half of Earth is tilted toward the sun. On that part of Earth, it is summer. On the part tilted away from the sun, it is winter.

Earth is divided into Northern and Southern Hemispheres by the equator. The **equator** is an imaginary line going all the way around Earth halfway between the North and South Poles. When the Northern Hemisphere is tilted toward the sun, the Southern Hemisphere is tilted away.

To see this process, follow the seasons shown in the diagram. When the Northern Hemisphere is tilted toward the sun, it is summer there. The number of hours of daylight is greater than the number of hours of darkness. The sun's rays strike part

When it is summer in the Northern Hemisphere . . .

. . . it is winter in the Southern Hemisphere.

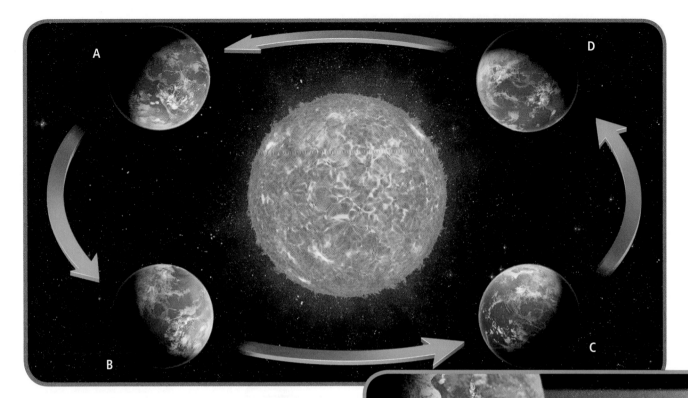

▲ The position of Earth in relation to the sun changes, depending on where Earth is in its orbit. During summer in the Northern Hemisphere [C], that hemisphere is tilted toward the sun. During spring [B] and fall [D], neither hemisphere is tilted toward the sun.

of the hemisphere directly, so the weather is warm. Even in Alaska, summer temperatures can reach 30°C (86°F).

As Earth continues in its orbit, the Northern Hemisphere begins to tilt away from the sun. It receives fewer hours of daylight and more hours of darkness in that hemisphere. The rays of the sun strike the Northern Hemisphere at more of an angle. The weather becomes much cooler.

The day with the greatest amount of daylight is called the *summer solstice* (SAHL•stis). In the Northern Hemisphere, that day is June 20 or 21. The winter solstice, the day with the least amount of daylight, is December 21 or 22.

Halfway between the solstices, neither hemisphere is tilted toward the sun. The

▲ During the Northern Hemisphere's summer, the number of hours of daylight is at its highest. During summer also, the sun's rays hit the Northern Hemisphere more directly, not at as great an angle as in winter. This causes more heating because the sun's rays don't spread out as much.

hours of daylight and darkness are about equal. These days are called the *equinoxes* (EE•kwih•nahks•uhz). In the Northern Hemisphere, the autumn equinox is September 22 or 23. The spring equinox is March 20 or 21.

 MAIN IDEA AND DETAILS What are the days called that have the most and the fewest hours of daylight?

Highs and Lows

Seasons at and near the North and South Poles are very different from seasons everywhere else. In the summer, the poles get six months of daylight and no darkness. Winter brings six months of darkness, with no daylight.

Even though the South Pole has a summer of nonstop daylight, it's never very warm. Sunlight that reaches Antarctica, even in the summer, is at a low angle and is spread out. This results in low temperatures all year.

At the equator, halfway between the poles, day and night last about 12 hours each all year. Temperatures stay about the same all year, too. The warmest places in the world are just south and north of the equator. Rain at the equator keeps temperatures from reaching highs like those in deserts such as the Sahara.

 MAIN IDEA AND DETAILS In Antarctica, why is it cold even in the summer?

The lowest temperature ever recorded on Earth, −89°C (−129°F), was at Russia's Vostok Station, in Antarctica, in 1983.

The highest temperature ever recorded on Earth, 58°C (136°F), was in Al Aziziyah, Libya, in the Sahara, in 1922.

1. MAIN IDEA AND DETAILS Draw and complete these graphic organizers.

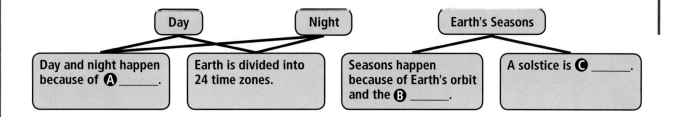

| Day | Night | Earth's Seasons |

| Day and night happen because of **A** _____. | Earth is divided into 24 time zones. | Seasons happen because of Earth's orbit and the **B** _____. | A solstice is **C** _____. |

2. SUMMARIZE Write a summary by answering the question in the lesson title.

3. DRAW CONCLUSIONS If Earth were not tilted on its axis, how might life be different?

4. VOCABULARY Use the words *revolve* and *rotate* to explain Earth's movements in space.

Test Prep

5. Critical Thinking A friend lives where there are 12 hours of daylight every day. Where does this person live, and how do you know?

6. What season is it in the Northern Hemisphere when the Southern Hemisphere tilts toward the sun?

A. fall   C. summer

B. spring   D. winter

Links

Writing

Narrative Writing

Living at a research station in Antarctica would be an unusual experience for most of us. Write a **story** telling what a week of summer vacation there would be like.

Math

Solve Problems

Use the highest and lowest temperatures ever recorded on Earth (see the previous page) to determine the range of temperatures on Earth.

Social Studies

Maya Calendar

Research the Maya calendar. Write a paragraph comparing that calendar with the calendar we use today. Draw a picture of the calendar to go with your paragraph.

 For more links and activities, go to www.hspscience.com

How Do Earth and the Moon Compare?

Fast Fact

The Moon Rocket The Saturn V Launch Vehicle shown here is 36 stories high. Sent into space by the launch vehicle, six Apollo missions landed on the moon. In 1969, Neil Armstrong was the first person to walk on the moon's cratered surface. In the Investigate, you'll make a model of craters being formed.

Making Craters

Materials
- newspaper
- aluminum pan
- apron
- large spoon
- $\frac{1}{2}$ cup water
- I cup flour
- safety goggles
- marble
- meterstick

Procedure

1. Copy the table.

2. Spread the newspaper on the floor. Place the pan in the center of the newspaper.

3. Put on the apron. Use the spoon to mix the water and most of the flour in the pan. Spread out the mixture. Lightly cover the surface of the mixture with dry flour to make a model of the moon's surface.

4. **CAUTION: Put on the safety goggles** to protect your eyes from flour dust. Drop the marble into the pan from a height of 20 cm. Carefully remove the marble.

5. Measure the width of the crater, and record it in the table. Repeat Step 4 two more times. Measure and record each time.

6. Now drop the marble three times from each of the heights 40 cm, 80 cm, and 100 cm. Measure and record the crater's width after each drop. Compare your results with those of your classmates.

Draw Conclusions

1. How did height affect crater size?

2. **Inquiry Skill** Scientists use models to study space. From using a model, what did you learn about how the moon's craters may have been formed?

Making Craters		
Trial	Height	Width of Crater
1	20 cm	
2	20 cm	
3	20 cm	
1	40 cm	
2	40 cm	
3	40 cm	

Step 3

Investigate Further

How would dropping objects of different sizes affect the size and shape of the craters? Plan and conduct a simple investigation to find out.

Reading in Science

 ES-3 Describe Earth in space

VOCABULARY
moon p. 40
crater p. 40
moon phase p. 43
eclipse p. 44
refraction p. 44

SCIENCE CONCEPTS
▶ how the moon and Earth are alike and different
▶ how the phases of the moon and solar and lunar eclipses happen

READING FOCUS SKILL

COMPARE AND CONTRAST Look for ways the phases of the moon are alike and different.

alike —— different

The Moon and Earth

If you stare at the moon at night, you may wonder what the surface of this silent, round object is like. A **moon** is any natural body that revolves around a planet. Earth and its moon are similar in several ways. Both are rocky and fairly dense. Both are made of many of the same elements, including aluminum, oxygen, calcium, silicon, and iron. Both the moon and Earth have craters. A **crater** is a low, bowl-shaped area on the surface of a planet or moon.

However, there are also important differences between the moon and Earth. One clear difference is size. The moon's diameter is about 3476 km (2160 mi), only about one-fourth of Earth's diameter.

The moon's pull of gravity is only about one-sixth that of Earth. A person who weighs 800 newtons (180 lb) on Earth would weigh only 133 newtons (30 lb) on the moon. The moon, unlike Earth, has almost no atmosphere and no liquid water. Temperatures on the moon can range

From space, the moon looks gray because of its rocks and dust. ▼

From space, Earth looks blue because of its oceans. There is no liquid water on the moon.

40

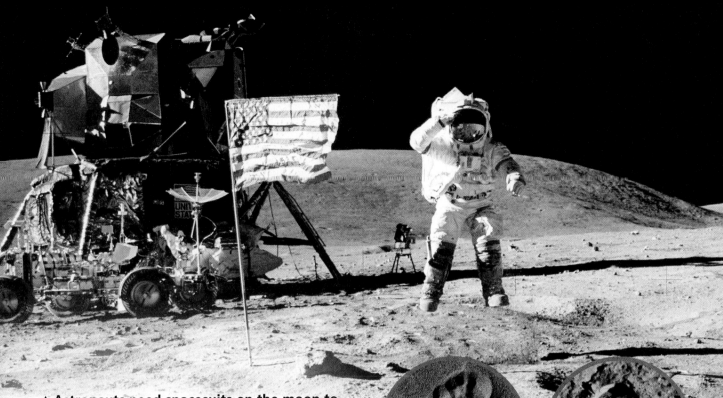

▲ Astronauts need spacesuits on the moon to provide air to breathe and to protect them from the extreme temperatures. The heavy suits and other equipment feel much lighter on the moon than on Earth because of the weaker gravitational pull of the moon.

from more than 100°C (212°F) during the day to −155°C (−247°F) at night. Earth's temperatures are much less extreme.

The moon's surface is covered with craters, many more than on Earth. The craters were made by objects falling from space, like the marbles in the Investigate.

Most objects that fall from space toward Earth burn up in the atmosphere before they reach the ground. The craters that do form on Earth are usually worn down by weathering. Objects that fall to the moon, though, do not burn up, because there is hardly any atmosphere. And there is no erosion, because of the lack of atmosphere and lack of water. As a result, craters last almost indefinitely.

COMPARE AND CONTRAST How is the moon's surface different from that of Earth?

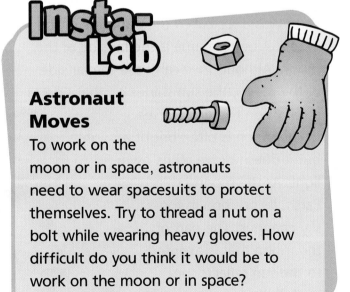

A footprint on Earth doesn't last long, but a footprint on the moon could last millions of years due to lack of erosion.

Insta-Lab

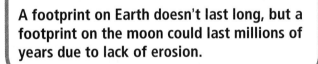

Astronaut Moves

To work on the moon or in space, astronauts need to wear spacesuits to protect themselves. Try to thread a nut on a bolt while wearing heavy gloves. How difficult do you think it would be to work on the moon or in space?

Phases of the Moon

On some nights, you may notice that the moon seems to have disappeared. On other nights, you see a large, white moon shining brightly. The moon, though, has not changed at all. Instead, the moon and Earth have moved.

In the Investigate in Lesson 1, you learned how Earth travels around the sun and how the moon travels around Earth at the same time. Earth orbits the sun in a slight ellipse. The moon's orbit around Earth is a slight ellipse, too. When the moon is closest to Earth, it is about 356,400 km (221,000 mi) away.

Both Earth and the moon rotate as they revolve, though at different speeds. The moon rotates more slowly. It completes a rotation every $29\frac{1}{2}$ Earth days. So a day on the moon is $29\frac{1}{2}$ Earth days long.

The moon rotates as it orbits Earth, but the same side of the moon always faces Earth. That's because one lunar cycle, from new moon to new moon, takes $29\frac{1}{2}$ days, the same amount of time the moon takes to complete one rotation.

The side of the moon we can't see from Earth was once called the dark side of the moon. A better name is the far side of the moon. Although we can't see the far side of the moon, the sun shines on that side as often as on the side we see.

The moon is often bright at night, but it doesn't give off its own light. As the moon orbits Earth, its position in the sky changes. The part of the moon that is exposed to the sun reflects the sun's light.

The Apollo 8 mission, in 1968, was the first space mission to carry people in orbit around the moon. While in orbit, the crew took pictures like this one of the moon's far side.

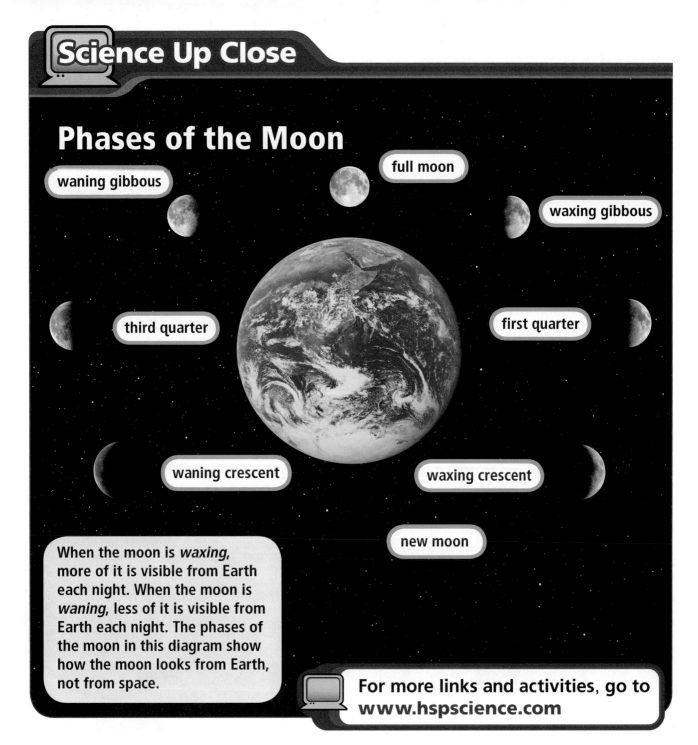

Phases of the Moon

waning gibbous

full moon

waxing gibbous

third quarter

first quarter

waning crescent

waxing crescent

new moon

When the moon is *waxing*, more of it is visible from Earth each night. When the moon is *waning*, less of it is visible from Earth each night. The phases of the moon in this diagram show how the moon looks from Earth, not from space.

 For more links and activities, go to **www.hspscience.com**

The way the moon looks from Earth changes daily. At any time, half of the moon is lit by the sun. But how much you see depends on the moon's phase. A **moon phase** is one of the shapes the moon seems to have as it orbits Earth. When Earth is between the moon and the sun, you see a full moon. When the moon is between Earth and the sun, you can't see the moon at all. This is called a new moon.

The cycle of phases of the moon takes $29\frac{1}{2}$ days. During the cycle, the visible portion of the moon changes gradually. Starting with a new moon, you see more and more of the moon each day until the full moon. Then you see less and less each day, until the next new moon.

COMPARE AND CONTRAST Contrast the appearance of the moon during a full moon and a new moon.

Eclipses

Objects in space block some of the sun's light, producing shadows. An **eclipse** occurs when one body in space blocks light from reaching another body in space.

Eclipses we see on Earth are solar eclipses and lunar eclipses. They are alike because both occur when Earth, the sun, and the moon line up. However, solar and lunar eclipses also differ.

A solar eclipse occurs when the moon—always a new moon—casts a shadow on Earth. In some places the moon seems to cover the sun, and the sky gets dark. Only the outer atmosphere of the sun is visible, as a bright glow around the moon. At other places, only part of the sun is covered.

A lunar eclipse occurs when the moon—always a full moon—passes through the shadow of Earth. Earth blocks the sun's light from reaching the moon, but the moon does not look black. Instead, it looks red. This is because Earth's atmosphere bends red light, which then reflects off the moon. Scientists call this bending of light **refraction**.

You might think that eclipses happen with every new or full moon. But the moon and Earth are not always in the proper alignment. Sometimes only a partial eclipse occurs. Partial solar and lunar eclipses each occur two to four times a year.

 COMPARE AND CONTRAST How do solar and lunar eclipses differ?

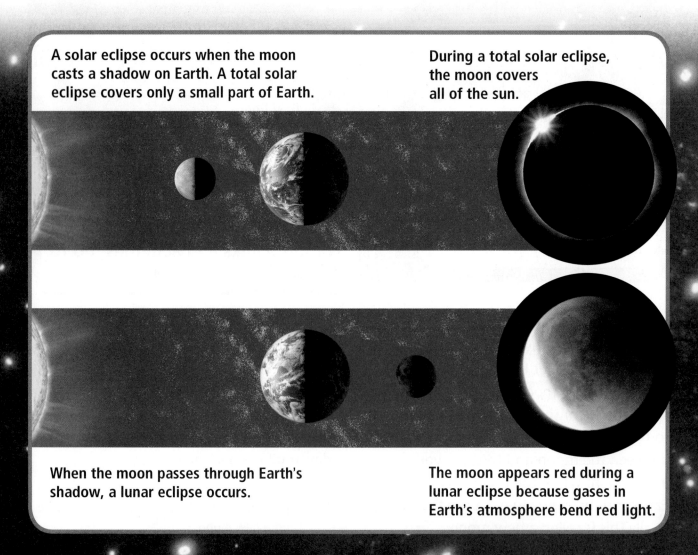

A solar eclipse occurs when the moon casts a shadow on Earth. A total solar eclipse covers only a small part of Earth.

During a total solar eclipse, the moon covers all of the sun.

When the moon passes through Earth's shadow, a lunar eclipse occurs.

The moon appears red during a lunar eclipse because gases in Earth's atmosphere bend red light.

Focus Skill

1. COMPARE AND CONTRAST Complete the diagram.

	Different	Alike
Earth and moon	atmosphere: Earth has an atmosphere. The moon does not. size: **A**_____ gravity: **B**_____ temperature: **C**_____	materials: **D**_____ surface features: Both the moon and Earth have craters.
New moon and full moon	appearance: **E**_____	phases: Both are phases of the moon.
Solar eclipse and lunar eclipse	positions of bodies in space: **F**_____	causes: Both pass through shadows of bodies in space.

2. SUMMARIZE Write two sentences that tell what this lesson is mostly about.

3. DRAW CONCLUSIONS How would the moon be different if it had liquid water?

4. VOCABULARY Explain in a sentence what a moon phase is.

Test Prep

5. Critical Thinking On a night when you see a full moon, where are the moon, sun, and Earth relative to each other in space?

6. Which of these are on the surfaces of both the moon and Earth?

   A. craters   **C.** oxygen
   B. liquid water   **D.** windstorms

Links

Writing

Narrative Writing

Think about the differences between the moon and Earth. Then write a **story** that describes the differences. Use as many descriptive words as you can.

Math

Use Fractions

During a full moon, you can see half of the moon's surface. During a first quarter, what fraction of the moon's surface can you see on a clear night?

Physical Education

Running to the Moon

The moon is about 355,000 km from Earth at its closest point. To get an idea of how far that is, run or walk 355 steps. Each step represents 1000 kilometers.

 For more links and activities, go to **www.hspscience.com**

Lesson 3

What Makes Up Our Solar System?

Fast Fact

Deep Space Close-Up Since the launch of the Hubble Space Telescope in 1990, people have studied and enjoyed many of the Hubble's amazing images, like this one of the Cone Nebula. Some of the objects shown in Hubble images are at a distance greater than 10 billion light-years (60 billion trillion mi). In the Investigate, you'll make your own telescope—though you won't see as far as with a telescope like the Hubble.

The Cone Nebula

Make a Telescope

Materials
- 2 sheets of construction paper
- tape
- modeling clay
- 2 convex lenses

Procedure

1. Roll and tape a sheet of construction paper to form a tube slightly larger in diameter than the lenses. Make a second tube just large enough for the first tube to fit inside it.

2. Slide most of the smaller tube into the larger tube.

3. Use some of the clay to hold one of the lenses in one end of the smaller tube. This will be the telescope's eyepiece.

4. Use clay to hold the other lens in the far end of the larger tube. This will be the lens closest to the object you are viewing.

5. Choose three distant objects to view. **CAUTION: Do not look at the sun.** Slide the smaller tube to focus on each object.

6. Observe each object twice, once without the telescope and once with it. Record each observation in a drawing.

Draw Conclusions

1. Compare the drawings made with and without the telescope. Why do they differ?

2. **Inquiry Skill** How was your observing similar to using a space telescope?

Step 1

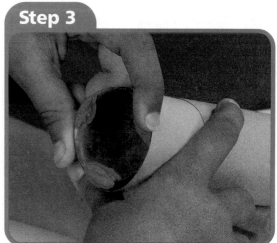

Step 3

Investigate Further

Use your telescope to observe the brightest object in the eastern night sky. List details you can see with the telescope but not without it.

VOCABULARY

star p. 48
solar system p. 48
constellation p. 49
planet p. 51
universe p. 54
galaxy p. 54

SCIENCE CONCEPTS

▶ what objects make up our solar system

▶ what other objects are in the universe

READING FOCUS SKILL

MAIN IDEA AND DETAILS Look for main ideas about planets and stars.

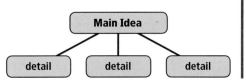

The Sun and Other Stars

One object that you can see in the sky without a telescope is the sun. But you should NEVER look directly at the sun. The sun is a **star**, a huge ball of very hot gases in space. The sun is at the center of our solar system. A **solar system** is made up of a star and all the planets and other objects that revolve around that star.

The sun is the source of much of the energy on Earth. Plants use energy from the sun to make food and store energy. Animals eat plants to use that food energy. When plants and animals die, they decay, or rot. Some that died long ago became fossil fuels, such as oil, that people use today.

The sun's features make it different from everything else in our solar system. The sun is huge: a million Earths could fit inside it.

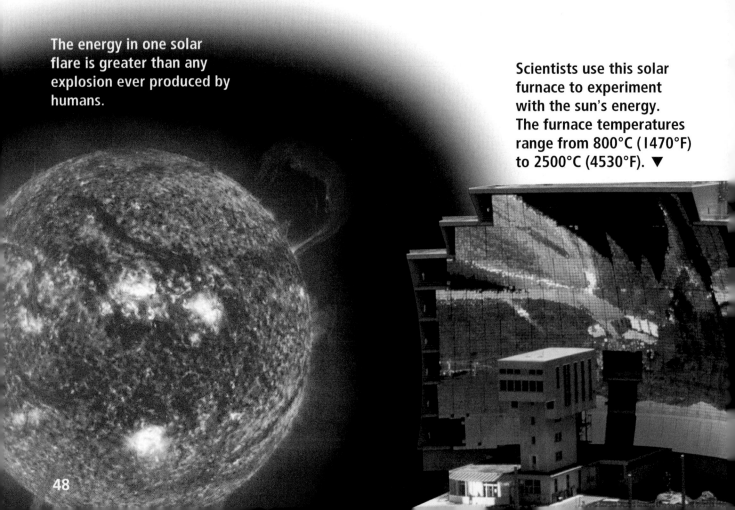

The energy in one solar flare is greater than any explosion ever produced by humans.

Scientists use this solar furnace to experiment with the sun's energy. The furnace temperatures range from 800°C (1470°F) to 2500°C (4530°F). ▼

▲ There are many ways to classify stars. A star can be classified according to its size, its brightness, its temperature, and its color.

The constellation Ursa Major, or the Great Bear, was named by the ancient Greeks. It contains a more familiar star pattern—the Big Dipper.

The glowing surface of the sun is what we see from Earth. On the sun's surface are sunspots visible from Earth. Sunspots are darker, cooler areas of the sun. They can produce brief bursts of energy called solar flares. Above the sun's surface is the corona. This area of hot gases extends about 1 million km (600,000 mi) out from the surface of the sun.

The sun is important to us because of its energy. But the sun is just one of billions of stars in the universe. Among all those stars, the sun is only average. It's a yellow star of medium size, medium brightness, and medium temperature.

One way scientists classify stars is by color. Star colors range from blue, white, and yellow to orange and red. The color of a star is a clue to its surface temperature. Blue stars are the hottest, and red stars are the coolest.

Another way scientists classify stars is by brightness. How bright a star appears depends on two factors. One is how far it is from Earth. The other is how bright it actually is.

Since ancient times, people have grouped stars into constellations. A **constellation** is a pattern of stars that is named after a religious or mythical object or animal. One set of constellations is visible from the Northern Hemisphere. Another set is visible from the Southern Hemisphere.

 MAIN IDEA AND DETAILS What are two ways scientists classify stars?

Mercury
diameter: 4900 km
(about 3040 mi)
distance from sun:
58,000,000 km
(about 36,000,000 mi)
length of year:
88 Earth days

Venus
diameter: 12,100 km
(about 7500 mi)
distance from sun:
108,000,000 km
(about 67,000,000 mi)
length of year:
225 Earth days

Earth
diameter: 12,700 km
(about 7900 mi)
distance from sun:
150,000,000 km
(about 93,000,000 mi)
length of year:
365.25 Earth days

Math in Science
Interpret Data

Weight on Different Planets

The pull of gravity at a planet's surface depends on the planet's diameter and on how much mass the planet has. The greater the planet's pull of gravity, the more you would weigh on its surface. Here are the weights on different planets for a person who weighs 100 pounds on Earth.

Planet	Weight (lb)
Mercury	37.8
Earth	100.0
Venus	90.7
Mars	37.7

Does Venus have a stronger or weaker pull of gravity than Earth?

Note: Diagrams not to scale.

*In 2006, Pluto was classified as a "dwarf planet."

The Inner Planets

Our solar system includes eight planets. A **planet** is a body that revolves around a star. A planet is held in its orbit by the gravitational force between the planet and the star.

Scientists divide the planets that orbit the sun into four inner planets and four outer planets. These groups are separated by the huge asteroid belt between Mars and Jupiter. The *asteroid belt* is a ring-shaped area where many small, rocky bodies, or asteroids, are located.

The four inner planets are rocky and dense. Mercury, which is closest to the sun, is about the size of Earth's moon. Like the moon, Mercury has almost no atmosphere and a surface covered with craters and dust. The side of Mercury facing the sun is hot—about 430°C (810°F). The side not facing the sun can become very cold, however—about −180°C (−290°F).

Venus is the brightest object in the night sky, after the moon. This planet is about the same size as Earth, and it is rocky. The similarities end there. Venus can become very hot, reaching about 460°C (860°F). It is even hotter than Mercury because Venus's thick atmosphere keeps heat from escaping.

Earth is the only planet to support life, because of its liquid water and atmosphere. Earth's atmosphere maintains temperatures in which living things can survive.

Mars is called the red planet because of its reddish soil. Its atmosphere is mostly carbon dioxide. Its valleys are evidence that Mars once had liquid water. Mars has the largest volcano in the solar system, and it has dust storms that can last for months.

 MAIN IDEA AND DETAILS What separates the inner planets from the outer planets?

Mars
diameter: 6800 km
(about 4200 mi)
distance from sun:
228,000,000 km
(about 142,000,000 mi)
length of year:
687 Earth days

The Outer Planets and Pluto

Beyond the asteroid belt are the four outer planets. In their order from the sun, they are Jupiter, Saturn, Uranus, and Neptune. They are called gas giants, because they are composed mostly of hydrogen and helium.

Jupiter is the largest planet in the solar system. It has rings and dozens of moons, including Ganymede, the largest moon in the solar system. There is a huge storm on Jupiter that has lasted for about 400 years. The storm has a name that describes its appearance—the Great Red Spot.

Saturn is best known for its rings, made of ice, dust, boulders, and frozen gas. The rings stretch about 136,200 km (84,650 mi) from the center of the planet. Like Jupiter, Saturn has dozens of moons.

Uranus also has many moons and rings. This planet rotates on an axis that is tilted much more than those of other planets. Compared with the other planets, Uranus looks like it is rolling on its side.

Neptune has several rings and moons and the fastest winds in the solar system. The winds can reach 2000 km/hr (1200 mi/hr)!

For almost 80 years Pluto was listed as the ninth planet in the solar system. In 2006, scientists met to form a new definition of a planet. They decided that a planet is a large round object in a clear orbit around a star. Because Pluto is not in a clear orbit, scientists removed it from the list of planets. They classified it as a "dwarf planet." The large asteroid Ceres, and the newly discovered object Eris, which orbits beyond Pluto, are also classified as "dwarf planets."

 MAIN IDEA AND DETAILS What are some characteristics of the gas giants?

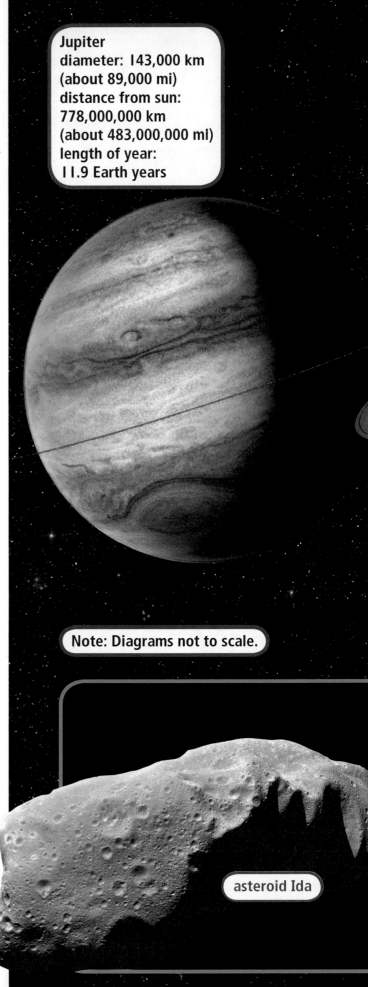

Jupiter
diameter: 143,000 km (about 89,000 mi)
distance from sun: 778,000,000 km (about 483,000,000 ml)
length of year: 11.9 Earth years

Note: Diagrams not to scale.

asteroid Ida

Pluto: a "dwarf planet"
diameter: 2300 km
(about 1400 mi)
distance from sun:
5,906,000,000 km
(about 3,670,000,000 mi)
length of year:
248 Earth years

Saturn
diameter: 120,000 km
(about 74,000 mi)
distance from sun:
1,427,000,000 km
(about 886,000,000 mi)
length of year:
29.4 Earth years

Uranus
diameter: 51,000 km
(about 32,000 mi)
distance from sun:
2,871,000,000 km
(about 1,784,000,000 mi)
length of year:
84 Earth years

Neptune
diameter: 49,000 km
(about 30,000 mi)
distance from sun:
4,498,000,000 km
(about 2,795,000,000 mi)
length of year:
165 Earth years

Asteroids and Comets

Both asteroids and comets orbit the sun. Asteroids are chunks of rock less than 1000 km (621 mi) in diameter. Comets have a small, solid, frozen core. As a comet nears the sun, however, its core begins to melt, forming a cloud of gas that is pushed into a long tail by energy from the sun. A comet's tail can be tens of millions of kilometers long.

comet Hale-Bopp

Beyond the Solar System

Look up on a clear night, and you may think you can see the universe. But what you see is only a small fraction of it. The **universe** is everything that exists—all the stars, the planets, dust, gases, and energy.

If it's dark enough where you live, you may see what look like ribbons of stars overhead. These ribbons are part of the Milky Way Galaxy, the galaxy that includes our solar system. A **galaxy** is made of gas, dust, and a group of stars, including any objects orbiting the stars. The Milky Way Galaxy has more than 100 billion stars and is one of the largest galaxies in the universe. Scientists estimate that the universe contains more than 100 billion galaxies.

Galaxies are classified by shape. There are four basic types: spiral, barred spiral, elliptical, and irregular. The Milky Way Galaxy is a spiral galaxy with a bulge of stars in the center and rotating arms around a disk. The sun is in one of the Milky Way Galaxy's spiral arms. The sun makes one complete turn around the center of the galaxy in about 200 to 250 million years.

A spiral galaxy can look like a giant pinwheel spinning through space. The arms wind around the center as the galaxy turns. ▼

The Hubble Space Telescope produced this image. Each bright spot is a galaxy containing countless stars. But even this image shows just one relatively small region of space. There are billions of galaxies in the universe.

A barred spiral galaxy is similar to a spiral galaxy, but the spiral arms extend from a bar of stars that stretches across the center. Elliptical galaxies make up about half of all galaxies. Their shapes range from almost a sphere to that of a flattened football. They do not seem to rotate. Irregular galaxies are groups of stars with no obvious shape.

Galaxies form groups known as clusters. The Milky Way Galaxy is one of about 30 galaxies in a cluster called the Local Group. There are thousands of galactic clusters in the universe.

Astronomers hypothesize that stars form in a nebula. A nebula is a huge cloud of hydrogen, helium, and tiny particles of dust. The matter of a nebula may clump together to form a *protostar*, a collection of gas clouds that starts reacting chemically. When a protostar is hot enough, it forms a star and begins to release energy in the form of heat and light.

Black holes are other, less understood, parts of the universe. A black hole is an object of extremely intense gravity. Black holes are so dense that even light gets pulled into them. Scientists have concluded that a black hole forms when a large star collapses into itself.

 MAIN IDEA AND DETAILS Describe the sun's position and movement in the Milky Way Galaxy.

A nebula may be composed of matter given off by an aging star. ▶

Rolling in Space

With supervision, sit in a desk chair that has wheels, lift up your feet, and try to move to another part of the room without touching the floor. How is the feeling you get the same as how you'd feel in space?

The Hubble Space Telescope took this image in 1994 of a huge spiral of dust being pulled into a black hole.

Space Exploration

In ancient times, people observed the sky and asked questions about what they saw. With the invention of the telescope in 1609, people first got a closer look into space. Early telescopes allowed astronomers to see details of the moon's surface, as well as moons around Jupiter. It was not until the mid-twentieth century, though, that people could launch vehicles into space.

The Russian satellite *Sputnik 1* was launched into Earth's upper atmosphere in 1957. A *satellite* is any body that orbits another. In the 1960s, Russian and United States spacecraft carried the first humans into space. In 1969, U.S. astronaut Neil Armstrong became the first person to walk on the moon.

Since the Apollo missions that flew astronauts to the moon from 1969 to 1972, much of space exploration has focused on other parts of the universe. In 1977, the United States launched the *Voyager 1* and *Voyager 2* space probes to study deep space. These robot vehicles have traveled to the edge of the solar system, past all the planets, and are still sending back information to Earth.

In 2004, the *Cassini* spacecraft reached Saturn. From its orbit around Saturn, *Cassini* has given scientists a wealth of information about the planet's famous rings.

Today's scientists use telescopes, satellites, and space probes to continue to explore space. All these devices are helping scientists understand more about our universe.

 MAIN IDEA AND DETAILS How has space exploration changed since the Apollo missions?

Two *Mars Rovers* landed on Mars in 2003. The six-wheeled rovers traveled over the surface of Mars collecting data, taking photographs, and analyzing Martian rocks and soil. ▶

In 1976, *Viking I* and *Viking 2* became the first space probes to successfully land on Mars.

1. MAIN IDEA AND DETAILS Draw and complete the graphic organizer.

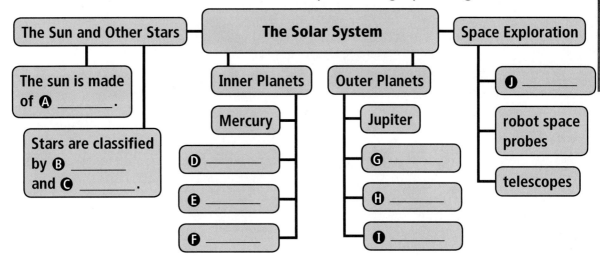

The Sun and Other Stars

The sun is made of **Ⓐ** _____.

Stars are classified by **Ⓑ** _____ and **Ⓒ** _____.

The Solar System

Inner Planets

Mercury

Ⓓ _____

Ⓔ _____

Ⓕ _____

Outer Planets

Jupiter

Ⓖ _____

Ⓗ _____

Ⓘ _____

Space Exploration

Ⓙ _____

robot space probes

telescopes

2. SUMMARIZE Using the graphic organizer, write a lesson summary.

3. DRAW CONCLUSIONS Why was it important for scientists to write a clear definition for a planet?

4. VOCABULARY How are *star, solar system,* and *galaxy* related?

Test Prep

5. Critical Thinking Why haven't scientists found life on other planets in the solar system?

6. Where is the asteroid belt?

   A. in the nebula

   B. in Saturn's rings

   C. between Jupiter and Mars

   D. between Earth and Venus

Links

Writing

Persuasive Writing
Should the United States increase the money spent for space exploration? Write a **letter** that tells your point of view. Include reasons that support your position.

Math

Multiply Numbers
An astronomical unit (AU) is about 149,600,000 km, the distance between Earth and the sun. If an object is 4 AU from Earth, how far away is it?

Literature

Space Poetry
Myra Cohn Livingston writes poetry about space. Read a book of her poetry, and write a paragraph about the poem you liked best.

For more links and activities, go to www.hspscience.com

Beyond the Shuttle

An elevator to space? A spaceship with engines so powerful that the vehicle can take off like an airplane and fly— not blast off—into orbit? Those might sound like the basis of an episode of Star Trek, but the ideas are currently under development by the National Aeronautics and Space Administration (NASA).

Taxi! Taxi!

On the top of NASA's wish list is a space taxi. The vehicle would ferry ten astronauts at a time to and from the International Space Station (ISS) beginning in 2010. NASA is spending $882 million to design a craft called the Orbital Space Plane.

The space plane is a shuttlelike craft that would sit on top of a rocket. The rocket would blast the plane into orbit. "It would not be a space shuttle replacement," Barry

Davidson of Syracuse University said of the space plane. "It would be the next-generation vehicle out there."

Within the next 15 years or so, scientists say, NASA will have to replace the three space shuttles—*Discovery*, *Atlantis*, and *Endeavour*—which were all built in the 1970s and early 1980s.

NASA might also replace the shuttles with a spacecraft that would be attached to the back of a large aircraft. Once both vehicles are airborne, the spacecraft would release itself and speed into orbit using a super-powerful jet engine called a ramjet or a scramjet. The ramjet or scramjet engine would propel the craft into orbit at ten times the speed of sound.

Sound Byte

Sound travels through air at about 340 meters (1100 feet) per second.

Next Stop, Space

Some scientists say the easiest way to get into space might just be by elevator. NASA scientists are currently working on a plan that would put a large satellite in orbit about 35,000 kilometers (21,748 miles) above the equator. The satellite would be programmed to constantly hover over the same spot on Earth's surface.

Scientists would attach to the satellite a very long cable and an elevator that could then be used to transport people and equipment into space. "We think we can have it up and operational in about 15 years," said scientist Bradley C. Edwards.

Think About It

1. Why is it a good idea to have a space plane that is easy to reuse?
2. Do you think it's important for people to keep exploring outer space? Why or why not?

Find out more! Log on to
www.hspscience.com

Flying High

Franklin Chang-Diaz knew from the age of 7 that he wanted to fly in outer space. Chang-Diaz was born in Costa Rica and moved to the

United States when he was 17. He studied hard in high school and college to become an expert in a type of rocket propulsion called plasma physics.

Chang-Diaz became an astronaut in 1980 when he joined the National Aeronautics and Space Administration (NASA). Since then, he has flown on seven space shuttle missions. Some of Chang-Diaz's missions have involved launching new types of satellites into orbit around Earth. The satellites give NASA information about our planet and the solar system.

Career Aerospace Engineer

Aerospace engineers produce amazing machines and engines that propel those machines. The engineers design, develop, and test every kind of flying machine, from an airplane the size of a warehouse, to a spacecraft that travels almost 20,000 miles an hour.

SCIENCE Projects

for Home or School

You Can Do It!

Materials
- 15-cm cardboard square
- protractor
- ruler
- drinking straw
- tape
- 20-cm piece of string
- metal washer

Quick and Easy Project

Navigating by the Stars

Procedure

1. Starting at one corner of the cardboard square, draw a line at an angle of 10° from an edge. Use the protractor and ruler to do this. Then draw lines at 20°, 30°, and so on to fill the square.

2. Tape the straw to the cardboard as shown.

3. At the point where all the lines meet, make a hole in the cardboard. Push the string through the hole, and tie a knot. Tie the washer to the other end of the string.

4. At night, look at a star through the straw. Measure the angle of the star by noting the angle of the string.

Draw Conclusions

The angle at which you see the North Star tells the latitude of where you are on Earth. What is the angle of the North Star where you live? What is the latitude where you live?

Design Your Own Investigation

A Change in the Days

You know that the seasons result from the tilt of Earth's axis as Earth moves around the sun. Design an investigation to find out how the amount of daylight changes because of Earth's movement. Plan to keep track of the amount of daylight each day for one week. Include a graph or table comparing the days.

Review and Test Preparation

Vocabulary Review

Use the terms below to complete the sentences. The page numbers tell you where to look in the chapter if you need help.

revolve p. 34	**eclipse** p. 44
orbit p. 34	**solar system** p. 48
equator p. 34	**constellation** p. 49
moon p. 40	**universe** p. 54
crater p. 40	**galaxy** p. 54

1. The path that Earth takes as it moves around the sun is its _____.

2. The sun is the center of our _____.

3. Everything that exists, including planets, stars, dust, and gases, is the _____.

4. Stars, gas, and dust make up our _____.

5. To travel in a path around another object is to _____.

6. Earth is divided into Northern and Southern Hemispheres by the _____.

7. When one body in space blocks light from reaching another body, there is an _____.

8. A bowl-shaped low place on a surface is a _____.

9. A natural body that revolves around a planet is a _____.

10. A pattern of stars is a _____.

Check Understanding

Write the letter of the best choice.

11. MAIN IDEA AND DETAILS Which detail explains why summers at the North Pole are cold?

A. Winters are long at the poles.

B. The North Pole is covered with ice.

C. Earth's orbit around the sun is elliptical.

D. The sun's rays are indirect at the North Pole.

12. COMPARE AND CONTRAST Which is a correct comparison of the moon and Earth?

F. They have similar gravitational force.

G. They both undergo weathering.

H. They both are rocky and dense.

J. They have similar atmospheres.

13. What does this illustration show?

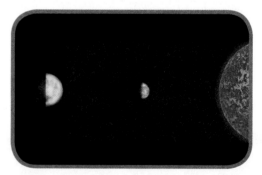

A. a full moon

B. a new moon

C. a waning moon

D. a waxing moon

14. Which is correct during summers in the Northern Hemisphere?

  F. Earth has its winter equinox.

  G. The Southern Hemisphere is tilted away from the sun.

  H. The Northern Hemisphere is not tilted toward the sun.

  J. Rays of the sun hit the equator more intensely than during the winter.

15. Which planet is labeled X?

  A. Earth

  B. Mars

  C. Mercury

  D. Venus

16. What determines the seasons on Earth?

  F. Earth's orbit and tilt

  G. the sun's speed and the orbit of the sun

  H. changing directions of Earth's orbit

  J. the position of the moon in relation to Earth

Inquiry Skills

17. How could you **use a model** to learn more about eclipses?

18. What tools do scientists use to **observe** deep space?

Critical Thinking

19. Explain how Saturn and Jupiter differ from the "dwarf planet" Pluto.

20. The moon is Earth's only natural satellite. We know now about many of the moon's characteristics.

  Part A Why do people sometimes refer to "the dark side of the moon"? Explain why this phrase is incorrect.

  Part B Think about the differences between Earth and the moon. Then make a plan for a settlement on the moon. Explain what settlers will need to take to the moon or change on the moon to make it suitable for life.

Chapter 2

Using Resources

Lesson 1 How Do People Use Soil and Water Resources?

Lesson 2 How Can People Conserve Resources?

Vocabulary

renewable resource
nonrenewable resource
pollution
conservation

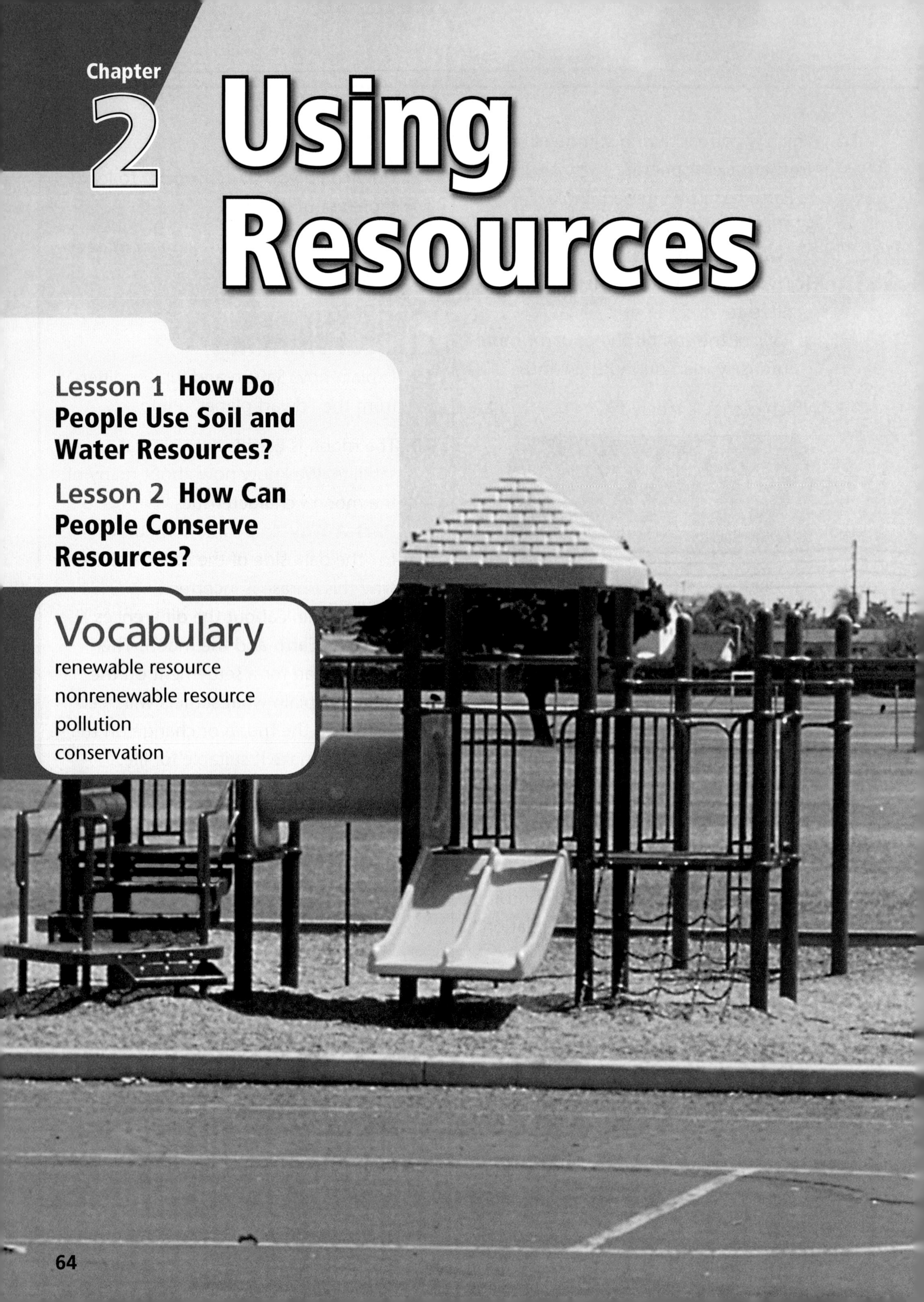

What do YOU wonder?

Milk bottles, grocery bags, plastic toys—all these things can be recycled to make playground equipment such as the kinds shown here. Why do you think many communities buy playground equipment made from recycled products?

How Do People Use Soil and Water Resources?

Lake Powell, Arizona

Cleaning Water

Materials
- spoon
- soil
- water
- 3 clear plastic cups
- 2 funnels
- cotton balls
- coffee filters
- charcoal
- pea-size gravel

Procedure

1. Stir one spoonful of soil into a cup of water until the water is cloudy.

2. Place a funnel in a clean cup. Think about how to clean the water with the materials you have. Then place two of the possible cleaners (cotton balls, coffee filters, charcoal, gravel) in layers in the funnel.

3. Pour the dirty water through the funnel. Observe the water after it has passed through the cleaners. Record your results.

4. Prepare a second cup of dirty water. Control variables by changing just one of the cleaners you used the first time.

5. Pour the dirty water through the funnel into a clean cup. Observe the water, and record your results.

6. Compare the cleaning systems.

Draw Conclusions

1. How do you think your water-cleaning systems compare to those used in community water treatment plants?

2. **Inquiry Skill** Identify the variable you tested with your two cleaning systems. Compare the effectiveness of the cleaners that varied.

Step 1

Step 3

Investigate Further

Plan and conduct an investigation in which you identify and control variables to find the best system to clean dirty water.

Reading in Science

VOCABULARY
renewable resource p. 68
nonrenewable
    resource p. 69
pollution p. 70

SCIENCE CONCEPTS
▶ what natural resources are
▶ what pollution is

READING FOCUS SKILL

MAIN IDEA AND DETAILS Look for details that support the main ideas.

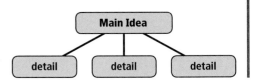

Natural Resources

You depend on natural resources every day. You breathe in air. You drink water found in nature and eat food grown in soil. The clothes you wear come from natural resources. Your bike, your CDs, your books, and your home were all made with natural resources. The light and heat in your home and the gasoline in your family car were produced using natural resources. Natural resources make life on Earth possible.

Some natural resources are reusable. One example is water, a resource that's essential for life. All the water people use is part of a natural water cycle. This cycle makes water usable again and again. Air is also reusable. Like water, it is a renewable resource.

A **renewable resource** is a resource that can be replaced within a human lifetime. A renewable resource is a reusable resource. Renewable resources can be used again and again—if we use them carefully.

How many renewable resources can you find in this photograph? ▼

Unfortunately, many resources can be used only once. They are nonrenewable. A **nonrenewable resource** is a resource that cannot be replaced within a human lifetime. Once it's used up, no one can wait for it to be replaced. Soil, for example, may take thousands of years to form. A large part of soil is weathered rock. The rock mixes with organic matter, water, and air. As the soil forms, it acquires nutrients that enable plants to grow. The richest soils are high in nutrients and are good for growing crops.

Many energy resources, such as coal and oil, are nonrenewable. It takes millions of years for coal to form from dead plants buried in Earth. Oil is nonrenewable because, like coal, it also takes millions of years to form.

Minerals, as well as metals, are nonrenewable, too. They occur in limited amounts in Earth's crust.

Even some plants are essentially nonrenewable resources. Trees such as fruit trees do grow quickly and may be replaced in a few years. But an old-growth forest contains trees that are hundreds of years old. Once these trees are cut down, they will not be replaced for hundreds of years to come.

 MAIN IDEA AND DETAILS What are three nonrenewable resources?

Wild animals are less important today as a resource, but 200 years ago, they were a primary food source for many people in North America. ▼

When people talk about rich soil, they mean soil with a lot of nutrients plants can use.

Air and Water Pollution

Some resources can be used again and again if people use them carefully. However, sometimes the use of resources leads to problems.

If you live near a city, you may have seen a hazy sky on what should have been a bright, sunny day. The haze may have been air pollution. **Pollution** is any change to the natural environment that can harm living organisms. Air pollution is one kind of pollution. Other kinds are water pollution and land pollution.

Most air pollution is caused by the burning of fuels such as coal and oil. Have you ever seen black smoke coming from a truck or bus? That's air pollution caused by burning diesel fuel. Like gasoline, diesel fuel comes from oil. When any fuel burns, it sends harmful substances into the air.

Air pollution can also appear as a yellow or brown haze called *smog*. Smog is a mixture of smoke, water vapor, and chemicals. It's usually produced by vehicles or factories.

Air pollution can cause acid rain. Vehicles and some energy stations release nitrous oxide, sulfur dioxide, and other chemicals into the air. These chemicals mix with water in the air and form acids. The acids fall to the ground as acid rain. Acid rain can kill fish when it falls into lakes, and it can damage trees and other plants. Acid rain can also damage buildings. The acid reacts with limestone and wears it away.

The biggest problems caused by air pollution are health related. Air pollution can irritate the eyes and cause breathing problems. Today, the United States has laws to control air pollution. The laws require vehicles and factories to release less of the substances that pollute the air.

Vehicles pollute less today than in the past, but the number of vehicles on the road today is greater than ever before. ▶

Air pollution in cities is not new. People in London have complained of air pollution since the 1600s.

Science Up Close

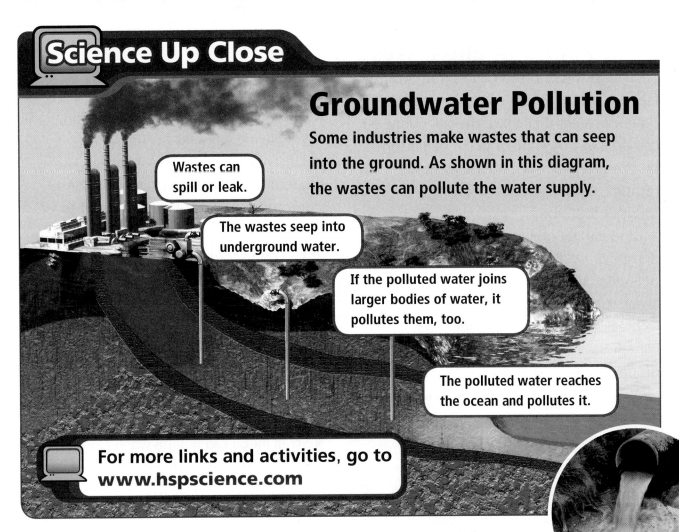

Groundwater Pollution

Some industries make wastes that can seep into the ground. As shown in this diagram, the wastes can pollute the water supply.

Wastes can spill or leak.

The wastes seep into underground water.

If the polluted water joins larger bodies of water, it pollutes them, too.

The polluted water reaches the ocean and pollutes it.

 For more links and activities, go to www.hspscience.com

Underground water supplies can also be polluted by materials that soak into the ground. ▶

Water pollution comes from harmful substances that enter the water cycle. Some of these substances come from factories and mines that dump wastes into rivers and lakes. The wastes can get into groundwater, too. Fertilizers and pesticides used by farmers and homeowners can also pollute groundwater.

Another water pollution source is sewage. *Sewage* is human waste that is usually flushed away by water. If sewage gets into the water supply that people use, it can make people sick.

There are laws to control some sources of water pollution. The laws require industries and cities to clean surface water when they finish using it.

⭐ **MAIN IDEA AND DETAILS** Where does most air pollution come from?

Insta-Lab

Traveling Pollution

Put three drops of red food coloring in half a glass of water. Observe the color of the water. Fill up the glass with water, and observe the color again. Then pour half of the water into another glass half filled with water. Observe the color. How does this process show how pollution spreads?

71

Land Pollution and Misuse

Some misuse of land comes from poor farming practices. For example, if farmers do not protect their land, the soil might be carried away by wind or water or poisoned by chemicals. Soil is a nonrenewable resource, and replacing it may take thousands of years.

Land can be polluted, too. Garbage in dumps or landfills can be a source of pollution. Many materials that are thrown away, such as plastics, take a long time to break down. Some garbage may contain harmful chemicals that seep into groundwater.

Wastes from industry can also harm the land and groundwater. Some poisonous wastes are buried in large containers or drums. If the drums leak, the poisons can seep into the ground. This causes land pollution and possibly water pollution.

People are working to stop land pollution and misuse. Most farmers use modern techniques to protect the land. Communities and companies can dispose of garbage, trash, and industrial wastes in ways that don't cause pollution. And governments spend millions of dollars removing poisons from the land. In the next lesson, you'll learn about other ways to prevent pollution and save natural resources.

 MAIN IDEA AND DETAILS What are some ways to solve the problem of land misuse?

◀ Scrap metal can pollute when it's left on the land. But some companies buy and reuse thousands of tons of scrap metal every year.

When land is left unplanted and unprotected like this, rainstorms can wash the soil away. ▼

1. **MAIN IDEA AND DETAILS** Draw and complete these graphic organizers by giving examples.

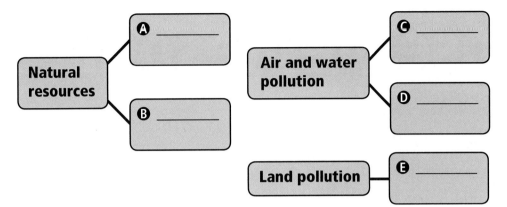

Natural resources
- Ⓐ _____
- Ⓑ _____

Air and water pollution
- Ⓒ _____
- Ⓓ _____

Land pollution
- Ⓔ _____

2. **SUMMARIZE** Use the graphic organizer to write a summary of this lesson.

3. **DRAW CONCLUSIONS** How can trees be both renewable and nonrenewable resources?

4. **VOCABULARY** Write a sentence that explains the meaning of the term *pollution*.

Test Prep

5. **Critical Thinking** How can farming have both positive and negative effects on the environment?

6. Which is a major cause of air pollution?
   - **A.** soil loss
   - **B.** farming
   - **C.** landfills
   - **D.** driving cars

Links

Writing

Narrative Writing
Write a **story** about how people use natural resources and change the environment. Share your story with your class.

Math

Solve a Problem
The Great Plains lost about 0.7 m of topsoil in the last 100 years. That left about 1.3 m of topsoil. How much will be left in another 100 years at this rate of loss?

Social Studies

Oil Spills
When a ship that carries oil breaks up, the result can be an oil spill. Research an oil spill, and report on the damage it caused to the environment.

For more links and activities, go to www.hspscience.com

How Can People Conserve Resources?

Fast Fact

Water, Water Growing plants in water—hydroponics—has a long history. Scientists think the ancient Babylonians sometimes grew plants this way, without soil. If people ever live on other planets, hydroponics will likely be the best way for them to grow vegetables. In the Investigate, you'll find out for yourself how to grow plants in water.

Growing Plants in Water

Materials
- scissors
- plastic food container with lid
- soft, absorbent cloth
- dry plant food
- measuring spoon
- water
- 1-liter bottle
- radish seeds

Procedure

1. Carefully use the scissors to cut a slit in the lid of the food container. Then cut a hole in the lid, large enough to pour water through.

2. Cut a rectangle of cloth that will fit through the slit and touch the bottom of the container when the lid is in place. The cloth should be long enough to allow about 2 cm of it to lie on top of the lid.

3. Push the cut cloth through the slit in the lid, leaving the end of the cloth on top.

4. Follow the instructions on the package of plant food to make 1 L of plant-food solution. Half-fill the container with the solution. Snap the lid closed on the container.

5. Place the seeds on the cloth.

6. Place the container in a sunny window. Add more plant food as necessary to keep the cloth moist.

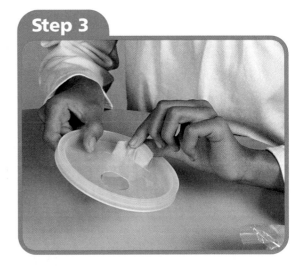

Step 3

Step 4

Draw Conclusions

1. Why do you need to use plant food to grow seeds without soil?

2. **Inquiry Skill** Draw a conclusion about why this method of growing plants would be useful in desert areas.

Investigate Further

Plan and conduct a simple investigation **for growing large plants without soil.**

VOCABULARY
conservation p. 77

SCIENCE CONCEPTS
▶ what conservation is
▶ how people can help in conservation efforts

 **READING FOCUS SKILL**

CAUSE AND EFFECT Look for ways that conservation decreases pollution.

cause ──▶ effect

The Three *R*s: Reduce, Reuse, Recycle

When you leave a room and turn out the lights, you're saving natural resources. When you wash out a cottage cheese container and use it again, you're saving resources. Every time you throw a newspaper in the recycling bin, you're also saving resources. All these actions are examples of conservation.

Reuse

Think twice before you throw out that milk container! Could you use it for another purpose?

Cut 5 minutes off your shower and save 20 gallons.

Reduce

Communities with a shortage of water or energy may require people to use less water or energy.

Recycle

Recycling a ton of newspaper saves 17 trees from being cut down.

Conservation is preserving or protecting natural resources. The actions described in the photos are examples of the three *R*'s—reduce, reuse, and recycle. The three *R*'s are effective ways to conserve natural resources. When you *reduce,* you cut down on the amount of resources used. Appliances such as clothes dryers, water heaters, air conditioners, and lamps use a lot of electricity. When you use appliances less, the need for energy resources such as coal goes down. This also means less pollution caused by burning fuels.

When you *reuse,* you use items again that might have been thrown out. For example, if you reuse plastic food containers, fewer resources are needed to make new containers.

Reusing often means using items for new purposes. For example, you can wash out milk cartons and juice bottles and use them as planters or bird feeders. As a result,

Insta-Lab

Search and Reuse

There may be things in your classroom that you've never thought of reusing. Look around the room, and identify an item you might throw out. Then think of a way the item can be reused. How can reusing the item help the environment?

the cartons and bottles are saved from the landfill and you have items you can use. Sometimes you can't use items anymore. You might give those items, such as toys and clothes you've outgrown, to a resale shop. Then other people can reuse them. Reusing items saves resources, reduces pollution, and saves space in landfills.

When you *recycle,* items are changed into a form that can be used again. Many resources can be conserved by recycling. For example, aluminum, glass, and paper can be ground up or melted down and used to make new glass, aluminum, and paper products. When people recycle, energy is saved, too. And as with reducing and reusing, recycling saves resources and reduces pollution.

 CAUSE AND EFFECT What are some of the effects of reusing items instead of throwing them out?

Math in Science
Interpret Data

For which material could recycling be improved the most?

Recycling Rates for Some Materials

Material (y-axis): Auto Batteries, Steel Cans, Yard Trimmings, Aluminum Cans, Paper and Paperboard, Plastic Drink Containers, Glass Containers, Tires

Percent Recycled (x-axis): 0, 20, 40, 60, 80, 100

Soil Conservation

A necessary resource for growing most crops is soil. How can this resource be protected? Reducing, reusing, and recycling are general ways to conserve resources, but there are some specific methods of soil conservation.

When farmers of long ago cleared fields to plant crops, they pulled out trees and native plants that kept the soil in place. Sometimes wind and water carried away the unprotected soil and left the land unsuitable for farming.

As a result, farmers had to learn ways to protect the soil. Farmers in windy areas use windbreaks. These are rows of trees or fences that stop the wind from carrying away soil. Another method farmers use to keep soil in place is contour plowing. This is the planting of crops along the curves of sloping land, not down the slopes. With this type of plowing, water cannot flow quickly downhill and carry soil with it.

Strip cropping also helps keep soil in place. In strip cropping, farmers plant strips of grass or clover between strips of crops. The thick mat of plants between the crops holds the soil and helps hold water.

◄ **One practice, called intercropping, involves alternating different crops. A tall crop is planted next to a low crop that grows well in the shade.**

Farmers lost millions of acres of soil in the 1930s. Government scientists then taught farmers contour plowing as a way to keep soil in place. ▼

In areas where the land is very steep, farmers use terracing to help conserve soil. They build up the soil to form level places. When terracing is completed, it can look like a series of steps going up a hill. Crops are then planted on the level areas. The result is that the soil is protected from being carried away by water running down the steep slopes.

Crop rotation is another way farmers conserve soil. Crop rotation is the changing of planted crops from year to year. When the same crop is planted year after year, the soil can lose important nutrients, such as nitrogen. These nutrients are often replaced by using chemical fertilizers. But by rotating crops, farmers can build up the soil's nutrients naturally. For example, corn takes nitrogen from the soil. Alfalfa, if grown after the corn, adds nitrogen to the soil. Avoiding chemicals in this way reduces the risk of land and water pollution.

A method called intercropping keeps soil healthy by reducing the need for pesticides. When farmers intercrop, they plant different crops near each other. This keeps some harmful insects from spreading, since many insects eat only one kind of crop.

 CAUSE AND EFFECT What is an effect of contour planting?

Crop rotation helps control pests. The pests die when the plants they eat are not being grown. ▶

Water Conservation

If you're in the middle of a heavy rainstorm, the idea that water needs to be conserved may sound strange. For much of the country, though, fresh water is a precious resource.

The western United States has often been threatened by drought. And the population in many western states is growing. This means more water users. Several years of drought and the growing population have led many people to believe that soon there will not be enough water for everyone.

As a result, governments, farmers, and others have begun to look for ways to conserve water. Some farmers have started growing crops that don't need much water. Others who once sprayed water onto their crops are now using drip irrigation. This method slowly drips water onto the ground. Less water is lost to evaporation.

Homeowners can conserve water by having a Xeriscape (ZIR•uh•skayp) instead of a lawn. Lawns require a huge amount of water, which isn't available in some areas. To conserve water, homeowners can plant native grasses, flowering plants, and shrubs that don't require as much water.

People can learn to conserve water in other ways, too. They can take shorter showers. They can remember not to leave faucets running. What else can you think of that would help conserve water?

 CAUSE AND EFFECT What has caused farmers to use drip irrigation?

Drip irrigation uses hoses with tiny holes that slowly release water.

Landscapes that conserve water can include flowering plants and shrubs as well as native plants. ▼

1. CAUSE AND EFFECT Draw and complete this graphic organizer.

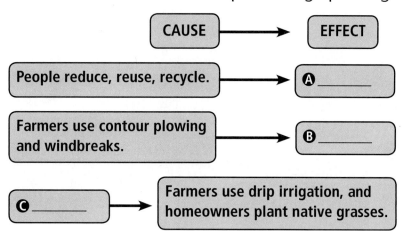

| CAUSE | | EFFECT |

People reduce, reuse, recycle. → **Ⓐ** _____

Farmers use contour plowing and windbreaks. → **Ⓑ** _____

Ⓒ _____ → Farmers use drip irrigation, and homeowners plant native grasses.

2. SUMMARIZE Write three sentences that summarize this lesson.

3. DRAW CONCLUSIONS Which of the three *Rs*—reduce, reuse, recycle— applies to landscapes that conserve water? Explain.

4. VOCABULARY Use the term *conservation* to explain how to save resources at home.

Test Prep

5. Critical Thinking How can a farmer and a factory owner conserve water?

6. Which of the following can conserve energy?
   A. crop rotation
   B. intercropping
   C. drip irrigation
   D. recycling newspaper

Links

Writing

Persuasive Writing
Write a **letter** to local government officials to persuade them to find ways of conserving energy resources.

Math

Display Data
Each day for a week, weigh the trash your class produces. At the end of the week, make a bar graph that shows the weight of the trash by day.

Health

Air Quality
Reducing, reusing, and recycling mean less pollution. Research the health problems caused by air pollution, and find out what you can do to protect yourself from air pollution.

 For more links and activities, go to www.hspscience.com

BUILDING THE FUTURE

What's holding your town together? More than likely it's a whole bunch of concrete. Concrete is the foundation for many buildings, houses, and garages and is used for sidewalks and roads. For many years, concrete has essentially remained the same: a mixture of cement, sand, and rocks.

Concrete can take the shape of any mold it is poured into and can dry to a smooth or rough finish, depending on what the builder needs. To help reinforce concrete, or make it stronger, builders add steel support bars to concrete mix before it dries. Steel-reinforced concrete can support more weight, so builders can construct bigger buildings.

Recently, however, scientists have come up with new formulas that make concrete stronger and more useful than ever.

New Materials

First developed in the early 1800s, modern concrete is made by mixing together cement (a product of limestone rock), water, sand, and gravel.

Modern building designs, however,

unique is that it is strong, even when it is very thin.

Another new type of concrete is translucent concrete, which allows light to come through it. With researchers providing new materials to builders, there's no telling what shapes buildings might take in the future.

New Ideas

Architects, people who design buildings, depend on concrete to make their drawings come to life. Without concrete, a skyscraper or a parking garage couldn't be built. With the new types of concrete, architects can expand their design ideas.

Think About It

1. What natural resources are used in making concrete?
2. Which would be better to use in building a house, concrete or wood? Why?

need new materials. To help make new designs a reality, researchers have developed new versions of concrete. Today, concrete can be flexible, different colors, and *translucent,* or see-through. It is strong enough to support the curves, spirals, and the round shapes given to buildings today.

One new type of concrete contains fibers that reinforce it without having to add steel bars. This new concrete does not chip or crack easily, and it is flexible. Another feature that makes it

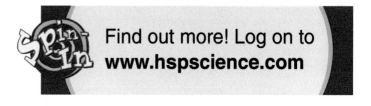

Find out more! Log on to
www.hspscience.com

THE INDIANA JONES OF GARBAGE

After 20 years spent studying garbage William Rathje has gotten used to the smell. He has been studying the garbage at landfills.

Rathje has examined landfills by looking at different layers of garbage, the way an archeologist studies the site of an ancient civilization. (He's even been called the "Indiana Jones of Garbage.")

One important discovery by Rathje is that most garbage is not decomposing but is still the same as when it was thrown away. For example, he has found newspapers that looked as good as the day they were first delivered—in the 1950s!

Rathje wants to remind people that trash does not just disappear. Recycling bottles, cans, and cardboard can help conserve natural resources.

Career   Forest Worker

The forests in the United States are an important natural resource. These woodlands provide recreational areas, as well as wood for building and other uses. Forest workers protect the forests by growing and planting new seedlings, fighting insects and diseases that attack trees, and helping to control soil erosion.

You Can Do It!

Materials
- plastic gloves
- shoe box
- plastic wrap
- tray
- soil
- small pieces of garbage: leaf, aluminum foil, plastic cup, bread, plastic bag, newspaper
- 50 mL of water

Make a Landfill

Procedure

1. **CAUTION: Put on the plastic gloves.** Line the shoe box with plastic wrap, and place the box on the tray.
2. Place a layer of soil in the bottom of the box. Place the pieces of garbage on the soil.
3. Cover the garbage with another layer of soil.
4. Water the model landfill with 50 mL of water.
5. After two weeks, put on the plastic gloves and remove the top layer of soil. Observe the pieces of garbage, and record your observations.

CLEAR FOOD WRAP

Draw Conclusions
Which garbage items were decomposing? What will happen to them over time? What will happen to the other items over time?

Conserving Soil

Collect twigs, rocks, or other materials you think could protect soil on a slope. On an aluminum pan, pack some soil into a hill shape, leaving room for water in the pan. Pour a cup of water down the slope. How much soil is carried away? Drain the water. Then design a system to hold the soil. You can mold the soil or use the materials you collected. Pour another cup of water down the slope. How much soil is carried away this time? Was your design successful?

Review and Test Preparation

Vocabulary Review

Use the terms below to complete the sentences. The page numbers tell you where to look in the chapter if you need help. You will use terms more than once.

renewable resources p. 68
nonrenewable resources p. 69
pollution p. 70
conservation p. 77

1. Resources that can be replaced in a human lifetime are _____.

2. The preserving or protecting of resources is _____.

3. Resources that cannot be replaced in a human lifetime are _____.

4. Waste products that can change the environment are _____.

5. The exhaust that comes out of a car is a form of _____.

6. Sunlight and fresh water are examples of _____.

7. Turning off a light when you leave a room is one way to practice _____.

8. The gasoline used to make a car run comes from _____.

Check Understanding

Write the letter of the best choice.

9. **MAIN IDEA AND DETAILS** Which detail tells how acid rain forms?
   A. Crop rotation causes pollution.
   B. Polluted water reaches the sea.
   C. Chemicals mix with water in the air.
   D. Sewage reaches the water supply.

10. **CAUSE AND EFFECT** What is an effect of a xeriscaped yard?
    F. Soil is preserved.
    G. Lawns are greener.
    H. Water is conserved.
    J. Crops are planted in terraces.

11. Which is an example of recycling?
    A. using less electricity
    B. melting aluminum to make new cans
    C. burying newspaper deep underground
    D. making a scoop from a milk container

12. Look at the picture. Which of the following resources will the person pollute first?
    F. air
    G. land
    H. surface water
    J. groundwater

13. What does the illustration show?

- **A.** the water cycle
- **B.** how water can become polluted
- **C.** how factories can be polluted
- **D.** the problems with landscaping

14. How would you recycle a glass jar?

- **F.** by using it again
- **G.** by not using it at all
- **H.** by melting it and making a new jar
- **J.** by making sure it is used efficiently

15. On which of the following would you be **most** likely to see this symbol?

- **A.** on a banana label
- **B.** on a juice container
- **C.** on a fertilizer spreader
- **D.** on a landscaped plot of ground

16. Which of these practices can homeowners use to conserve water?

- **F.** contour plowing
- **G.** Xeriscape landscaping
- **H.** strip cropping
- **J.** recycling

Inquiry Skills

17. Draw a conclusion about why manufacturing industries may have more problems controlling pollution than other kinds of businesses have.

18. How might you **control variables** in an experiment about landscaping techniques?

Critical Thinking

19. Explain how you can reduce, reuse, and recycle to avoid wasting plastic shopping bags.

20. Suppose you're a farmer who has just bought a farm. The land is in a drought area, and much of it is hilly.
Part A How can you use this land in ways that conserve both soil and water?
Part B How do farmers misuse land?

Bellefontaine
Outlier

OHIO

Columbus

Dayton

Ohio River

Ohio's Highest Point

The last Ice Age ended about 10,000 years ago. It left behind many land features you can see today. A huge glacier began near Hudson Bay. It spread out across Canada and carved out the Great Lakes. The ice was hundreds of feet thick—in places, thousands of feet thick! Ice covered much of North America. You may already know that glaciers caused some landforms in Ohio. There was one place in western Ohio, however, that changed the direction of the glaciers. Campbell Hill, in Logan County, is the highest point in Ohio. It stands about 470 m (1550 ft) above sea level.

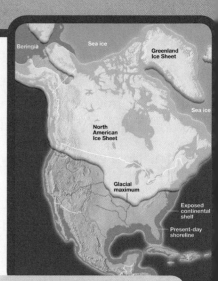

Beringia
Sea ice
Greenland
Ice Sheet
Sea ice
North
American
Ice Sheet
Glacial
maximum
Exposed
continental
shelf
Present-day
shoreline

Glaciers were stopped by the sun as they spread south. Once the ice at the edge of a glacier melts faster than the glacier spreads, the glacier stops advancing.

The Bellefontaine Outlier

How did one hill remain standing while glaciers flattened so much of the rest of the state? Campbell Hill is made of a different kind of rock. The area is called the Bellefontaine Outlier. The rock in this area was not eroded like the rock around it. It formed an "island" of rock and stood about 30 m (100 ft) higher than the nearby land. The front edge of the glacier split into two parts when it reached this rock. The rock was eventually covered with ice. But it remained higher than the rest of the state.

This is the edge of a continental glacier.

What the Glaciers Left Behind

There is almost no place in Ohio that was not changed by glaciers. Even places that were not covered by ice were affected. Melting ice formed many streams. These streams helped produce fertile plains. The waterways the ice formed, including Lake Erie and the Ohio River, are vital to the state. Glaciers also built hills and ridges of gravel and sand.

Ridges of sand and gravel left behind by the glaciers are quarried for construction.

Two-thirds of Ohio is covered by rich soils. These soils built up on top of the wide, flat plains formed by the glaciers. People farm these rich lands. Farm products from Ohio are sold all over the world.

Farm products often leave Ohio on barges. Many raw materials arrive that way, too. Factories and assembly plants in Ohio use the materials to produce steel, cars, appliances, and other products.

People also use the gravel and sand left by the glaciers. They use these materials in construction, such as in building roads. To get to the gravel and sand, people dig into the hillsides and ridges. They then load the gravel and sand into trucks and take these materials to places where they are needed.

Waterways formed by glaciers carry goods from Ohio to the rest of the world.

Think and Do

1. SCIENCE AND TECHNOLOGY All over Ohio, people use technology to quarry, or dig out, sand and gravel. How does that technology influence the quality of life in Ohio? Write a paragraph to explain your ideas.

2. SCIENTIFIC THINKING Sketch a map of Ohio. On the map, show the farthest reach of the most recent glaciers. Then list the ways the glaciers affected the landscape of Ohio, and tell how these effects are important to people in Ohio today.

Coal Cleanup

Wayne National Forest covers about 97,000 hectares (240,000 acres) in southeast Ohio. It is divided into three parts in 12 counties. The forest actually has an area of about 338,000 hectares (834,000 acres). But much of the land is still privately owned. The rolling hills are beautiful. People camp, hike, fish, and picnic there. It is a wonderful place to enjoy nature.

Digging for Riches

Wayne National Forest is the only national forest in Ohio. It was once home to many coal mines, but no one knows how many there were. That's because they are all beneath the ground. These old mines can be dangerous to people, and they can harm the environment. In some places, abandoned coal mines have caved in. People are working to solve the many problems caused by old coal mines.

About 150 years ago, miners began digging shafts into the ground and bringing coal to the surface. Coal from Ohio provided fuel for new industries. It helped make the United States grow. More than 2 billion tons of coal were mined in Ohio.

Wayne National Forest is in the foothills of the Appalachian Mountains. It is beautiful at all times of the year.

Cleanup Isn't Easy

Even though coal brought many benefits to Ohio, coal mines have damaged the environment. Acid seeps into streams from old mines. Some of the streams even have an orange color. Piles of waste block the streams. In places, water that is needed on the surface drains into old mines. All of these things have hurt animals and plants that live near the streams. They can also harm people who live nearby.

In Wayne National Forest, more than 29,000 hectares (72,000 acres) of land was damaged. Cleaning up the damage is a huge task. Teams of scientists, workers, and volunteers try to fix the problems in one area at a time. On the surface, chemical kits are used to test the acid levels in streams. People add lime to the water to try to make it less acidic.

Piles of low-grade coal and other waste from mines are called "gob" piles. Gob piles erode easily. They add harmful chemicals to streams. Earth-moving machines are used to remove the old coal. Then the shape of the land is changed so chemicals no longer run into streams.

"Gob" piles of waste from coal mines are a problem in Wayne National Forest. Runoff from the piles pollutes streams.

Seepage from old mines has turned some streams orange. The water may be so acidic that it kills fish downstream.

Researchers check the quality of the water in streams. They can then add chemicals to improve water that has too much acid.

Think and Do

I. SCIENCE AND TECHNOLOGY Choose one of the problems caused by old coal mines. Find out how scientists are trying to solve the problem. Draw a flowchart to show what caused the problem, what harm it does, and how people are trying to solve the problem.

2. SCIENTIFIC THINKING What signs might tell a scientist that a stream has too much acid in it? Write a paragraph to describe the clues that a person might notice first.

ST-1 Investigate technology impact; **ST-3** Explain how solutions may cause problems; **ES-5** Explain ways to conserve limited resources

91

Salt Mines

Many people are surprised to learn that there is a huge salt mine beneath Lake Erie. Deep below the water, 600 km (400 mi) of roads wind through a city of salt. It is the same kind of salt that you would put on food. However, it has things in it that are not good to eat. So the salt from the Cleveland Salt Mine helps make Ohio's roads safer in the winter. This is where highway crews get the salt that is spread on icy roads.

Salt from an Ancient Ocean

Have you ever heard of the Bonneville Salt Flats in Utah? The salt flats came from an inland sea that dried up. The salt beneath Lake Erie formed in a similar way. Millions of years ago, a shallow ocean covered most of what is now Ohio. Over many years, the water evaporated. The salt was left behind. Some layers are 15 m (50 ft) deep. Over time, the layers of salt were covered by sediment. Eventually, the salt was buried deep beneath the surface.

The salt was first discovered at the end of the 1800s. People were drilling for natural gas when they hit huge deposits of rock salt. In the 1950s, miners dug a shaft about 530 m (1750 ft) into the salt. The shaft starts on an island in Cleveland's harbor. The mine covers 8 sq km (3 sq mi) beneath Lake Erie.

As salt is mined, large rooms are formed deep underground. The roofs are supported by thick pillars of salt.

This is what the salt from the Cleveland Salt Mine looks like when it is mined.

Inside the Cleveland Salt Mine

Today, the Cleveland Salt Mine produces about 2.5 million tons of salt each year. First, machinery digs under a wall of salt. Then, holes are drilled into the salt and explosives are put into the holes. At night, explosions loosen the rock salt. In the morning, the loose salt is scooped up and put on conveyor belts, which move it to an underground mill. At the mill, the salt is broken into smaller pieces. Finally, giant lifts take it to the surface. Each lift is so big that it can carry about 20 tons of salt.

The Cleveland Salt Mine has been operating since the 1950s. It produces nearly 2.5 million tons of salt each year. The salt is used on highways in Ohio and throughout the Midwest.

The mine is a maze of rooms and tunnels. It is never too hot or too cold so far below the ground. Huge fans are used to move fresh air into the mine and the exhaust from machines out of the mine. This keeps the miners safe and comfortable.

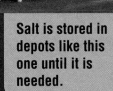

Salt is stored in depots like this one until it is needed.

At the surface, the salt is shipped all over Ohio and piled in storage depots. When snow falls, the salt is loaded onto trucks. The salt trucks roll out and spread salt on the roads. The salt helps melt snow and ice, making winter travel safer.

The next time you see a salt truck at work, think about the mine under Lake Erie. Remember the people who work day and night beneath the lake to get salt to your town. The salt came a long way—from an ancient sea to your local roads.

Salt trucks spread salt whenever snow falls or the roads are icy. The salt melts the snow and ice and makes roads safer.

Think and Do

1. **SCIENCE AND TECHNOLOGY** The Cleveland Salt Mine is deep underground. No sunlight reaches the mine. Wind and rain cannot be felt there. How does the mine use technology to keep the miners safe and comfortable? Write a paragraph to explain your answer.

2. **SCIENTIFIC THINKING** Make a list of the main parts of the Cleveland Salt Mine. Then make a flowchart that shows the whole journey of salt to Ohio's roads. Begin with how rock salt formed at the bottom of an ancient sea. End with salt being spread on the roads after a snowstorm.

Where Did the Salt Come From?

Materials

- beaker or measuring cup
- 100 mL warm water
- $\frac{1}{2}$ cup salt
- spoon or other stirring utensil
- pencil
- string or thread
- paper clip or other weight
- plastic wrap

Procedure

1. Tie the string to the pencil. Tie the weight to the other end of the string.

2. Place the pencil over a beaker of salt water, and let the string and weight hang down into the beaker.

3. Place plastic wrap over the top of the beaker, and set the beaker aside. Observe what happens to the string over the next several days.

Draw Conclusions

1. What happened to the string?

2. How could you use this model to explain the formation of large deposits of salt from seawater? How might the salt become concentrated in one area?

A Look at Water Pollution

Materials
- newspapers
- shallow clear plastic box
- sand
- water
- dropper tube that is open on both ends
- spray bottle
- food coloring and a dropper
- clock

Procedure

1. Spread newspapers over a table top or your desk. Fill the plastic box about halfway with sand. Use a little water to make the sand damp.

2. Push some of the sand into one corner of the box to make a sand hill. Smooth it down to make a low area (a lake bed) in the opposite corner.

3. Pour water into the "lake" until it is about half as high as the sand hill.

4. Push the dropper tube down into the sand hill. Push until the tip is about 1 cm below the surface of the hill. This will be a way to add "pollution," as if from an old coal mine, that is seeping into the water supply.

5. Add a dropper of food coloring to the tube. What happens?

6. Use the spray bottle to make the sand hill damp, as if it is raining. Spray for 2 or 3 minutes.

7. Record the flow of pollution in the sand hill. Use the table below to record what you observe.

What you observe

Model before spraying	
After 15 minutes	
After 30 minutes	
After 1 hour	
After 2 hours	

Draw Conclusions

1. Describe how seepage from an old coal mine could affect a lake far downhill from the mine.

2. Would the lake become more or less polluted if the seepage was on the surface? Explain your answer.

SI-3 Communicate investigation results; **SI-6** Explain experimental variances; **SK-1** Explain how new information changes conclusions

95

UNIT B

Life Sciences

 The Chapters and features in this unit address these Grade Level Indicators from the Ohio Academic Content Standards for Science.

Chapter **3**

Energy and Ecosystems

LS-1   Describe the role of producers in the transfer of energy entering ecosystems as sunlight to chemical energy through photosynthesis.

LS-2   Explain how almost all kinds of animals' food can be traced back to plants.

LS-3   Trace the organization of simple food chains and food webs.

Chapter **4**

Ecosystems and Change

LS-5   Support how an organism's patterns of behavior are related to the nature of that organism's ecosystem, including the kinds and numbers of other organisms present, the availability of food and resources, and the changing physical characteristics of the ecosystem.

LS-6   Analyze how all organisms, including humans, cause changes in their ecosystems and how these changes can be beneficial, neutral or detrimental.

Chapter **5**

World Ecosystems

LS-4   Summarize that organisms can survive only in ecosystems in which their needs can be met. The world has different ecosystems and distinct ecosystems support the lives of different types of organisms.

Unit B Ohio Expeditions

The investigations and experiences in this unit also address many of the Grade Level Indicators for standards in Science and Technology, Scientific Inquiry, and Scientific Ways of Knowing.

OHIO

Columbus

Yellow Springs

Ohio River

TO: rashid@hspscience.com

FROM: traveler@hspscience2.com

RE: EcoCamp at Yellow Springs

Dear Rashid,

Next summer, let's go to EcoCamp at Yellow Springs! The camp is run by the Glen Helen Ecology Center. We'll be with a small group. We'll walk along the Little Miami River where there are waterfalls. We'll see the beautiful mineral springs. We'll also see the Raptor Center, which helps injured birds. Raptors are hunting birds with great eyesight, strong claws, and sharp beaks. They are very important to the ecosystem. Sounds like fun. Hope you can join me there.

Marcus

Living Things Interact

All living things interact with each other and with their physical environment. Human activity can sometimes pollute the physical environment. Living things in the ocean can suffer greatly from pollution. How can visible pollution be removed from water? For example, can certain materials be used to filter polluted water? Plan and conduct an experiment to find out.

Chapter

3 Energy and Ecosystems

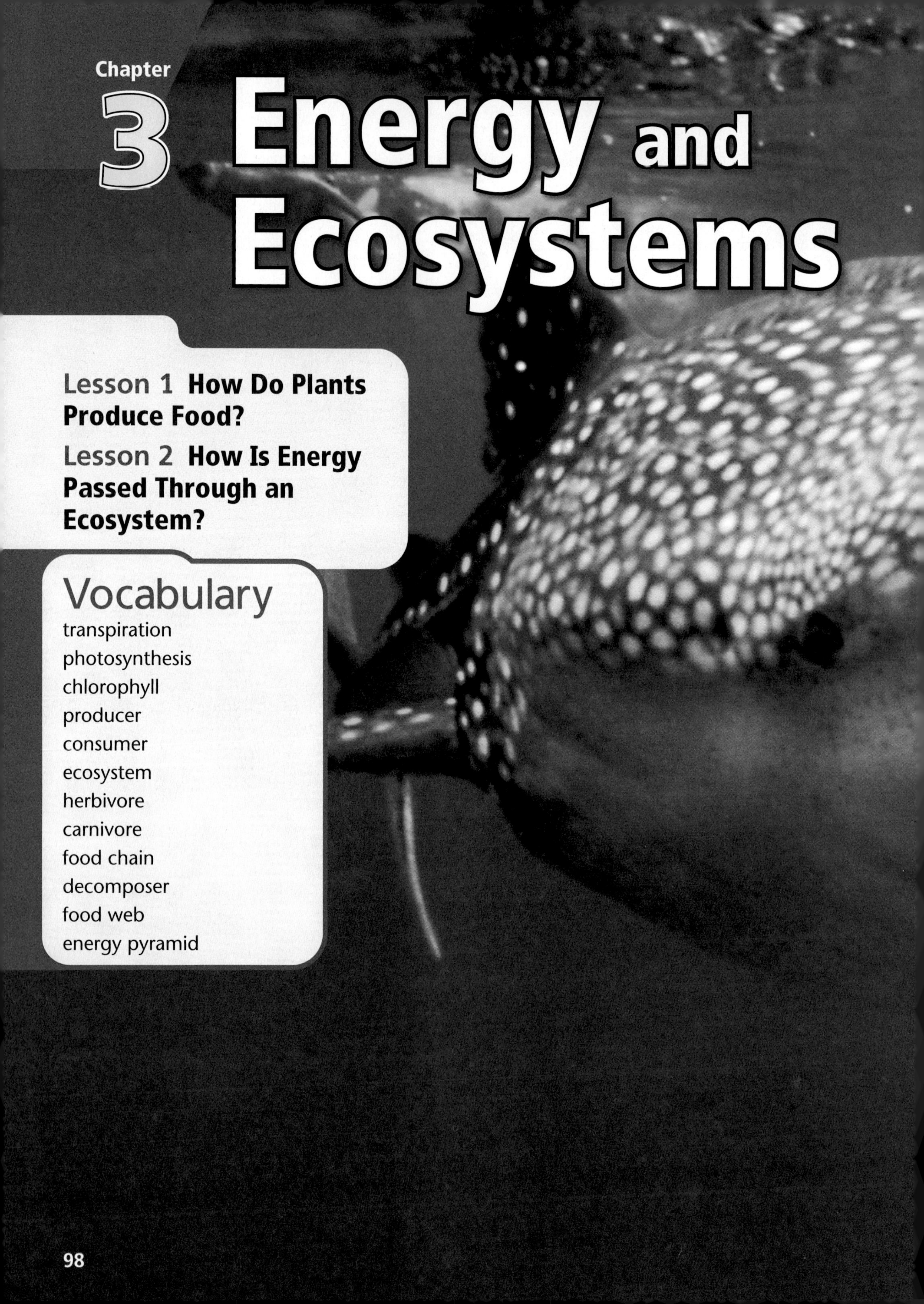

Lesson 1 **How Do Plants Produce Food?**

Lesson 2 **How Is Energy Passed Through an Ecosystem?**

Vocabulary

transpiration
photosynthesis
chlorophyll
producer
consumer
ecosystem
herbivore
carnivore
food chain
decomposer
food web
energy pyramid

What do YOU wonder?

Whale sharks are the largest of all sharks, growing up to 15 m (50 ft) long. They also have the largest mouths, as you can see. What do you think a huge shark like this one eats? Where does it get the energy it needs?

99

How Do Plants Produce Food?

Fast Fact

Working Plants These flowers and trees produce some of the oxygen you breathe. They also take carbon dioxide out of the air. In the Investigate, you will observe that a plant takes in carbon dioxide.

Using Carbon Dioxide

Materials
- safety goggles
- 2 plastic cups
- water
- dropper
- bromothymol blue (BTB)
- 2 test tubes with caps
- *Elodea*
- funnel
- plastic straw

Procedure

1. **CAUTION: Wear safety goggles.** Fill one cup about two-thirds full of water. Use the dropper to add BTB until the water is blue.

2. Put the straw into the cup, and blow into it. **CAUTION: DO NOT suck on the straw. If the solution gets in your mouth, spit it out and rinse your mouth with water.**

3. Observe and record changes in the water.

4. Put the *Elodea* in one test tube. Use the funnel to fill both test tubes with the BTB solution. Cap both tubes.

5. Turn the tubes upside down, and put them in the empty cup. Place the cup on a sunny windowsill. Predict what changes will occur in the test tubes.

6. After 1 hour, observe both tubes and record your observations.

Step 2

Step 5

Draw Conclusions

1. What changes did you observe in the BTB solution during the activity?

2. **Inquiry Skill** Scientists use what they know to predict what will happen. After you blew into the water, how did your observations help you predict what would happen next?

Investigate Further

Plan and conduct an experiment to test the effect of sunlight on the changes in the BTB solution. Predict what will happen. Then carry out your experiment.

Reading in Science

VOCABULARY
transpiration p. 103
photosynthesis p. 104
chlorophyll p. 104
producer p. 106
consumer p. 106

SCIENCE CONCEPTS
▶ how leaves use carbon dioxide and give off oxygen
▶ how the parts of plants make food by means of photosynthesis

READING FOCUS SKILL

MAIN IDEA AND DETAILS Look for details about how plants make and store food.

```
        Main Idea
      /     |     \
 detail   detail   detail
```

Plant Structures

You are probably familiar with the basic parts of plants. These parts include roots, stems, and leaves. Some of those parts produce food for the plant.

Roots Roots have two main jobs. They anchor plants, and they take in water and nutrients. Tubes in the roots carry water to the stems. The roots of some plants, such as carrots, also store food.

Different plants have different types of roots. For example, the roots of desert plants spread out just below the surface to catch any rain that falls. Some plants, like the dandelion, have one main root to reach water deep underground.

Stems Stems support a plant and enable its leaves to reach the sunlight. Stems also contain tubes that carry water and nutrients to the leaves. Other tubes carry food to all parts of the plant. The stems of some plants, such as sugar cane, store food.

Just as plants have different roots, they also have different stems. Small plants tend to have flexible, green stems. Most of these plants live for just one year. Larger plants and

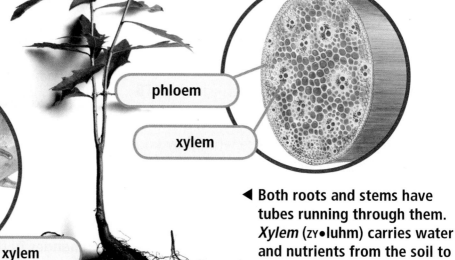

phloem

xylem

xylem

phloem

◀ Both roots and stems have tubes running through them. *Xylem* (ZY•luhm) carries water and nutrients from the soil to the leaves. *Phloem* (FLOH•em) carries food from the leaves to other parts of the plant.

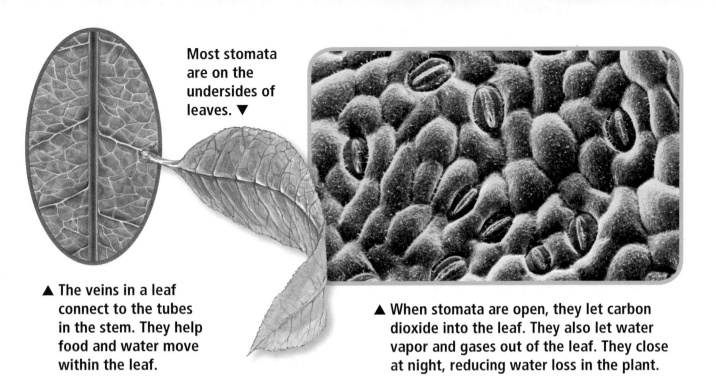

Most stomata are on the undersides of leaves. ▼

▲ The veins in a leaf connect to the tubes in the stem. They help food and water move within the leaf.

▲ When stomata are open, they let carbon dioxide into the leaf. They also let water vapor and gases out of the leaf. They close at night, reducing water loss in the plant.

trees need more support. They usually have stiff, woody stems, and live for many years.

Leaves Leaves have one main job—to make food for the plant. A leaf can be as small as the head of a pin, or it can be wide enough to support a frog on the surface of a pond. Some leaves are very specialized. The leaves of the Venus' flytrap are able to catch food for the plant. They snap shut when an insect lands on them. Then the leaves help digest the insect.

Most leaves are thin and have several layers of cells. The outer layer, called the *epidermis* (ep•uh•DER•mis), keeps the leaf from drying out. The upper epidermis is often covered with a layer of wax. This helps keep water in. The lower epidermis has many small openings called *stomata*.

Stomata usually open during the day so the leaf can take in carbon dioxide to make food. Stomata close at night to keep the plant from drying out. The loss of water through leaves is called **transpiration**.

Just below the upper epidermis is a closely packed layer of cells in which most

of the food is made. Just above the lower epidermis is a spongy layer of cells. Air spaces among these cells contain carbon dioxide, oxygen, and water vapor.

Veins, which connect to the tubes in the stems, are found in the center of most leaves. In broad leaves, the veins have many branches. They bring the water needed to make food to cells throughout the leaf.

 MAIN IDEA AND DETAILS What is the main job of each plant part?

Insta-Lab

Moving Out
Partially break five toothpicks, leaving the halves connected. Arrange them in a grouping, as shown. Wet the center of the grouping with several drops of water. How does this activity show the way water moves through plants?

Photosynthesis

Plants make food in a process that uses water from the soil, carbon dioxide from the air, and energy from sunlight. This process, called **photosynthesis**, produces food for the plant and releases oxygen into the air.

Recall that plant cells contain organelles called chloroplasts. Cells with chloroplasts are found in the inner layers of leaves on most plants. Only cells with chloroplasts can make food.

Chloroplasts contain a green pigment, or coloring matter, called chlorophyll (KLAWR•uh•fil). **Chlorophyll** enables a plant to absorb light energy so that it can produce food. It also makes plants green. Plants contain small amounts of other pigments as well. In autumn, many plants stop producing chlorophyll, so you can see the other pigments. This is what makes some leaves change color in autumn.

Photosynthesis begins when sunlight hits the chloroplasts. The energy absorbed by the chlorophyll causes water and carbon dioxide to combine to form sugar—the food that plants need to live and grow.

Oxygen is produced as a byproduct of photosynthesis. It is released into the air through the stomata. About 90 percent of the oxygen you breathe is produced during photosynthesis by plants and plantlike protists. Plants also help you by taking carbon dioxide, which your body does not need, out of the air.

 MAIN IDEA AND DETAILS What does a plant need for photosynthesis?

Science Up Close

Photosynthesis

Sunlight provides energy for plants to make food.

Plants take in carbon dioxide from the air.

After making food, the leaves release oxygen through their stomata.

Chlorophyll absorbs energy from sunlight. The plant needs this energy, along with carbon dioxide and water, to make food.

The food made by the plant is stored in the plant's leaves, stems, seeds, and—in some plants—roots.

Plant roots take in water, which is necessary for photosynthesis.

For more links and activities, go to www.hspscience.com

It All Starts with Plants

All organisms need energy to live and grow. That energy comes from food. Plants are called **producers** because they produce, or make, their own food. Animals can't make their own food, but they need energy from food to survive. When animals eat plants, the animals receive the energy that's stored in those plants. The word *consume* means "to eat," so we call animals that eat plants or other animals **consumers**.

You are a consumer. For example, when you eat a salad, you take in the energy stored in the lettuce leaves and carrot roots. When you eat strawberries, you get the energy that was stored in the fruit and seeds of the strawberry plants.

In fact, you and every animal on Earth depend on plants. Even animals that eat only other animals depend on plants. Without plants, animals such as deer and rabbits, which eat only plants, would starve. Then animals such as wolves, which eat deer and rabbits, would have nothing to eat. They, too, would starve.

The energy from sunlight moves from plants, to animals that eat plants, to animals that eat other animals. Without sunlight, every living thing on Earth would die.

 MAIN IDEA AND DETAILS Define the terms *producer* and *consumer*.

These bison get the energy they need by eating grasses. Without plants, the bison couldn't survive.

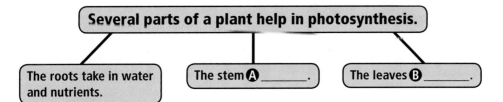

 1. MAIN IDEA AND DETAILS Draw and complete the graphic organizer.

> **Several parts of a plant help in photosynthesis.**
>
> - The roots take in water and nutrients.
> - The stem **A** _____ .
> - The leaves **B** _____ .

2. SUMMARIZE Write two sentences that explain what this lesson is about.

3. DRAW CONCLUSIONS What would happen if all plants had the same kind of roots?

4. VOCABULARY Make a crossword puzzle, including clues, using this lesson's vocabulary terms. Then exchange puzzles with a partner, and solve his or her puzzle.

Test Prep

5. Critical Thinking How would Earth's atmosphere change if plants stopped carrying out photosynthesis?

6. Which gas do plants need for photosynthesis?
  A. carbon dioxide
  B. carbon monoxide
  C. nitrogen
  D. oxygen

Links

Writing

Narrative Writing

Write a **myth** that "explains" a concept in this lesson, such as why plants have roots, why some leaves change color in the fall, or why animals depend on plants. Illustrate your story.

Math

Make a Table

Suppose you want to conduct a two-week experiment to see how different amounts of sunlight affect five sunflower seedlings. Make a table that you could use to record your results.

Language Arts

Word Meanings

Identify the parts of the word *photosynthesis*. Explain how the parts' meanings relate to the fact that plants make their own food. Then list at least three other words that have one of the word parts found in *photosynthesis*.

 For more links and activities, go to www.hspscience.com

How Is Energy Passed Through an Ecosystem?

Fast Fact

Bear Chow Bears eat just about anything. A bear weighing 91 kg (200 lb) can eat more than 13 kg (29 lb) of salmon in one day. Or it might eat nearly 32 kg (70 lb) of berries or apples. In the Investigate, you will classify and order organisms that eat one another.

Ordering What Eats What

Materials
- index cards
- markers
- pushpins
- bulletin board
- yarn

Procedure

1 You will be assigned an organism. On an index card, draw it, write its name, or do both.

2 Do some research to classify your organism. Is it a producer, a plant-eating consumer, or a meat-eating consumer? Is it a consumer that eats both plants and meat? Or is it an organism that gets its energy from the remains of dead organisms?

3 Work with members of your group to put your cards in an order that shows what eats what.

4 Pin your team's cards in order on the bulletin board. Connect your cards with yarn to show what eats what. Then use yarn to show which of your team's organisms eat organisms from other teams.

Draw Conclusions

1. Classify each organism on your group's cards. In which group does each belong?

2. **Inquiry Skill** When scientists order things, they better understand relationships between them. Could you put your team's cards in another order? Why or why not? Which card must always be first? Which card must always be last?

Step 1

Step 4

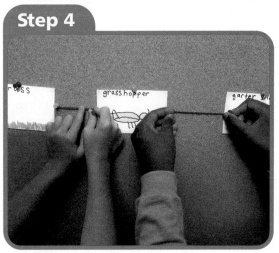

Investigate Further

Draw the order of organisms that eat one another in the ocean. Share your drawing with the class.

Reading in Science

VOCABULARY
ecosystem p. 110
herbivore p. 110
carnivore p. 110
food chain p. 111
decomposer p. 111
food web p. 112
energy pyramid p. 115

SCIENCE CONCEPTS
▶ how food energy is passed from plant to animal to animal in an ecosystem
▶ how food chains make up food webs

READING FOCUS SKILL
SEQUENCE Look for the order of events in the transfer of energy.

Energy Transfer

You read that plants make their own food through the process of photosynthesis. So do a few other organisms, such as algae and lichens (LY•kinz). Plants are the main producers in most land ecosystems.

An **ecosystem** (EE•koh•sis•tuhm) includes all the organisms in an area and the environment in which they live. All the organisms shown in the photos on these two pages are part of a tundra ecosystem. An ecosystem includes many kinds of organisms. Each organism has its own *niche*, or role in an ecosystem.

Some tundra animals, like caribou, eat plants and other producers. The food energy stored in the reindeer moss is transferred to the caribou. An animal that eats plants or other producers is an **herbivore**. Herbivores are also called first-level consumers.

Other tundra animals, such as wolves, don't eat plants. They get their energy by eating other animals, like caribou. Food energy stored in the caribou is transferred to the wolf. An animal that eats mainly other animals is a **carnivore**. Carnivores are also called second-level consumers.

Reindeer moss, a lichen, makes food by photosynthesis. The food energy is stored in the organism.

The caribou gets its energy by eating reindeer moss.

Some animals, called *omnivores,* eat both plants and other animals. Omnivores can be first-level or second-level consumers. The bear shown on the first page of the chapter is an omnivore. So are most people.

In another ecosystem, a large carnivore, such as a hawk, might eat a smaller carnivore, such as a snake. That makes the hawk a third-level consumer. Each time something eats something else, food energy is transferred from one organism to the next. The transfer of food energy between organisms is called a **food chain**.

When plants and animals die, what happens to the food energy stored in their remains? The remains are broken down and the food energy is used by decomposers. A **decomposer** is a consumer that gets its food energy by breaking down the remains of dead organisms. Decomposers can be animals, such as earthworms. Many decomposers are fungi. Others are single-celled organisms—protists or bacteria.

Decomposers use some of the nutrients as food. The rest become mixed into the soil. Then plant roots can take up these nutrients. In this way, decomposers connect both ends of a food chain.

You know that all the organisms in an ecosystem depend on producers to make food. Then food energy is transferred through the ecosystem from one consumer level to another. All along the way, decomposers get energy from the remains of dead organisms. Any nutrients not used are returned to the soil.

 SEQUENCE **What can happen next to food energy taken in by a second-level consumer?**

The wolf gets the energy it needs by eating caribou.

When the moss, caribou, and wolf die, decomposers break down their remains. Then the reindeer moss and other producers can take up any remaining nutrients.

Food Webs

You know that most animals eat more than one kind of food. For example, a hawk might eat a mouse that ate seeds. The same hawk might also eat a small snake that ate grasshoppers and other insects. The insects, in turn, might have eaten grass. An organism, such as the hawk, can be a part of several food chains. In this way, food chains overlap. A **food web** shows the relationships among different food chains.

Carnivores eat herbivores, omnivores, and sometimes other carnivores. Carnivores also

Prairie Food Web

The producers in this prairie ecosystem include grasses, clover, and purple coneflowers. First-level consumers, or herbivores, include insects, mice, ground squirrels, and bison. Second-level and third-level consumers—carnivores— include spiders, snakes, and hawks. The decomposers that you can see are mushrooms. What you can't see are the millions of single-celled decomposers. They are in the soil, helping recycle nutrients.

Pond Food Web

In this pond ecosystem, the producers include water plants and algae. Here the first-level consumers, or herbivores, include insects and tadpoles. Second-level and third-level consumers include fish. Some of the birds, such as ducks, are herbivores, while others are carnivores. The turtle is an omnivore, eating insects, tiny fish, and plants. The water is full of decomposers, such as snails, worms, and single-celled protists.

limit the number of animals below them in a food web. For example, without snakes, the number of mice in the prairie ecosystem would keep increasing. In time, the mice would eat all the available food. Then the mice would starve, and so would hawks, which eat mice.

Organisms in an ecosystem depend on one another for survival. A change in the number of one kind of organism can affect the entire ecosystem!

SEQUENCE If all the mosquitoes in a pond died, what might happen next?

Energy Pyramid

Not all the food energy of plants is passed on to the herbivores that eat them. Producers use about 90 percent of the food energy they produce for their own life processes. They store the other 10 percent in their leaves, stems, roots, fruits, and seeds.

Animals that eat the producers get only 10 percent of the energy the producers made. These herbivores then use for their life processes 90 percent of the energy they got from the producers. They store the other 10 percent in their bodies.

The owl is a third-level consumer. It takes a lot of grass, locusts, and snakes to provide the owl with the energy it needs.

Owl

The snakes are second-level consumers. They pass on to the owl only 10 percent of the energy they receive from the locusts.

Snakes

Math in Science
Interpret Data

Suppose the grasses at the base of this energy pyramid produce 100,000 kilocalories of energy. How many kilocalories would be passed to each of the other levels?

The locusts are first-level consumers. They pass on to the snakes only 10 percent of the energy they receive from the grasses.

Locusts

The grasses are producers. They pass on to the locusts only 10 percent of the energy they produce.

Grasses

An **energy pyramid** shows that each level of a food chain passes on less food energy than the level before it. Most of the energy in each level is used at that level. Only a little energy is passed on to the next level.

Because each level passes so little energy to the next, the first-level consumers need many producers to support them. In the same way, the second-level consumers need many first-level consumers to support them. This pattern continues up to the top of the food chain.

That's why the base of an energy pyramid is so wide. That's also why only one or two animals are at the top of the pyramid.

Most food chains have only three or four levels. If there were more, a huge number of producers would be needed at the base of the pyramid! Sometimes, things in the environment may cause the number of organisms at one level of the pyramid to change. Then the whole food chain is affected. Suppose a drought kills most of the grasses in an area. Then some of the first-level consumers will starve. Many second-level and third-level consumers will go hungry, too.

Suppose people cut down a forest to provide space for houses. The second-level and third-level consumers may not be able to find enough small animals to eat, so they may leave that ecosystem. With fewer carnivores to eat them, the number of small animals will increase over time. If there isn't enough food for their larger numbers, many will starve.

When a change in numbers occurs at any level of a food chain, the entire chain will be affected.

 SEQUENCE What can happen to a food chain if the number of second-level consumers increases?

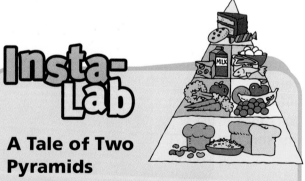

A Tale of Two Pyramids

Compare the energy pyramid with this pyramid that was once used to classify foods. How are they alike? How are they different? Who are the consumers at each level of the food pyramid?

Natural Cycles

Most ecosystems depend on the water cycle to provide plants with the water they need for photosynthesis. Other cycles affect ecosystems, too.

For example, nitrogen also has a cycle. Nitrogen compounds are important for all living organisms. Nitrogen is a gas that makes up most of Earth's atmosphere. Before nitrogen gas can be used as a nutrient, it must be changed to a form that plants can take up through their roots.

Some nitrogen is changed, or fixed, by lightning. Lightning burns air, producing nitrogen-rich compounds that dissolve in rain. Plant roots can absorb these compounds. Bacteria found in some plant roots also change nitrogen gas into compounds that plants can use.

When a plant or animal dies and decays, nitrogen returns to the soil. Animal wastes also contain nitrogen. Decomposers change these wastes and the remains of organisms into the nitrogen compounds plants need.

Carbon and oxygen also have a cycle. You learned that plants use carbon dioxide to make food and that they release oxygen as a byproduct. Plants and animals use this oxygen and release more carbon dioxide.

Carbon is stored in organisms, too. Burning wood, coal, and natural gas releases carbon dioxide into the air.

 SEQUENCE What part do decomposers play in the nitrogen cycle?

Plants use nitrogen compounds to grow.

A small amount of nitrogen is "fixed" by lightning.

Animals eat plants that contain nitrogen compounds.

Animal wastes and decaying matter release nitrogen back into the soil.

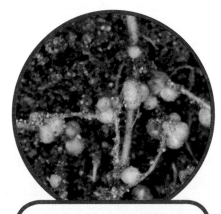

Bacteria in nodules (NAH•joolz), or lumps, on some plant roots change nitrogen into a form plants can use.

1. SEQUENCE Draw and complete this graphic organizer. Put the organisms in an order that forms a food chain, ending with a decomposer.

bear	**grass**	**grasshopper**	**mushroom**	**salmon**

(A) _____ → (B) _____ → (C) _____ → (D) _____ → (E) _____

2. SUMMARIZE Write a summary of this lesson, beginning with this sentence: *Energy moves through an ecosystem.*

3. DRAW CONCLUSIONS What is your role in a food chain or a food web? Explain your answer.

4. VOCABULARY Write a sentence for each of this lesson's vocabulary terms. Leave a blank space in each sentence for the term. Have a partner fill in the correct terms.

Test Prep

5. Critical Thinking What is your favorite food? What level of consumer are you for that food?

6. Which of these is **not** essential in a food chain?

   A. decomposer
   B. first-level consumer
   C. producer
   D. second-level consumer

Links

Writing

Expository Writing
Imagine that you have discovered an animal that was thought to be extinct. Write a **paragraph** that describes the animal and explains how it fits into a food web in its ecosystem.

Math

Solve a Problem
An eagle ate 2 fish and received 20 kilocalories of energy. The fish had eaten many insects. How many kilocalories were produced by the plants that the insects ate?

Social Studies

Food Choices
In some parts of the world, meat protein is scarce. Find out what kinds of insects some people eat to add protein to their diets. Present a report to share what you learn.

For more links and activities, go to www.hspscience.com

Trash Man

Chad Pregracke grew up on the banks of the Mississippi River. He spent summers fishing, sailing, water-skiing, and canoeing. When Pregracke was 15, he started working with his brother, a commercial shell diver.

Like a modern-day Tom Sawyer and Huck Finn, the brothers spent their nights camping on river islands and their days combing the pitch-black river bottom for clamshells.

During their travels, Pregracke noticed that the riverbanks were lined with trash. "We're talking refrigerators, barrels, tires. There was this one pile of 50 or 60 barrels that had been there for [more than] 20 years. ... I saw there was a problem, basically in my backyard. And I wanted to do something about it," explained Pregracke.

Taking Action

In addition to collecting clamshells, Pregracke started picking up garbage. He

also wrote letters to local companies requesting donations to launch a river cleanup. When he started in 1997, Pregracke single-handedly cleaned 160 kilometers (100 miles) of the Mississippi River shoreline with community donations and a grant from a local corporation.

Since then, Pregracke's project has grown. He now has a ten-person crew, a fleet of barges and boats, and thousands of volunteers to help keep the Mississippi and other rivers in the United States clean. "There's been a lot of accomplishments, and I've had a lot of help," said Pregracke. "But I feel like I'm just getting started."

Phantom Garbage

Although Pregracke has hauled tons of garbage from the Mississippi, the river is still polluted by a type of waste that can't be picked up with a forklift: runoff.

Rainwater either soaks into the ground or flows over Earth's surface as runoff. Runoff transports ground pollution to rivers, oceans, lakes, and wetlands. Many of the pollutants in runoff come from oil, antifreeze, and gasoline leaked by automobiles; pesticides sprayed on lawns; and fertilizers spread on fields. Other water pollutants include heavy metals, such as iron, copper, zinc, tin, and lead; oil from spills; and sewage.

Water pollution can cause human health problems and harm aquatic ecosystems.

An ecosystem is a community of living things and its environment.

Think About It
1. How might runoff pollution affect your drinking water?
2. What can you do to help keep rivers clean?

Did You Know?

• The majority of Americans live within 10 miles of a polluted body of water.

• Water pollution has caused fishing and swimming to be prohibited in 40 percent of the nation's rivers, lakes, and coastal waters.

• Your own daily habits can help reduce water pollution. For more information, visit the U.S. Environmental Protection Agency's water website for kids.

Find out more! Log on to
www.hspscience.com

Looking for Trouble

Most people think of marine biologists as swimming in the open ocean, studying whales or sharks. Fu Lin Chu is a marine biologist, but the animals she studies are usually a lot smaller than a whale and can be found in the creeks and shallow areas of the Chesapeake Bay, on the east coast of the United States.

Chu works at the Virginia Institute of Marine Science. She spends most of her time studying shellfish and how they are affected by their environment. This is especially important research in the Chesapeake Bay region, where oysters, a type of shellfish, are in trouble because of pollution and overfishing.

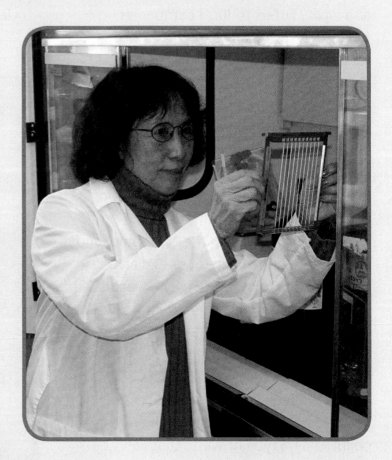

Career Lab Technician

When water samples from field research are sent to the laboratory, they are not just thrown under a microscope and analyzed. Samples have to be catalogued, prepared, and tested. Lab technicians usually are given specific instructions by scientists about how to test or analyze a sample.

Quick and Easy Project

Materials
- clover plant
- trowel
- outside faucet or hose

Clover's Secret

Procedure

1. Find in a field a clover plant at least 15 cm (6 in.) tall. Get permission to dig it up.
2. Use the trowel to dig up the soil around the plant. Then carefully lift the roots out of the soil.
3. Gently shake the loose soil off the roots. Then use water to rinse off the rest of the soil.
4. Look for light-colored lumps on the roots. These lumps are nodules. They contain bacteria that change nitrogen gas from the air into nitrogen compounds that plants can use.

Draw Conclusions

How does nitrogen gas reach the nodules? Are the bacteria in the nodules helpful or harmful? Explain. How do the nodules affect any plants growing around the clover plant?

Design Your Own Investigation

Sweaty Leaves

You read in Lesson 1 that plant leaves can lose water vapor through their stomata. How could you use a green plant and a plastic bag to show that this happens? Design an experiment. Write down the steps you will use to carry it out. Then do your experiment. Be sure to get permission before using someone else's plant. After observing what happens and recording your findings, draw some conclusions about your results.

3 Review and Test Preparation

Vocabulary Review

Use the terms below to complete the sentences. The page numbers tell you where to look in the chapter if you need help.

producers p. 106   **decomposers** p. 111
herbivores p. 110   **food web** p. 112
food chain p. 111   **energy pyramid** p. 115

1. To survive, all consumers rely on _____.

2. Nutrients are returned to the soil by _____.

3. Animals that eat producers are _____.

4. Grass-insect-songbird-hawk is an example of a _____.

5. The fact that each level of a food chain passes on less food energy than the level before it is shown in an _____.

6. The relationship among different food chains in an ecosystem is a _____.

Check Understanding

Write the letter of the best choice.

7. Which of the following is the process in which stomata release water from a leaf?
   A. chlorophyll
   B. photosynthesis
   C. respiration
   D. transpiration

8. Which of the following is the substance that enables a leaf to use sunlight to produce food?
   F. chlorophyll
   G. photosynthesis
   H. respiration
   J. transpiration

9. How much energy is passed from each level of an energy pyramid to the next?
   A. 10 percent
   B. 20 percent
   C. 80 percent
   D. 90 percent

10. **SEQUENCE** To which group do herbivores pass their energy?
    F. first-level consumers
    G. plants
    H. producers
    J. second-level consumers

11. **MAIN IDEA AND DETAILS** What is the source of all food energy on Earth?
    A. decomposers
    B. herbivores
    C. producers
    D. carnivores

12. Which process produces most of the oxygen in Earth's atmosphere?
    F. burning
    G. photosynthesis
    H. respiration
    J. transpiration

13. Which of these is **not** a consumer?

   A. caribou   **C.** owl

   B. mouse   **D.** reindeer moss

14. The relationships between organisms in an ecosystem can be shown in many ways. Which way is shown here?

   F. energy pyramid

   G. food chain

   H. food pyramid

   J. food web

15. Which gas does photosynthesis produce?

   A. ammonia

   B. carbon dioxide

   C. nitrogen

   D. oxygen

16. Which of the following must plants have for photosynthesis?

   F. soil   **H.** warmth

   G. stems   **J.** water

Inquiry Skills

17. Which three of the organisms below should be **classified** in the same group? Explain your answer.

18. Kendra will perform an experiment in which she cuts the stem of a sunflower and then puts the stem into the soil. **Predict** what will happen, and explain why.

Critical Thinking

19. Not all producers are plants. Some protists are also producers. How can you tell by looking at a protist whether it is a producer?

20. The diagram shows a sequence involving four organisms.

grass → grasshopper → snake → hawk

   Part A What does the direction of the arrows tell you?

   Part B If this were part of a food web, would more arrows point toward the second-level consumer or away from the second-level consumer? Explain.

Chapter 4

Ecosystems and Change

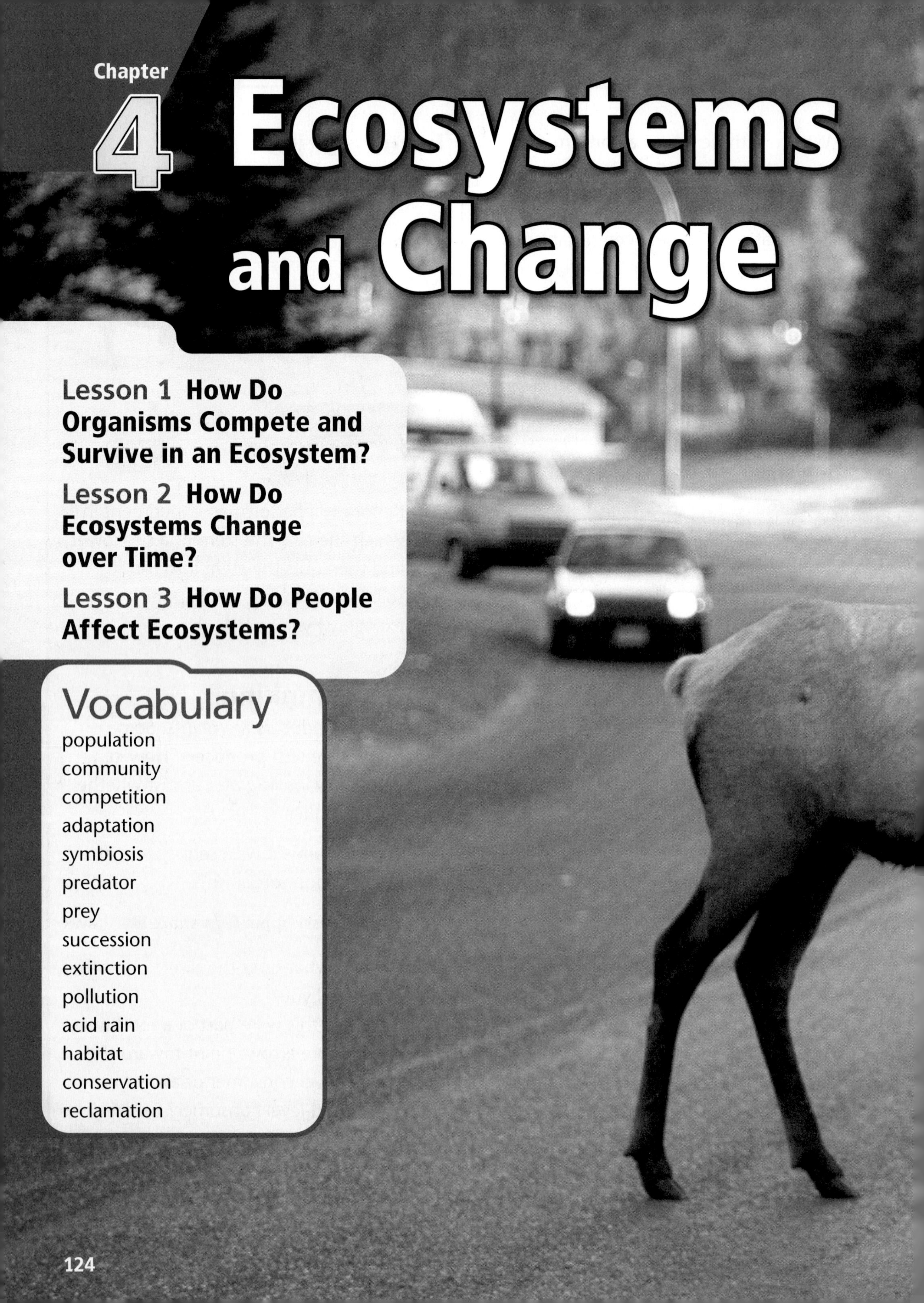

Lesson 1 **How Do Organisms Compete and Survive in an Ecosystem?**

Lesson 2 **How Do Ecosystems Change over Time?**

Lesson 3 **How Do People Affect Ecosystems?**

Vocabulary

population
community
competition
adaptation
symbiosis
predator
prey
succession
extinction
pollution
acid rain
habitat
conservation
reclamation

What do YOU wonder?

Many animals share their ecosystems with people. Here an elk is searching for food and water in a neighborhood. How might the neighborhood—a dramatic change in the natural ecosystem of elk— affect the survival of these animals?

How Do Organisms Compete and Survive in an Ecosystem?

Fast Fact

That's Fast! This chameleon's tongue shoots out at about 22 km/hr (14 mi/hr)! This enables the chameleon to catch fast-moving insects. It can even zap insects more than one and a half body lengths away. In the Investigate, you'll find out how some insects avoid being captured, even by chameleons.

Using Color to Hide

Materials
- hole punch
- red, blue, green, and yellow sheets of acetate
- large green cloth
- clock or watch with a second hand

Procedure

1. Make a table like the one shown.

2. Using the hole punch, make 50 small "insects" from each color of acetate.

3. Predict which color would be the easiest and which would be the hardest for a bird to find in grass. Record your predictions.

4. Spread the green cloth on the floor, and randomly scatter the insects over it.

5. At the edge of the cloth, kneel with your group. In 15 seconds, each of you should pick up as many insects as you can, one at a time.

6. Count the number of each color your group collected. Record the data in the table.

7. Repeat Steps 5 and 6 three more times. Then total each column.

Step 2

Number of Insects Found				
	Red	Blue	Green	Yellow
Hunt 1				
Hunt 2				
Hunt 3				
Hunt 4				
Total				

Draw Conclusions

1. Which color did you predict would be easiest to find? Which color was collected most often? Least often? Why?

2. **Inquiry Skill** Scientists predict what they expect to happen and then observe what happens. Predict what might happen to green insects if the grass turns brown.

Investigate Further

Predict how different body shapes might help insects hide in grass. Then plan an investigation to test your prediction.

VOCABULARY
population p. 128
community p. 128
competition p. 129
adaptation p. 129
symbiosis p. 130
predator p. 132
prey p. 132

SCIENCE CONCEPTS
▶ how populations depend on and compete with one another
▶ how adaptations help plants and animals compete

READING FOCUS SKILL
MAIN IDEA AND DETAILS Look for details about how organisms interact.

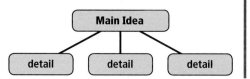

Interactions in Nature

In the last chapter, you learned about different kinds of ecosystems. You also learned that ecosystems include many kinds of plants and animals. All the organisms of one kind in an ecosystem are called a **population**. For example, a pond ecosystem might have populations of frogs, waterlilies, insects, duckweed, and protists.

Populations living and interacting with each other form a **community**. Each population in a community has a niche. For example, in a pond community, some insects eat plants. Then frogs eat insects.

Another part of an ecosystem is the physical environment, which includes the sun, air, and water. The soil and climate are also part of the environment. Populations interact with the environment. Plants grow in sunlight and take water and nutrients from soil. Fish and frogs live in water that birds and other animals drink.

To survive, each population needs a certain amount of food, water, shelter, and space. The challenge of meeting these

As this water hole dries up, many organisms compete for water.

Competition can take many forms. These moray eels compete for shelter in a coral reef.

Counting the Survivors

This graph shows the average number of young produced and the number that survive the first year. What can you say about survival rates compared to the numbers of young produced?

Survivors

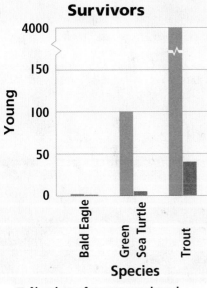

(Bar graph showing Young on the vertical axis with values 0, 50, 100, 150, 4000 and Species on the horizontal axis: Bald Eagle, Green Sea Turtle, Trout)

- ■ Number of young produced
- ■ Number of young that survive the first year

After sea horses hatch, they are on their own. Many starve or are eaten by other fish. Sea horses have as many as 1000 young, which helps increase their chances of survival.

Some animals have few young but take care of them after birth. This care helps the young survive.

needs leads to **competition**, a contest among populations with the same niche.

Populations often compete for the same sources of food. For example, alligators and snapping turtles both eat fish. When there isn't much food, individuals of the same population compete with each other.

In winter, deer compete with each other for food.

Too little food leads to increased competition. Increased competition limits the number of organisms that can share an ecosystem. For this reason, food is a *limiting factor*. It limits the size of a population.

To survive and compete in an ecosystem, animals have developed many kinds of adaptations. An **adaptation** is a characteristic that helps an organism compete in an ecosystem. A turtle survives the winter by burrowing into the mud. A tiger's coloring enables it to sneak up on prey. Some plants smell so bad that animals won't eat them. All of these characteristics are adaptations.

MAIN IDEA AND DETAILS What do organisms compete for in an ecosystem?

129

Mistletoe sends its roots into the tree on which it grows. It takes nutrients from the tree. The mistletoe benefits, but the tree is harmed.

▲ The barnacles on this humpback whale eat scraps the whale misses. The barnacles benefit, but the whale is not affected.

Symbiosis

Populations don't always compete with each other. Sometimes a relationship between organisms helps each of them meet basic needs. A relationship between different kinds of organisms is called **symbiosis** (sim•by•OH•sis).

There are three kinds of symbiosis. In the first kind, both organisms benefit. For example, some ants take care of tiny insects called aphids. The ants guide the aphids to leaves. Then the ants protect the aphids while the aphids eat. When an ant rubs an aphid, the aphid gives off a sweet liquid. The ant drinks this liquid. This relationship, called *mutualism*, helps both the ant and the aphid.

In the second kind of symbiosis, only one organism benefits. The other isn't affected. An example is the relationship between sharks and small fish called remoras. A remora attaches itself to the shark by using a sucker on its head. Being near a shark protects the remora. The remora also eats scraps from the shark's meals. The remora benefits, and the shark isn't affected much. This relationship is called *commensalism*.

Some bacteria in your large intestine have this kind of relationship with you. They feed on the food in your intestine without harming you. Other bacteria help supply you with vitamin K. This relationship is an example of mutualism. You provide food, and the bacteria help keep you well. You both benefit.

In the third kind of symbiosis, called *parasitism*, one organism benefits but the other is harmed. The organism that benefits is called a *parasite*. The organism that is harmed is called a *host*. Parasites steal food from hosts or harm them in some other

▲ The birds on this rhino are eating insects that bother the rhino. The birds get dinner, and the rhino gets relief from the insects. Both benefit.

way. Some parasites release chemicals into the host. In time, these chemicals may kill the host.

Viruses and many one-celled organisms—such as bacteria, some protists, and some fungi—are parasites. They cause diseases such as polio, measles, and influenza. During the Middle Ages, a parasite caused an illness called the Black Plague, which killed about one-third of the population of Europe.

Bacteria and viruses spread as long as they can find hosts. Vaccinations can stop the spread of some of these parasites. When the parasites can't find new hosts, they die.

Roundworms and tapeworms are parasites that live in their hosts' intestines. They absorb food from their hosts, harming or killing them.

The sea lamprey is also a parasite. This eel attaches itself to a fish. Unlike the remora, the lamprey drills a hole into the fish and sucks its blood. The wound often becomes infected.

 MAIN IDEA AND DETAILS Give examples of the three kinds of symbiosis.

Human Symbiosis
With a partner, think of human activities that are examples of symbiosis. Then act out your examples. Have classmates classify the types of symbiosis being acted out.

131

Predator-Prey Relationships

To survive, animals must eat. They must also avoid being eaten. An animal that eats other animals is called a **predator**. For example, hawks and wolves are predators. Animals that are eaten, such as mice and rabbits, are called **prey**.

It's easy to see why predators need prey. However, prey need predators, too. Otherwise, prey populations would grow very large. Then the prey would have to compete with each other to meet their basic needs. Many would end up starving.

The number of prey and the number of predators are closely related. Any change in one leads to a change in the other. For example, if a prey animal's food supply increases, it will be easier for more prey to survive long enough to reproduce. More prey means more food for predators, so the number of predators goes up, too.

On the other hand, a drought might kill much of the grass and other plants in an ecosystem. Then the number of prey that eat the plants is likely to drop. Soon the ecosystem will have fewer predators, too.

Predators help keep the number of prey in balance. For example, wolves keep the deer in some ecosystems to a manageable number. If there were too many deer, they might eat all of the available food. Then more deer would die of starvation than from the attacks of wolves.

 MAIN IDEA AND DETAILS What symbiotic relationship is most like a predator-prey relationship?

The cheetah's markings keep it hidden until it gets close to its prey—an antelope. Then the predator's speed enables it to chase down its prey. ▼

1. MAIN IDEA AND DETAILS Draw this graphic organizer, and add the missing details.

> **Organisms depend on and compete with one another.**
>
> | Two examples of mutualism: Ⓐ_____ _____ | Four things that organisms compete for to meet their needs: Ⓑ_____ _____ _____ _____ |

2. SUMMARIZE Write a summary of this lesson by using the vocabulary terms in a paragraph.

3. DRAW CONCLUSIONS A certain forest is home to a large number of hawks. What does this tell you about the number of mice and other small animals that live there?

4. VOCABULARY Use the lesson vocabulary terms to create a quiz that uses matching.

Test Prep

5. Critical Thinking What are three of the populations in an ecosystem near you?

6. Which of these is an adaptation that helps a skunk defend itself against predators?

A. its stripe   **C.** its odor

B. its tail   **D.** its size

Links

Writing

Expository Writing
You have discovered a new kind of organism in a rain forest. Write a brief **description** explaining how this organism meets its needs. Include any symbiotic relationships it has.

Math

Solve a Problem
For a certain fish, only 5 of every 100 eggs hatch and survive to adulthood. If this fish lays 5000 eggs, how many will become adults?

Health

Parasites
Learn more about the parasites that affect people, such as tapeworms or the viruses that cause smallpox or influenza. Then, in an oral or written report, share what you learned.

 For more links and activities, go to **www.hspscience.com**

2

How Do Ecosystems Change over Time?

Fast Fact

Missing Marshes Many of the world's ecosystems are changing. Salt marshes like this one are quickly disappearing. By 2025, two-thirds of Africa's farmable land will be too dry for growing crops. In the Investigate, you'll model how an ecosystem can change from a pond into dry land.

Observing Changes

Materials
- ruler
- potting soil
- plastic dishpan
- water
- duckweed
- birdseed

Procedure

1. Make a model of a pond by spreading 5 cm of potting soil in the dishpan. Dig out a low space in the center, leaving 1 cm of soil. Pile up soil around the low space to make sides about 10 cm high.

2. Slowly pour water into the low spot until the water is 4 cm deep. Put duckweed in the "pond."

3. Sprinkle birdseed over the soil. Do not water it. Make a drawing or take a photograph to record how your pond looks.

4. After three or four days, measure and record the depth of the water in the pond. Record how the pond looks now.

5. Sprinkle more birdseed over the soil, and water it lightly.

6. Wait three or four more days, and observe how your pond has changed. Measure and record the depth of the water. Compare your three observations.

Step 1

Step 3

Draw Conclusions

1. What caused the changes you observed?

2. **Inquiry Skill** Scientists often make models and observe changes, just as you did. Which of the changes you observed might occur in a real pond? What other changes do you think might occur in a real pond?

Investigate Further

Make a model of another ecosystem, such as a forest floor. If possible, include some insects. Observe and record the changes that take place over time.

VOCABULARY
succession p. 136
extinction p. 140

SCIENCE CONCEPTS
▶ how changes in ecosystems affect the organisms there
▶ how these changes can cause the extinction of some organisms

READING FOCUS SKILL

CAUSE AND EFFECT Look for the causes of changes in ecosystems.

| cause | → | effect |

Primary Succession

Ecosystems change every day, but the changes are usually too slow to be noticed. Some organisms die out, while others start to thrive. A gradual change in the kinds of organisms living in an ecosystem is called **succession**. Unlike the changes you observed in the Investigate, succession in nature can take thousands of years.

What causes succession? One cause is a change in climate. When a region becomes drier, for example, some of the organisms that live there will no longer be able to meet their needs. If fewer plants survive in the dry climate, herbivores will have to move to find food or they'll die. A loss of herbivores leads to a loss of predators. Meanwhile, plants and animals that can live with less water begin to thrive. They will slowly replace the organisms that cannot live in the drier climate.

Succession can also be caused by the organisms living in an ecosystem. For example, a large herd of deer can kill many trees by eating too many leaves. Then the deer and other animals in the ecosystem

Primary Succession

① At the edge of a pond, plants trap soil in their roots. As the plants die and decay, the soil gains nutrients.

② More plants begin to grow in the rich new soil at the edge of the pond. The pond is starting to get smaller.

can no longer find enough food or shelter. To survive, they must move to a new area. With fewer small animals to eat, the predators also leave or die. Because fewer trees shade the forest floor, plants that thrive in the sun begin to grow. Much of the ecosystem has changed.

Adding new plants or animals to an ecosystem is another cause of succession. For example, a vine called *kudzu* has taken over many ecosystems of the southern United States. Kudzu was brought to the United States from Japan in 1876. Farmers were paid to plant it because, they were told, kudzu could control erosion and feed animals.

The climate of the South was perfect for kudzu. It could grow 30 cm (1 ft) a day! Soon this vine was everywhere. It killed whole forests by climbing on trees and preventing sunlight from reaching the trees' leaves. In 1972, kudzu was declared to be a weed. By then, it had affected many ecosystems in the South by changing both the plants and the animals that lived there.

Succession can be primary or secondary. *Primary succession* begins with bare rock. The first plants to grow, such as lichens (ɪʏ•kinz), are called *pioneer plants*. Lichens can grow without soil, and they can survive harsh conditions. As they grow, lichens produce chemicals that help weather the rock they grow on. In time, a thin layer of soil forms, allowing mosses to grow.

As mosses grow and die, they add nutrients to the thin soil. Soon grass seeds begin to sprout. Then birds and other animals come to eat the grasses and their seeds. The animals' droppings add more nutrients to the soil. When the soil is deep enough and rich enough, larger plants, including trees, begin to grow. In time, the ecosystem becomes stable, and changes stop. The result is known as a *climax community*.

 CAUSE AND EFFECT What are three causes of succession?

The pond ecosystem continues to grow smaller, while the land ecosystem grows larger.

Small shrubs now grow where the pond was. In time, they will be replaced by larger trees.

Secondary Succession

Rebirth of a Forest

1. Fire destroys all the organisms living above ground.

2. Roots that survive underground and seeds blown in by the wind begin to sprout, forming new plants.

Secondary Succession

Secondary succession helps rebuild damaged ecosystems. This kind of succession occurs in places that already have soil. It often happens after a forest fire or a volcanic eruption has destroyed the original ecosystem.

Primary succession is a very slow process. Secondary succession is not. It happens quickly because soil is already there and the soil usually contains many seeds. Animals and wind bring in more seeds. Some roots of original plants survive underground, and they start sending up new shoots. In secondary succession, as with primary succession, the first plants are hardy. But

they don't have to be as hardy as those growing on bare rock. The soil is deep enough for strong roots, and ashes from burned trees add nutrients to the soil.

You might have heard about eruptions of Mount St. Helens in Washington State. This volcano exploded on May 18, 1980, covering the mountain with a thick layer of ash and mud. Yet by the summer of 1981, the mountainside bloomed with pink fireweed flowers. A few years later, shrubs began to grow there. Many insects, birds, and other animals have already returned. Now you can find young fir trees on the mountain's slopes. Even with more eruptions, a mature forest will one day cover Mount St. Helens again.

3. New growth appears among the blackened tree trunks. Many insects and other small animals return to the forest.

 For more links and activities, go to www.hspscience.com

Where secondary succession occurs, there is also some primary succession. Secondary succession cannot occur without primary succession. You can find bare rock after a volcanic eruption. Fire, followed by erosion of the soil, also uncovers bare rock. Lichens would begin growing on the rock. Mosses would grow next, and so on, until the ecosystem of the bare rock would be the same as that restored by secondary succession. But this may take hundreds of years. Remember, primary succession happens very slowly.

CAUSE AND EFFECT What is the main result of primary succession and of secondary succession?

Insta-Lab

Regrowth
Make a drawing showing regrowth of a climax community in an area that has had a fire, a flood, a volcano, or other natural disaster. Be sure to include several stages of secondary succession in your drawing.

139

Extinction

Sometimes changes in an ecosystem cause the extinction of an entire species. **Extinction** is the death of all the organisms of a species.

Many organisms can adapt to slow changes in an ecosystem. But some cannot. When an environment changes, some organisms living in it will die. Plants and some animals can't move to other ecosystems to meet their needs.

A species with just a few small populations in different places is more likely to become extinct than a species with many large populations. A population that lives in a small area, such as on a remote island, is in more danger than a population spread out over a large area. Any change in the island environment could wipe out an entire population.

An environmental change can be so great that it affects many populations of different species. You might know that most dinosaurs became extinct about 65 million years ago. But did you know that more than 70 percent of all the other organisms on Earth were also wiped out? This mass extinction was probably due to a drastic change in the worldwide climate.

Some scientists hypothesize that the cause may have been a huge meteorite. It may have thrown up a dust cloud so big that it blocked out the sun. Some plants died, followed by many herbivores and most carnivores. Of course, most changes in ecosystems are more gradual.

Many human actions, too, can lead to extinctions. You'll learn more about that in the next lesson.

 CAUSE AND EFFECT How can a change in climate cause extinctions?

Beginning 40,000 years ago, thousands of plants and animals became trapped in tar that rose to Earth's surface. Fossils of nearly 200 kinds of organisms, including saber-toothed cats, have been identified in the La Brea tar pits in California. ▼

Saber-toothed cats became extinct about 11,000 years ago. The cause was probably climate change or hunting.

Focus Skill

1. CAUSE AND EFFECT Draw and complete these graphic organizers. For B–D, describe three causes of the same effect.

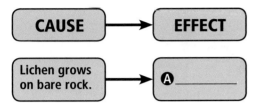

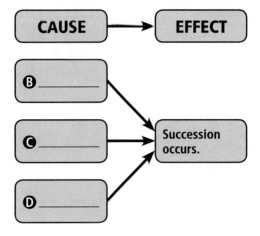

2. SUMMARIZE Write two sentences to summarize this lesson.

3. DRAW CONCLUSIONS How are pioneer plants different from plants in a climax community?

4. VOCABULARY Write a paragraph using each vocabulary term twice.

Test Prep

5. Critical Thinking Describe ways that people affect succession.

6. Which of these is the final result of secondary succession?

   A. adaptation

   B. rebuilt ecosystem

   C. competition

   D. final extinction

Links

Writing

Narrative Writing

Choose a wild area or park near you. Write a **description** of its present stage of succession. Describe how human activities have influenced its natural succession.

Math

Make an Estimate

Florida is 65,700 sq mi in area. Texas covers 268,600 sq mi. Florida has 111 species in danger of extinction. Texas has 91. Which state has more endangered species per square mile?

Art

Succession

Use any kind of media to illustrate the stages of primary or secondary succession. Set the succession in a certain climate, and research the plants that should be shown.

 For more links and activities, go to www.hspscience.com

Lesson **3**

How Do People Affect Ecosystems?

Fast Fact

Too Much Paper! More than 40 percent of the trash in this landfill is paper! Despite widespread recycling programs, paper is still the most common item tossed in the trash. Unfortunately, paper buried in a landfill is very slow to decay. Newspapers can still be read 40 years after they were buried. In the Investigate, you'll explore how human actions can affect other parts of our ecosystems.

142

Observing Effects of Fertilizer

Materials
- marker
- 4 jars with lids
- pond water
- dropper
- liquid fertilizer

Procedure

1. Use the marker to number the jars 1–4.

2. Fill each jar with the same amount of pond water.

3. Use the dropper to put 10 drops of liquid fertilizer in Jar 1, 20 drops in Jar 2, and 40 drops in Jar 3. Do not put any fertilizer in Jar 4.

4. Put the lids on the jars, and place them in a sunny window.

5. Observe the jars every day for two weeks, and record your observations.

Step 1

Draw Conclusions

1. Which jar had the most plant growth? Which had the least? What conclusion can you draw about fertilizer and plant growth?

2. As organisms die and decay in water, they use up the oxygen in the water. Which jar do you infer will eventually contain the least amount of oxygen? Explain your answer.

3. **Inquiry Skill** Scientists identify and control variables in their experiments so they can observe the effect of one variable at a time. Which variables did you control in setting up the four jars? Which variable did you change?

Step 3

Investigate Further

Suppose you want to study the effect of sunlight on fertilizer in pond water. Plan an experiment that will identify and control the variables. Then carry out your experiment.

VOCABULARY
pollution p. 144
acid rain p. 144
habitat p. 145
conservation p. 146
reclamation p. 148

SCIENCE CONCEPTS
▶ how people's actions can change the environment
▶ how the environment can be protected and restored

READING FOCUS SKILL

MAIN IDEA AND DETAILS Look for details about how people damage ecosystems.

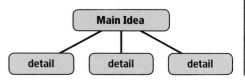

Damaging Ecosystems

In the Investigate, you observed how fertilizer affects pond water. You observed that it speeds up plant growth. But isn't plant growth a good thing?

In time, plants in water will die. As they decay, they will use up oxygen in the water. Without oxygen, any fish living there will also die. The decaying fish will use up still more oxygen.

Decaying organic matter can pollute water. **Pollution** is any waste product that damages an ecosystem. Chemicals used on crops and lawns also pollute water. Heavy rain carries them from the fields to streams, rivers, and lakes.

Air can be polluted, too. Burning fossil fuels, such as coal, oil, and gas, is a major cause of air pollution. Certain chemicals in fossil fuels mix with water vapor in the air. The combination produces acids. When these acids fall to Earth with rain, we call it **acid rain**.

Acid rain can damage trees, crops, and other plants. It has made many bodies of clean-looking water acidic. Acidic water affects organisms differently. For example, it might kill all the small fish in a pond but not harm the larger fish. Then that pond's food chain would be affected.

A strip mine can pollute the groundwater as well as the land.▼

This bear now has to share its ecosystem with people.

144

Trash threatens wildlife in many ways. Animals can get cut by broken glass or snared by plastic drink-can holders. Small animals can even get trapped inside containers.

▲ Every year, snowmobiles add tons of pollutants to the air in places such as Yellowstone National Park.

Ecosystems can also be damaged by changing them. For example, most of our prairie ecosystems have been turned into farms. Prairies once had many communities. Now most of them are used to grow only one crop.

People fence off many ecosystems. This reduces the size of habitats or forces animals to share habitats with people. A **habitat** is an area where an organism can find everything it needs to survive. Fences make it hard for animals to migrate, or move, to different habitats. Fences also cut through hunting grounds of predators such as mountain lions and wolves.

When people cut down forests for timber, they destroy habitats. Habitats are also destroyed when people fill wetlands to make space for houses and shopping malls.

Sometimes people introduce organisms from other regions, such as the kudzu vine

you read about. These organisms crowd out native plants and animals, changing and often damaging the ecosystem.

 MAIN IDEA AND DETAILS What are three ways that people damage ecosystems?

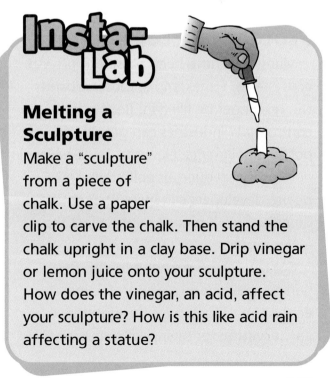

Insta-Lab

Melting a Sculpture

Make a "sculpture" from a piece of chalk. Use a paper clip to carve the chalk. Then stand the chalk upright in a clay base. Drip vinegar or lemon juice onto your sculpture. How does the vinegar, an acid, affect your sculpture? How is this like acid rain affecting a statue?

▲ Beach walkovers help protect the fragile ecosystem of the dunes.

Protecting Ecosystems

Many laws have been passed to protect ecosystems. For example, most wetlands can no longer be filled in. Regulations control how industries can get rid of possible pollutants. New cars must have devices that reduce air pollution. And before developers can build, they must describe how a project might affect the environment.

But laws alone are not enough. Each person can have a role in protecting ecosystems. One way is through the **conservation**, or saving, of resources.

Conservation of resources includes three actions: reduce, reuse, and recycle.

Reduce means "use fewer resources." For example, if you walk or ride your bike instead of riding in a car, you save gasoline. Opening windows instead of turning on an air conditioner helps reduce the amount of coal burned to produce electricity. Burning gasoline and coal also causes acid rain.

Reuse means "use resources again, instead of throwing them away." For example, you can give outgrown clothes and toys to a charity. That way, someone else can use them. You can also use glasses and dishes that can be washed and used again and again. That saves plastic and paper that would be thrown away.

Some items can be reused for a new purpose. For example, a plastic drink bottle can be reused as a planter, a bird feeder, or a funnel. Reusing items saves resources and space in landfills, too.

Recycle means "collect used items so their raw materials can be used again." For example, glass, paper, aluminum, and some plastics can be ground up or melted and made into new products. And recycling often uses less energy than producing the same items from new resources.

Most glass can be recycled. Recycled glass melts at a lower temperature than the resources used to make new glass. Recycling glass requires 30 percent less energy than making new glass.

Nearly all kinds of paper can be recycled. Making new paper from old paper uses 20 percent less energy than making paper from trees. However, paper coated with wax, foil, or plastic is too costly to recycle.

Recycling aluminum helps a lot. Recycling just two cans saves the energy equal to a cup of gasoline. Making a can from recycled aluminum uses only 4 percent of the energy needed to make a can from new resources.

Plastics make up about 10 percent of our waste. Some kinds of plastic are hard to recycle. However, soft-drink bottles are easy. The recycled bottles can be used to make carpeting, boards, new bottles, and many other products.

Reducing, reusing, and recycling save resources and energy. These actions reduce pollution and help protect ecosystems.

MAIN IDEA AND DETAILS List six ways you can help protect ecosystems.

Juice boxes are hard to recycle because most contain paper, plastic, and aluminum. Pouring juice from a large container into a glass means fewer juice boxes end up in landfills.

Discarded batteries can leak pollutants into the soil. In some states, it is illegal to put batteries in the trash. Instead, use rechargeable batteries.

Old newspapers take up about 13 percent of all the space in landfills. Yet they are easy to recycle into new paper.

Restoring Ecosystems

Damaged ecosystems are not always lost. Some can be cleaned and restored. The process is called **reclamation**. But reclamation is costly and takes time.

Removing pollutants is often part of reclamation. We now know that wetlands can help filter pollutants out of water. Yet the United States has lost most of its wetlands. In the 1970s, builders were filling in 500,000 acres of wetlands a year.

Now the rate of wetland loss has slowed. Many programs are helping to protect remaining wetlands or even to restore them.

For example, many wetlands have been restored along Florida's Gulf Coast. The bays of Fort DeSoto Park, near St. Petersburg, Florida, had become clogged with soil. The water quality was poor. The plants and animals were struggling to survive. Now the water moves freely. This change has also improved water quality in wetlands nearby.

Fragile ecosystems are being restored across the nation. Perhaps there is a reclamation project near you.

 MAIN IDEA AND DETAILS Why are wetlands important in reclamation?

This area used to be a strip mine. The first step in reclaiming a strip mine is removing mining wastes. Then soil must be added to provide a base for trees and plants. Reclamation of a large strip mine can take many years and cost millions of dollars. ▼

1. MAIN IDEA AND DETAILS Draw and complete this graphic organizer by adding three details to support the main idea.

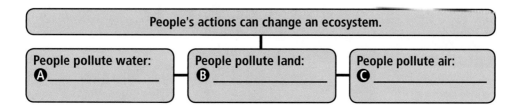

People's actions can change an ecosystem.

| People pollute water: Ⓐ_____ | People pollute land: Ⓑ _____ | People pollute air: Ⓒ _____ |

2. SUMMARIZE Write one sentence that describes three ways people affect ecosystems.

3. DRAW CONCLUSIONS How is conservation different from reclamation?

4. VOCABULARY Make up quiz-show answers for the vocabulary terms. See if a partner knows the correct questions for the answers, such as "What is pollution?"

Test Prep

5. Critical Thinking What specific things can people do to avoid the need to restore an ecosystem?

6. Which of these is a cause of acid rain?

A. burning forests

B. burning fuels

C. runoff from farmers' fields

D. decaying organisms in the water

Links

Writing

Persuasive Writing
Some people think recycling is not worth the effort. Write a **letter** for your school or community newspaper, urging readers to recycle. Try to motivate them to help protect ecosystems.

Math

Make a Pictograph
Make a pictograph showing U.S. recycling rates: cardboard, 70%; newspaper, 60%; aluminum cans, 49%; soft-drink bottles, 36%; glass, 22%.

Literature

Life Preservers
Read about the life of a well-known naturalist, such as Rachel Carson, Henry David Thoreau, John Burroughs, or John Muir. In a written or oral report, share what you learned.

For more links and activities, go to **www.hspscience.com**

Technology

Saving the
EVERGLADES

What blood is to the human body, water is to Florida's Everglades. And over the past half-century, the Everglades have been slowly and steadily bleeding to death. In 2001, the federal government passed the Everglades Restoration Act to stop the bleeding and save the Everglades. The restoration will cost more than $8 billion and continue for 30 years.

River of Grass

The Everglades is a slow-moving river that is less than 30 centimeters (1 foot) deep and 80 kilometers (50 miles) wide and covers millions of acres from Lake Okeechobee to Florida Bay. In 1947, the federal government established Everglades National Park. In 1948, Congress ordered the U.S. Army Corps of Engineers to drain large parts of the Everglades outside the park.

The corps began construction on a series of dams and canals that drained hundreds of thousands of acres. That changed the natural flow of water and eventually funneled 6.4 billion liters (1.7 billion gallons) of fresh water into the ocean every day. Builders put up new housing developments, and even whole cities, on drained areas of the Everglades.

The canals and other artificial barriers prevented some animal species from migrating. Drainage caused the populations of some wading birds, for instance, to plummet by 90 percent. Chemical and sewage runoff from Florida's growing towns and factories also spilled into natural areas, killing both animals and plants.

Undoing the Damage

The Everglades Restoration Act is aimed at restoring the Everglades to its natural state. One important part of the plan calls for the removal of dams, dikes, and flood-control gates that stop or slow the flow of water. The act also aims to improve water treatment plants. Those plants clean wastewater coming from farms and towns near the Everglades. The improved plants will allow less-polluted water to flow into the Everglades.

Many people, from environmental groups to private citizens, applaud the

The Whole World Is Watching

This is the first time the restoration of an entire ecosystem has been tried.

plan, saying it is a major step in stopping the destruction of a great natural resource.

Think About It

1. Why would the government want to drain wetlands such as the Everglades?
2. Why might it be harmful to change the flow of water in the Everglades?

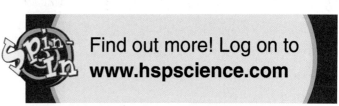

Find out more! Log on to
www.hspscience.com

Working on the River

Most field trips allow students to see cool sights or visit historical places. However, Portia Johnson recently had a chance to spend a day up to her knees in mud helping to protect an important river in Virginia. Portia and her classmates were part of a project organized by the Friends of the Rappahannock.

During the project, students planted seedlings from the school's nursery along eroded sections of the river. The trees will help to keep the riverbank's soil in place and slow down erosion.

The Rappahannock River runs about 184 miles through Virginia until it empties into the Chesapeake Bay. This river is an important source of water and habitat for many plants and animals.

152   SK-6 Identify scientific work

You Can Do It!

Quick and Easy Project

Plant Power

Materials
- 2 pots filled with soil
- 6 beans
- water
- flour

Procedure
1. Plant 3 beans in each pot, and water both pots in the same way.
2. Mix some flour and water until it forms a thick batter.
3. Pour the batter into one pot, covering the soil with a thick layer.
4. Put both pots at a sunny window.
5. Observe the pots for 10 to 14 days. Water the uncovered pot when the soil feels dry.

Draw Conclusions
What conclusion can you draw from your observations? What variable did you test? What does this experiment tell you about plants' role in restoring damaged ecosystems?

Design Your Own Investigation

Taking Out the Trash

Which kinds of trash decay quickly in a landfill, and which kinds take up space for a long time? Form a hypothesis. Then check your hypothesis by designing an investigation and carrying it out. For example, you might make a model of a landfill and bury different kinds of trash in it. Be sure to ask for permission before you start your investigation. Also, wear plastic gloves when you check your results.

Review and Test Preparation

Vocabulary Review

Use the terms below to complete the sentences. The page numbers tell you where to look in the chapter if you need help.

competition p. 129   **succession** p. 136
adaptation p. 129   **extinction** p. 140
predators p. 132   **conservation** p. 146
prey p. 132   **reclamation** p. 148

1. Grasses replace mosses in a process called _____.

2. Recycling is one kind of _____.

3. The number of organisms in a population is limited by _____.

4. A hummingbird's long beak is an _____.

5. Cleaning up polluted water is an example of _____.

6. Earthworms can be _____.

7. The death of all earthworms would be an _____.

8. Big cats are usually _____.

Check Understanding

Write the letter of the best choice.

9. How can we reduce the amount of acid rain that falls?
   A. by driving less
   B. by restoring wetlands
   C. by planting more trees
   D. by cleaning up polluted water

10. What forms a community?
    F. symbiotic relationships
    G. several populations
    H. an ecosystem
    J. succession

11. Which of these is usually in the last stage of succession?
    A. bushes   **C.** mosses
    B. lichen   **D.** trees

12. **CAUSE AND EFFECT** Which of these could possibly lead to an extinction?
    F. adaptation   **H.** reclamation
    G. pollution   **J.** symbiosis

13. **MAIN IDEA AND DETAILS** Which statement is most accurate?
    A. All ecosystems change in a way that is often gradual.
    B. People cause all the changes in ecosystems.
    C. Succession is a cause of change in ecosystems.
    D. Competition is the main cause of change in ecosystems.

14. Which of these is **not** a predator or prey?

   F. corn

   G. alligator

   H. ant

   J. antelope

15. Which of these is **not** a result of human actions?

   A. acid rain

   B. conservation

   C. extinction

   D. symbiosis

16. What is shown in the photo below?

   F. competition

   G. extinction

   H. succession

   J. symbiosis

Inquiry Skills

17. In an experiment, you water one plant with a certain amount of plain water. You water an identical plant with the same amount of a mixture of vinegar and water. You put both plants in a sunny window. Which **variables are you controlling** in this experiment?

18. Suppose the number of organisms in one population in a community suddenly increases. **Predict** what might happen, and explain why.

Critical Thinking

19. Explain how recycling is like mutualism.

20. Study the photograph below, and answer both questions.

Part A What concept from this chapter does the photograph illustrate?

Part B What organisms probably grew here before this photograph was taken? What kinds of organisms will grow here next?

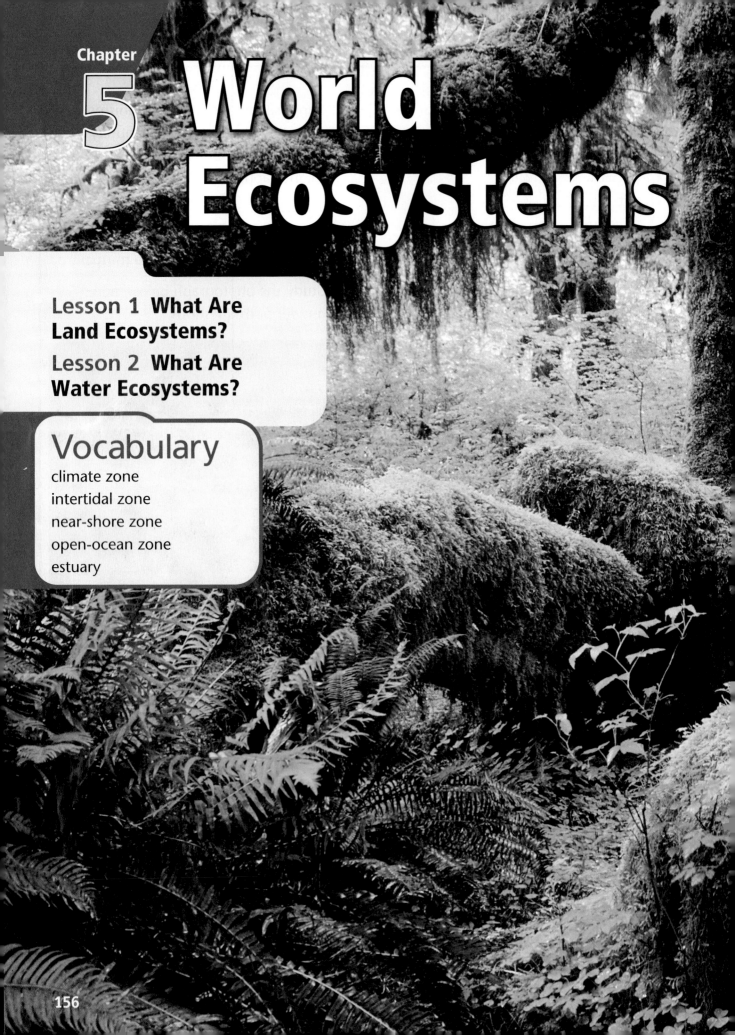

Lesson 1 **What Are Land Ecosystems?**

Lesson 2 **What Are Water Ecosystems?**

Vocabulary

climate zone
intertidal zone
near-shore zone
open-ocean zone
estuary

What do YOU wonder?

This temperate rain forest is in Olympic National Park, in Washington. Temperate rain forests occur along the Pacific coast, from Alaska to Oregon. How are they different from tropical rain forests?

What Are Land Ecosystems?

Fast Fact

So Many Names! Grasslands provide food for many of the world's people and animals, including these bison. However, a grassland ecosystem has different names in different places. In the United States, we call it a prairie. In South Africa, it's called a *veld*. In South America, tropical grasslands are called *savannas*, but temperate grasslands are called *pampas*. Grasslands are called *steppes* in Eurasia. In the Investigate, you will match land ecosystems, including grasslands, to climates.

Climates and Ecosystems

Materials
- map of climate zones of North America
- map of ecosystems of North America
- markers or colored pencils

Procedure

① On the map of climate zones, color the climates as shown in the first table.

② On the map of ecosystems, color the ecosystems as shown in the second table.

③ Compare the green areas on both maps. How do areas with a warm, wet climate compare to areas of tropical rain forest? Compare other ecosystems and climate zones that are the same color.

Draw Conclusions

1. How do areas on the climate map compare to areas of the same color on the ecosystem map?

2. If an area is too wet to be a desert and too dry to be a forest, predict what ecosystem you might expect to find there.

3. **Inquiry Skill** When scientists compare sets of data, they can draw conclusions about relationships between them. For example, needle-leafed trees are the dominant plants of the taiga. Broad-leaved trees are the dominant plants of the deciduous forest. Draw conclusions about the water needs of conifers compared to those of broad-leaved trees.

North American Climate Zones

Area	Climate	Color
1	More than 250 cm rain; warm all year	green
2	75–250 cm rain or snow; warm summer, cold winter	purple
3	20–60 cm rain or snow; cool summer, cold winter	blue
4	10–40 cm rain or snow; warm summer, cold winter	orange
5	Less than 10 cm rain; hot summer, cool winter	yellow
6	250 cm snow (25 cm rain); cold all year	brown

North American Ecosystems

Area	Ecosystems	Color
A	Tropical rain forest	green
B	Deciduous forest	purple
C	Taiga	blue
D	Grassland	orange
E	Desert	yellow
F	Tundra	brown

Investigate Further

Make a map combining climate zones and ecosystems. Draw conclusions about areas where climate and ecosystem don't match exactly.

VOCABULARY
climate zone p. 160

SCIENCE CONCEPTS
▶ how different ecosystems support different organisms
▶ how organisms adapt to their ecosystems

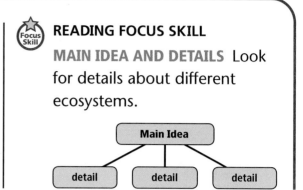

READING FOCUS SKILL

MAIN IDEA AND DETAILS Look for details about different ecosystems.

Earth's Land Ecosystems

Suppose you travel to a region far from your home. The first thing you might notice is the weather. Is it hotter or colder than where you live? Is it wetter or drier? Next, you might notice the plant and animal life. Is it different from the plant and animal life in your region?

If the weather and the living organisms are different, you are in a different ecosystem. As you saw in the Investigate, ecosystems roughly match up with climate zones. A **climate zone** is a region in which yearly patterns of temperature, rainfall, and the amount of sunlight are similar throughout. Wind patterns, landforms, and

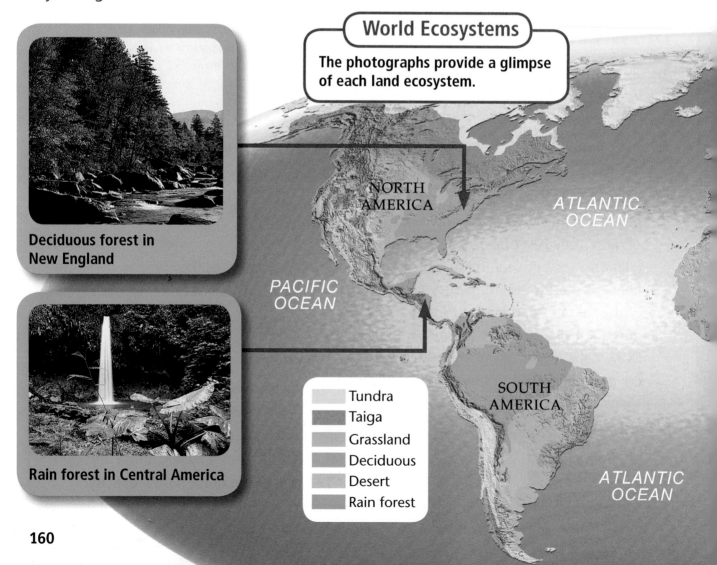

Deciduous forest in New England

Rain forest in Central America

World Ecosystems

The photographs provide a glimpse of each land ecosystem.

NORTH AMERICA

ATLANTIC OCEAN

PACIFIC OCEAN

SOUTH AMERICA

ATLANTIC OCEAN

Tundra
Taiga
Grassland
Deciduous
Desert
Rain forest

closeness to large bodies of water help determine climate zones as well.

Earth has six major land ecosystems. They are tropical rain forest, deciduous forest, grassland, desert, taiga (TY•guh), and tundra. Each ecosystem occurs in several places on Earth. You saw this in the Investigate.

Organisms can only live in ecosystems where their needs can be met. Food, water, and shelter are three such needs. Some organisms have adaptations for living in certain climate zones. For example, some organisms can live in only one desert ecosystem. The collared lizard lives only in North American deserts. The frilled lizard lives only in Australian deserts.

Parts of an ecosystem may have different organisms. The type of soil, for example determines where certain plants will grow. The plant life, in turn, helps determine the kinds of animals that live there.

 MAIN IDEA AND DETAILS What factors affect where an organism lives?

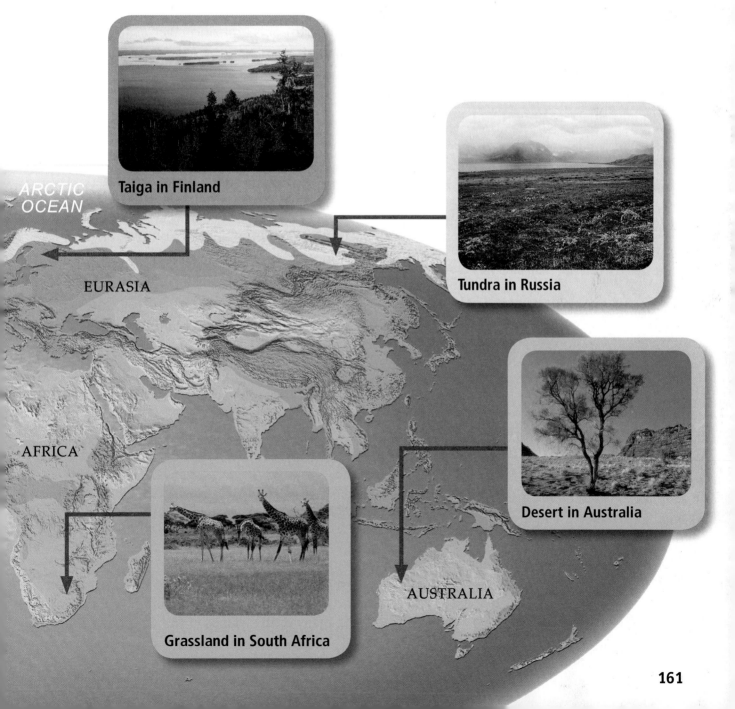

Taiga in Finland

ARCTIC OCEAN

Tundra in Russia

EURASIA

AFRICA

Desert in Australia

AUSTRALIA

Grassland in South Africa

Tucanette

Tropical Rain Forests

You can get an idea of what it feels like to be in a tropical rain forest by walking through a greenhouse. Tropical rain forests are found near the equator. There, Earth receives direct sunlight most of the year, so temperatures are always warm. The climate of tropical rain forests is also very wet. It rains almost every day.

The strong sunlight and warm, wet climate provide ideal growing conditions for a variety of plants. Tropical rain forests have about half of all the different kinds of plants on Earth. This amazing *diversity,* or variety, of life is one characteristic of tropical rain forests.

Producers in a rain forest are found in three layers. The tallest trees form the upper layer. Slightly lower, a second layer of trees forms a canopy, or roof, of leaves and tree branches. Under the canopy are a few shorter trees and many vines, orchids, and ferns. Very few plants live on the rain-forest floor because very little sunlight can shine down through the thick canopy.

The animal life in a tropical rain forest is just as diverse as the plant life. Many animals spend most of their lives in the canopy. Reptiles, amphibians, mammals, insects, fish, and birds all do well in a rain forest. The food webs they form are the most varied and complicated of all the ecosystems.

 MAIN IDEA AND DETAILS What is the climate like in a rain forest?

◄ **In North America, tropical rain forests occur from southern Mexico through Panama, on many of the islands in the Caribbean Sea, and in Hawai`i.**

Deciduous Forests

The leaves of many broad-leafed trees turn yellow, orange, or red before they drop. These trees are deciduous. That means they shed their leaves each year. Trees are the dominant plants in deciduous forests. This ecosystem occurs where there are moderate temperatures and moderate amounts of rainfall. Every continent except Africa and Antarctica has deciduous forests.

The varying amounts of sunlight Earth's surface receives at different times of the year cause changes of seasons in deciduous forests. The seasonal changes, in turn, cause a yearly cycle of plant growth. Warm temperatures in the spring and summer allow plants to grow and bloom. During the winter, temperatures often fall below freezing. The growing season in deciduous forests lasts about eight months.

Several layers of plants can be found in deciduous forests. The tallest trees—oaks, maples, and hickories—form a thin canopy of leaves. Unlike the tropical rain forest, this canopy lets in enough sunlight for a layer of small trees and shrubs to grow. Mosses, lichens, and ferns grow beneath the shrubs.

The different layers of plants provide a variety of animal habitats. Many species of insects and birds live in the canopy. Rabbits, skunks, deer, and chipmunks are the herbivores of the forest floor. Toads, lizards, and snakes also live on the forest floor. Foxes, coyotes, hawks, and a few other small carnivores prey on the herbivores.

 MAIN IDEA AND DETAILS What characteristic of deciduous trees is most obvious?

White-tailed deer

Deciduous forests in North America occur mostly from southeastern Canada through the mountains of northern Georgia and west to the Mississippi River.

Grasslands

Imagine a sea of grass rippling in the wind like ocean waves. The tall grasses stretch to the horizon. This is what you might have seen 200 years ago on the prairies, or grasslands, of North America. Grasslands are found on all continents except Antarctica. Temperatures are moderate, rainfall is light, and grasses like big bluestem are the dominant plants.

Grasses have several adaptations that help them live without much rain. Their long, slender leaves slow water loss. Their roots grow just below the surface of the soil, and they spread out to absorb the rain that does fall. The few trees found in grasslands usually grow along streams and rivers, where they can get more water.

Many small animals, such as rabbits, prairie dogs, gophers, badgers, rats, mice, snakes, and insects, live in grasslands. Herds of larger herbivores, such as deer and bison, are also found in North American grasslands.

Grasslands play a major role in world agriculture. Farmers grow wheat, corn, rice, and other grains—all types of grasses. These grains are used to make animal feed, cereal, and flour. North American grasslands produce so much food that they are sometimes called the breadbasket of the world. Grasslands are also used to graze livestock, such as cattle and sheep, which provide most of the animal products people eat.

 MAIN IDEA AND DETAILS How are grasses adapted to the grassland climate?

North American grasslands stretch from central Canada through Texas and into Mexico. ▼

Burrowing owl

164

Deserts in North America reach from the interior of southwestern Canada through northern Mexico.

Jackrabbit

Deserts

If you ever watch old westerns on TV, you know what a desert looks like. If you visit the Sonoran Desert in Arizona, you will find that the sun shines nearly every day, it doesn't rain very often, and the soil and air are both very dry. Because deserts receive very little water, only a few kinds of plants can grow there.

Most deserts are very hot on summer days, but temperatures can drop below freezing on winter nights. Some deserts have no water at all. In others, streams or lakes form after the few, but heavy, thunderstorms. However, they don't last very long.

Desert plants have adaptations that help them conserve water. The cactus plants of North American deserts store water in their thick stems. Their roots lie close to the surface of the soil, so they can quickly absorb water from infrequent rains. Unlike the cactus, desert bushes, such as the mesquite (mes•KEET), don't store water. Instead, their roots grow up to 15 m (about 50 ft) long to reach underground sources of water.

Desert reptiles, such as snakes and lizards, have tough, scaly skins that help prevent water loss. Some small mammals get all the water they need from the plants they eat. Most desert animals hide during the heat of the day. They come out to hunt for food at night, when it is cooler.

MAIN IDEA AND DETAILS Give an example of a desert organism, and tell how it has adapted to a dry climate.

The taiga in North America stretches from Alaska across central Canada to the Atlantic Ocean.

Canada lynx

Taiga

You can travel for miles in the taiga and see nothing but evergreen trees. The taiga extends in a broad belt across Europe, Asia, and North America. Taiga winters are too long for most deciduous trees to survive. A few grow in the taiga, but only near lakes and streams.

Evergreens, which include pines, firs, spruces, and hemlocks, are adapted to the taiga. The most important adaptation is their needlelike leaves. A waxy covering protects needles from the cold and limits the amount of water loss. Evergreens don't shed their needles all at once, so they can make food all year.

Unlike deciduous forests, the taiga has only two layers. The trees form an almost solid canopy. The forest floor is always covered with a thick mat of dead, dry needles. Even during a heavy rain or snow, much water is caught and held in the canopy. Mosses and lichens are usually the only organisms that grow below the canopy, either on the forest floor or on the trunks of trees.

On the taiga, the diversity of life changes from season to season. Mosquito and fly populations increase during the summer months. Birds return from the south to eat them and to breed. Owls, warblers, and woodpeckers live in the taiga year-round. Snowshoe hares and mice do, too. Lynxes, weasels, and wolves prey on these mammals. Bears may also live in the forest, eating nuts, leaves, and small animals.

 MAIN IDEA AND DETAILS What adaptation helps evergreens keep their leaves all year?

Tundra

The tundra is a rolling plain spreading across Greenland and the northern parts of Europe, Asia, and North America. It also covers the southern tip of South America and a small part of Antarctica.

Low temperatures and long winters in the tundra prevent trees from growing. Only smaller plants that send out roots in dense, shallow mats can survive. Large plants cannot survive because the soil just below the surface stays frozen all year. In the spring, the soil above this *permafrost* layer thaws a little. A few small plants grow in this mud, low to the ground and away from the strong winds.

The tundra is so far from the equator that the sun disappears below the horizon in the fall and may not rise for months.

Many tundra animals, such as birds, caribou, and musk oxen, migrate into the taiga for the winter. Those that remain, such as the arctic fox and arctic hare, have thick white coats that help them blend into the snowy landscape.

In contrast, the sun shines all night during the tundra summer. The constant light allows plants to sprout, grow, and bloom in only a few weeks. Herds of caribou and musk oxen return to graze, and birds come back to their summer nesting grounds.

 MAIN IDEA AND DETAILS Describe winter in the tundra.

Insta-Lab

Leaf Me Alone!

Use a hand lens to compare a leaf from a deciduous tree with needles from an evergreen. How are they alike and different? How is each one adapted to the climate where it grows?

Grizzly bear

In North America the tundra is limited to northern Alaska and Canada and to the higher peaks of the Rocky Mountains.

Comparing Ecosystems

Starting at the poles and moving toward the equator, ecosystems occur in this order: tundra; taiga; deciduous forest, grassland, or desert; and tropical rain forest.

Ecosystems are in this order because the corresponding climate zones occur in this order. At the equator the sun is directly overhead most of the year, and the number of hours of daylight varies only a little. This climate zone receives more solar energy than other zones, so it is warmer. It is also wetter, so tropical rain forests can grow there.

As you move toward the poles, each climate zone receives a little less energy from the sun. Near the poles, sunlight reaches Earth at a sharp angle during the summer. No sunlight reaches those areas during the winter. With so little solar energy available, tundra develops.

In temperate climates, the kind of ecosystem depends on the amount of water available. Zones near large bodies of water have enough moisture for deciduous forests. Zones farther from water have only enough moisture for grasslands or deserts.

Variations in landforms also affect climate. High elevations, such as the Rocky Mountains, may have taiga on their slopes and tundra on their peaks. When the wind forces moist air over a mountain, the air cools, and moisture condenses into clouds. The moisture then falls to Earth as rain or snow. By the time the air reaches the other side of the mountain, it is dry. Deserts also occur in these areas, called *rain shadows*.

 MAIN IDEA AND DETAILS What determines the order of climate zones and ecosystems?

The Atacama Desert in northern Chile is the world's driest place. Some areas receive no rain for as long as 20 years at a time. ▼

Math in Science
Interpret Data

Why is it difficult to put these ecosystems in order by amount of rainfall?

Amount of Rainfall

Ecosystem	Yearly Precipitation
Tropical rain forests	250 cm (about 100 in.)
Deserts	10 cm (about 4 in.)
Grasslands	10–40 cm (about 4–16 in.)
Deciduous forests	75–250 cm (about 30–100 in.)
Taiga	20–60 cm (about 8–24 in.)
Tundra	25 cm (about 10 in.)

Wai'ale'ale in Hawai'i is the world's wettest place, with about 725 cm (285 in.) of rain a year.

1. **MAIN IDEA AND DETAILS** Draw and complete the graphic organizer. Identify two adaptations of plants or animals to each ecosystem.

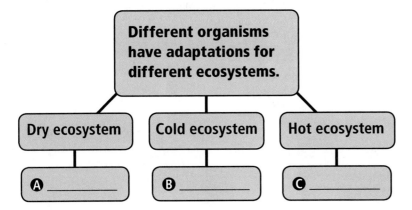

Different organisms have adaptations for different ecosystems.

Dry ecosystem

Cold ecosystem

Hot ecosystem

Ⓐ _____

Ⓑ _____

Ⓒ _____

2. **SUMMARIZE** Write two sentences that tell what this lesson is mainly about.

3. **DRAW CONCLUSIONS** What would happen to a grassland if its annual rainfall increased greatly?

4. **VOCABULARY** Write a paragraph about climate zones as well as ecosystems, including the order in which they occur, starting at the poles.

Test Prep

5. **Critical Thinking** The map of Earth's ecosystems shows definite borders between them. What might you actually see at these borders?

6. Which ecosystem has the greatest diversity of plants and animals?
   A. deciduous forest
   B. desert
   C. taiga
   D. tropical rain forest

Links

Writing

Persuasive Writing
Write a **travel brochure** to convince readers to visit an ecosystem where people do not often vacation, such as the tundra. Describe the interesting things they might see there.

Math 9÷3

Solve a Problem
About 25 acres of rain forest are being destroyed every 10 seconds. About how many acres of rain forest is Earth losing every minute? Every hour?

Social Studies

Read Maps
Have a partner assign you a map location by latitude and longitude. Find that location. Then research the ecosystem and write a short report of your findings.

 For more links and activities, go to www.hspscience.com

2

What Are Water Ecosystems?

Fast Fact

Protect Earth's Reefs Coral reefs are probably the most diverse saltwater ecosystems on Earth. Because of their great diversity, they are able to survive most natural disturbances. But they are threatened by many kinds of human activity. One way to protect coral reefs is to learn more about them. In the Investigate, you will learn about a freshwater ecosystem.

Observing Interactions

Materials
- bucket
- collecting net
- large jar
- aquarium or second large jar
- air pump and short piece of plastic tubing

Procedure

1. With your class, visit a stream or pond in your community.

2. Use the bucket and the net to scoop up sand or soil, water, water plants, and water animals, including insects.

3. Back in your classroom, pour the water with the organisms in it into a container. Then transfer the soil or sand from the bucket to the aquarium.

4. Next, gently pour the water with the organisms into the aquarium.

5. Set up the air pump. Observe your water ecosystem and record your observations.

Draw Conclusions

1. List all the living and nonliving things in this ecosystem.

2. What interactions did you observe between organisms? Between organisms and the nonliving parts of the ecosystem?

3. **Inquiry Skills** Scientists learn about living and nonliving things by looking for similarities. Then they classify things into groups. In what ways can you classify the organisms in your ecosystem? Compare your classification system with those of other students.

Step 2

Step 3

Investigate Further

By observation or inference, gather data about what eats what in another local ecosystem, such as a field. Then make a food web to show how food energy flows from one organism to another.

Reading in Science

LS-4 Summarize importance of habitats;
LS-5 Relate organism's behavior to nature of ecosystem

VOCABULARY
intertidal zone p. 172
near-shore zone p. 173
open-ocean zone p. 173
estuary p. 176

SCIENCE CONCEPTS
▶ about three types of water ecosystems
▶ how organisms meet their needs in water ecosystems

(Focus Skill) READING FOCUS SKILL
CAUSE AND EFFECT Look for what causes different kinds of water ecosystems.

cause ⟶ effect

Saltwater Ecosystems

How many kinds of water ecosystems do you know? The three main kinds are saltwater, freshwater, and brackish water.

Like organisms on land, those that live in water are adapted to their ecosystems. Each water ecosystem offers different amounts of nutrients and oxygen. Each also offers different amounts of sunlight, and the temperature of the water varies in each ecosystem. So does any movement of the water—waves, tides, and currents.

The saltwater ecosystem of the ocean has three life zones. Each zone has its own conditions. The **intertidal zone** is at the ocean's edge. There, waves lap the shore. Tides rise and fall. Tides and waves provide

Science Up Close

Intertidal Zone

Near-Shore Zone

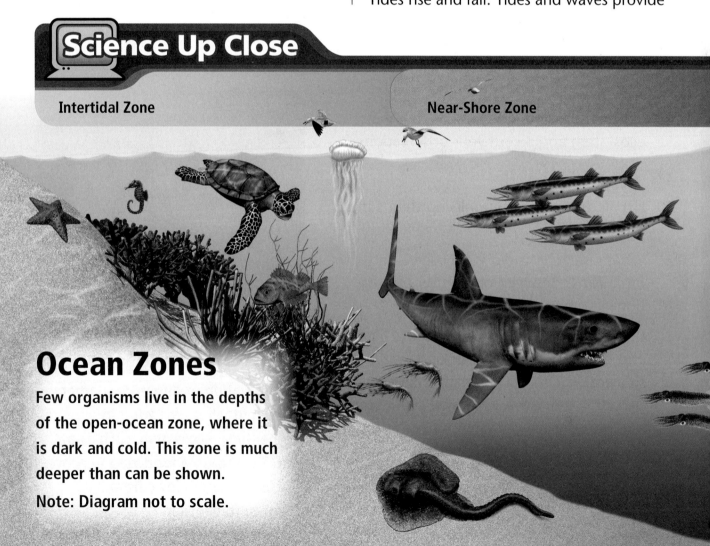

Ocean Zones

Few organisms live in the depths of the open-ocean zone, where it is dark and cold. This zone is much deeper than can be shown.

Note: Diagram not to scale.

172

a constant supply of oxygen and nutrients. But they also mean that sometimes the water disappears.

Animals in the intertidal zone include sea stars, sea urchins, clams, and crabs. Many can live both in water and in moist sand.

Beyond the breaking waves is the **near-shore zone**. It extends out to waters that are about 200 m (about 600 ft) deep. Rivers that empty into the ocean provide most of the nutrients for this zone. The water is fairly calm here. Schools of fish feed on large numbers of protists (algae)—the main producers. Oysters, worms, and other organisms on the ocean floor rely on a steady "rain" of dead organisms from above for their food. There are few producers near the bottom. Because of the lack of sunlight, no photosynthesis can occur.

The **open-ocean zone** includes most of the ocean. Here, the water is very deep, but most organisms live near the surface. Trillions of microscopic algae, or *phytoplankton* (FY•toh•plangk•tuhn) are the producers of the open-ocean food chains. Tiny herbivores, called *zooplankton* (ZOH•plangk•tuhn), graze on the protists. In turn, small fish eat zooplankton. These fish are then eaten by larger fish, such as tuna and sharks, and by dolphins.

Each zone includes organisms that are adapted to life there. They survive because they can meet all their needs in that zone.

 CAUSE AND EFFECT Why do few producers live near the bottom of the near-shore zone?

For more links and activities, go to **www.hspscience.com**

Open-Ocean Zone

0 m–30 m

30 m–200 m

greater than 200 m

Ecosystems like this one along the Lake Erie shoreline have been affected by human activities, such as shipping, steel making, and other industries.

This is South Bass Island in Lake Erie. Its freshwater ecosystem is being studied at Stone Laboratory, part of Ohio State University. ▶

Freshwater Ecosystems

Lakes, ponds, streams, rivers, swamps, and marshes are all freshwater ecosystems. The plants and animals in these ecosystems are adapted to life in fresh water only. They can't survive in salt water.

Freshwater plants include duckweed, waterlilies, cattails, and many different grasses. Many kinds of algae also live in freshwater. Trout, bass, catfish, frogs, crayfish, and turtles are a few of the more common freshwater animals.

Water temperatures and the speed at which the water moves, if it moves at all, determine the kinds of organisms that live in a freshwater ecosystem.

In streams and rivers, the water moves fast. Fewer plants and animals can live in fast-moving water than in the still waters of lakes and ponds. The plants and animals that do live in rivers often have adaptations for anchoring themselves to the bottom. For example, algae attach themselves to rocks, while insects and crayfish often live under rocks.

Like oceans, the Great Lakes also have life zones. In shallow lakes, like Lake Erie, sunlight reaches the bottom, so many water plants and algae grow. They provide both food and shelter for animals living in and near the water.

Few plants grow in the deeper lakes, like Lake Superior, because little sunlight reaches the bottom. However, small organisms do live in the mucky bottom, feeding on decaying matter. Fish in the deeper lakes feed on these organisms.

Swamps are a type of freshwater wetland. The water can be up to 30 centimeters (1 ft) deep, although some swamps dry up during summer months. The main plants of swamps are trees and shrubs. Swamp animals include snakes and frogs, but foxes, raccoons, and bears may wander through.

Most wetlands in Ohio are freshwater marshes. Marsh plants must be able to live with their stems partly underwater. Few trees can survive here, but grasses thrive. Many ducks and other birds make their homes in marshes, as do raccoons, otters, and beavers.

 CAUSE AND EFFECT How does the speed of the water affect freshwater ecosystems?

The Cuyahoga River in northeast Ohio is a clean, nearly wild river. Back in the late 1960s, the river contained so much trash and oil that part of it caught fire. ▼

Insta-Lab

Going, Going....
Your teacher will mark off a series of "wetlands" on the classroom floor. As "birds," you and your classmates will "migrate" south to escape the icy winter. The number on a die or spinner will tell you how far you travel each day. But you must stop on a wetland every night. What happens if developers build on some of the wetlands, and they disappear?

Estuaries

Brackish water is a mixture of fresh water and salt water. It is usually found in an **estuary,** a place where a freshwater river empties into an ocean. The water in an estuary contains huge amounts of nutrients, making estuaries among the most productive ecosystems on Earth. Salt marshes and mangrove swamps are two types of estuaries. There are also freshwater estuaries, where creeks or rivers empty into large lakes.

All estuaries have changing water conditions. At high tide, salty water flows into some estuaries. At low tide, they fill with fresh water or become mud flats. Organisms in these estuaries have adaptations that allow them to survive in both fresh water and salt water.

The water in most estuaries tends to be calm and shallow. Sunlight easily reaches the bottom, so many plants grow there. Millions of fish, shellfish, and birds start their lives in estuaries. These habitats offer plenty

▲ **Old Woman Creek, on the south shore of Lake Erie, is one of Ohio's few remaining estuaries.**

of food, shelter, and few large predators. Estuaries also help prevent coastal flooding and shoreline erosion.

Now people recognize both the beauty and importance of estuaries. That may save the few remaining ones from fill-and-build development that has destroyed many of these important ecosystems.

 CAUSE AND EFFECT What causes estuaries to be productive ecosystems?

Tall grasses are the main plants in salt marshes. These plants are able to live in brackish water because they get rid of salt through pores in their leaves. ▼

Reading Review

1. CAUSE AND EFFECT Copy and complete the graphic organizer.

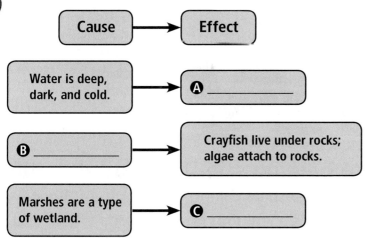

| Cause | → | Effect |

Water is deep, dark, and cold. → **A** _____

B _____ → Crayfish live under rocks; algae attach to rocks.

Marshes are a type of wetland. → **C** _____

2. SUMMARIZE Write a summary of this lesson.

3. DRAW CONCLUSIONS What kinds of adaptations allow organisms to live in estuaries?

4. VOCABULARY Use this lesson's vocabulary words to make a crossword puzzle. Use definitions for the clues.

Test Prep

5. Critical Thinking How might an organism be adapted to living in a river?

6. Which ocean zone is deepest?
   A. estuary
   B. intertidal
   C. near-shore
   D. open-ocean

Links

Writing
Descriptive Writing
Describe a water ecosystem near your home or one you have visited. Explain how the plants and animals that live in this ecosystem are adapted to it.

Math
Display Data
Make a circle graph showing the forms of water on Earth:
97 percent—salt water
 2 percent—ice
 1 percent—fresh water

Social Studies
Protecting Ecosystems
In 2004, Big Darby Creek in Ohio was named one of America's most endangered rivers. Find out what is being done to protect this river. Then write a letter to local citizens, enlisting their help.

 For more links and activities, go to www.hspscience.com

177

On the Prowl

Cameras are helping scientists count jaguars.

A sleek, spotted jaguar sneaks along the thick forest floor. As it passes a fig tree, there is a whirring noise. A flashing light and click follow. A camera has just snapped the cat's photograph.

No person was behind the camera's lens. The camera was triggered by motion and heat from the passing cat.

A Narrowing Range

Scientists from the Wildlife Conservation Society in New York have placed about 30 such cameras in trees throughout the tropical forest of Belize (beh•LEEZ). That is a country in Central America.

The forest is also the site of the world's first jaguar reserve. A reserve is an area set apart for a special purpose. At the reserve in Belize, jaguars are protected and can safely roam.

Belize has a healthy number of jaguars. The wildlife group estimates that about 14 jaguars live within a 143 square-km (55-square-mile area) there. The cameras are helping researchers count the number of jaguars within certain areas of Belize and other places where jaguars roam.

"Camera trapping" will help scientists because jaguars are hard to study. Despite the cats' hefty size, their mysterious nature and the thick jungle where they live make them difficult to spot.

178

A camera snaps a photograph of a passing jaguar.

The map shows how the range of jaguars has changed.

KEY
- Where jaguars live now
- Where jaguars used to live

"The cameras help researchers determine how many cats are out there and where they make their homes," jaguar expert Kathleen Conforti told WR.

The researchers will use that information to help protect the endangered animals. They want to conserve, or save, the jaguars' habitat. A habitat is the area where the animal naturally lives.

The actions of people have caused a decline in the animal's range. The cutting down of trees has destroyed some of the jaguar's habitat.

THINK ABOUT IT

1. How might the loss of trees affect how jaguars live?
2. How might equipment such as cameras help protect endangered animals around the world?

What a Roar

- Jaguars, which are carnivorous, can grow up to 1.8 meters (6 ft) long and weigh up to 136 kilograms (300 pounds).
- Jaguars are the third-largest cats, after tigers and lions.
- The cats usually live alone and are very territorial. That means they protect their habitat from other jaguars.
- In Spanish, this cat's name is *el tigre,* which means "the tiger."

Find out more! Log on to
www.hspscience.com

WORKING WITH ELEPHANTS

In India, adult Asian elephants have no natural enemies. However, humans have killed many elephants. Now elephants are close to dying out. Raman Sukumar wants to save them.

Sukumar studied how building changes elephant habitats. New dams, roads, and railways force elephants closer to towns. He also studied elephant deaths. He found that illegal hunting has killed many elephants.

Sukumar has found ways to help humans and elephants live together. Areas of the wild are being linked. Elephants can move safely from one area to the next. They don't have to go through farms or towns. Farmers now use different types of fences so that elephants will not eat crops.

Career Paleontologist

If you like digging, then you may want to become a paleontologist. These scientists study the fossils of ancient animals and plants. As a result, paleontologists can figure out why some species disappeared long ago while other species still exist today.

You Can Do It!

Materials
- a small potted plant, such as coleus or a sunflower seedling
- a small potted cactus plant
- water
- tablespoon

Quick and Easy Project

Trading Ecosystems

Procedure
1. Place both plants in a sunny spot. Draw how each plant looks.
2. Water the cactus plant often, keeping the soil moist at all times.
3. Give the other plant a tablespoon of water once a week.
4. Draw how both plants look at the end of three days, six days, and ten days.

Draw Conclusions
How did each plant change during your investigation? What caused these changes? What does this experiment tell you about the needs of each plant? How did their ecosystems not meet those needs?

Design Your Own Investigation

How Much Is Too Much?

Design an experiment to determine how much water a certain kind of plant needs. First, write a hypothesis about how much water the plant needs. Then write how you will find out whether that amount of water is right for that kind of plant. Which variables will you control? Which variable will you change? How will you record the data and share your results? If possible, carry out your investigation.

Vocabulary Review

Use the terms below to complete the sentences. The page numbers tell you where to look in the chapter if you need help.

climate zone p. 160
intertidal zone p. 172
near-shore zone p. 173
open-ocean zone p. 173
estuary p. 176

1. The part of the ocean that extends to a depth of about 200 m (600 ft) is called the _____.

2. The part of the ocean where organisms must be able to live in both water and moist sand is called the _____.

3. An ecosystem where fresh water and salt water mix is an _____.

4. The deepest part of the ocean is the _____.

5. A region that has similar yearly patterns of temperature, rainfall, and sunlight is called a _____.

Check Understanding

6. Which ecosystem has a frozen layer of soil year-round?
   A. deciduous forest
   B. polar region
   C. taiga
   D. tundra

7. Which of these is NOT a characteristic of an ecosystem?
   F. its animals
   G. its climate
   H. its location
   J. its plants

8. **MAIN IDEA AND DETAILS** Which ecosystem has the most different kinds of plants?
   A. deciduous forest
   B. grasslands
   C. taiga
   D. tropical rain forest

9. **CAUSE AND EFFECT** Where would you expect to find brackish water?
   F. where the ocean is deepest
   G. where a river empties into an ocean
   H. near a tropical rain forest
   J. in the ocean's near-shore zone

10. What is shown in the photo below?

   A. intertidal zone
   B. near-shore zone
   C. open-ocean zone
   D. stream

11. Which ecosystem changes the most from one season to the next?

F. deciduous forest

G. desert

H. grasslands

J. tropical rain forest

12. Which of these is a freshwater ecosystem?

A. estuary

B. ocean

C. pond

D. taiga

13. Which of these does NOT characterize a climate zone?

F. amount of rainfall

G. amount of sunlight

H. kinds of animals

J. range of temperatures

14. Which of these ecosystems requires the fewest adaptations from the organisms that live there?

A. estuary

B. grasslands

C. taiga

D. tundra

15. Which statement is NOT true?

F. Animals that live in the taiga can adapt to cold temperatures.

G. An animal living in one part of the taiga can live in any part of the taiga.

H. Some animals migrate between the taiga and the tundra.

J. Some birds are able to live in the taiga year-round.

16. Which ecosystem is characterized in this photo?

A. deciduous forest

B. grasslands

C. tropical rain forest

D. taiga

Inquiry Skills

17. Select two places on Earth that you would like to visit, and explain why. **Classify** each by its ecosystem.

18. Write a brief paragraph in which you **compare** the climate and plant and animal life found in a desert and in a tropical rain forest.

Critical Thinking

19. Explain how climate affects the kinds and numbers of organisms in a land ecosystem.

20. Study the map in Lesson 1 and answer both questions.

Part A: What are the main land ecosystems in North America?

Part B: What factors cause many different ecosystems to occur on the same continent?

Oak Openings

OHIO

Toledo

Columbus

Ohio River

National Center for Nature Photography

West of Toledo is a place called Oak Openings. There are more rare species found there than anywhere else in Ohio. In Oak Openings the land is diverse, with prairies, sandy fields, swamps, and forests. It is home to many types of plants and animals. This makes Oak Openings a great place to take pictures. And the National Center for Nature Photography is located there.

Photography for Everyone

The Center shows the works of famous nature photographers. It also features Ohio photographers, like Tom Anderson, a local photographer. He has taken many bird pictures there.

The National Center for Nature Photography offers classes in nature photography.

Oak Openings is a good place to take pictures of wildlife.

The Center teaches classes in nature photography. One class takes pictures of water birds. Another focuses on fall leaves. There is something for everyone.

Photographs help keep track of endangered species.

Photography and Science

There is a lot of art in nature. Beautiful photographs are a form of art. But nature photos are also used in science. Taking photos is a type of observation. Observation is basic to science.

A photograph can be a record of a plant or animal. It is different from a drawing or a description of an organism. Photos show what living things really look like. Photos also record things about habitats where organisms live.

Photos may be useful as records in the future. Human activities threaten many environments. Because of this, some organisms may be gone some day. Photographs are records of these organisms.

Taking photos of living things is easy. They are all around. It is important to have respect for them when taking photos. Scientists making observations have to be careful. They must not harm organisms being studied.

So go out and take some nature photos! Those pictures may be part of tomorrow's scientific record.

Photographs can record information about an organism, such as this pheasant, in its environment.

Think and Do

I. SCIENCE AND TECHNOLOGY In the past, scientists killed animals to study them. Since the development of photography, they don't have to do that. What are the advantages and disadvantages of studying animals with photography? Write a paragraph to explain your ideas.

2. SCIENTIFIC THINKING How might taking photographs be a more reliable method of recording observations than written descriptions? Which could be looked at again in several months and give the same results? Which is likely to allow others to repeat the original work?

Retreating glaciers helped form Clifton Gorge.

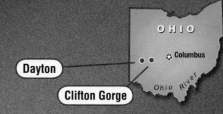

Clifton Gorge

Erosion can be a destructive force. But can erosion ever be beautiful? The answer is *yes*. Take Clifton Gorge, for example. The 108-hectare (269-acre) area includes dramatic waterfalls, rock formations, and overhanging cliffs. It is home to many interesting plants and animals. Clifton Gorge is a National Nature Landmark.

Clifton Gorge is located about 48 km (30 mi) east of Dayton. It is part of the larger John Bryan State Park. This may be the most scenic park in western Ohio. Glaciers formed Clifton Gorge. The large flow of meltwater eroded the nearby rock. The river carved the gorge out of limestone and dolomite, a limestone-like rock.

Plant Life in the Gorge

The shape of the gorge resulted in cool, moist areas. This is good for many plant species. Canada yew, mountain maple, and hemlock are among the trees found there. More than 100 different trees and shrubs grow in and around the gorge. One of Clifton Gorge's main attractions, though, is its variety of wildflowers. There are more than 340 species of wildflowers in and around the gorge.

The running water of the river shaped the rocks and the path of Clifton Gorge.

Clifton Gorge is home to a great variety of plant life.

186

The Wildflowers of Clifton Gorge

Clifton Gorge is beautiful all year long, but the spring is special because of the wildflowers. Among the many flowers are hepatica, Virginia bluebell, and shooting star. These are the first to bloom in the spring. Many other types of wildflowers are found in the gorge. They include eastern columbine, golden alexander, and jack-in-the-pulpit.

Other wildflowers found in and around the gorge are bellworts, wild ginger, and Dutchman's breeches. Some of the wildflowers found in the gorge, like the snow trillium, are rare. Many people come to Clifton Gorge just to see the snow trillium. The species is threatened, and there are few places to see it in Ohio.

Clifton Gorge and John Bryan State Park have many hiking trails. Hiking there can be a scientific expedition. As a trained observer would do, remember to respect the plants and animals you see. Take pictures, take notes, and make drawings, but don't pick the flowers. Clifton Gorge is one of Ohio's natural treasures. Help keep it beautiful for everyone.

The wildflowers of Clifton Gorge attract many visitors every spring. This is hepatica.

The rare and endangered snow trillium can be observed in Clifton Gorge.

Think and Do

I. SCIENCE AND TECHNOLOGY Clifton Gorge has been named a National Nature Landmark. Why do you think this was necessary? How does a decision like this relate to human activity and technology? Write a paragraph to explain your ideas.

2. SCIENTIFIC THINKING What would you need if you were to make a scientific expedition to Clifton Gorge? Make a list of everything you should take. Think about what you would like to observe. Decide how you might communicate your observations to your classmates.

 LS-4 Summarize importance of habitats; **ST-1** Investigate technology impact; **SI-1** Select and use appropriate tools

187

The Ohio State Reptile

The black racer snake is found mostly in the eastern and southern parts of Ohio.

OHIO
Columbus

Black racer, the Ohio state reptile

Many people are afraid of snakes. Although some snakes are dangerous, most are not. In fact, almost all snakes benefit humans. They do this by eating pests that destroy crops. Among these destructive pests are rodents and insects.

In 1995, the Ohio Legislature recognized this fact. It declared the black racer snake to be the state reptile. The black racer is commonly found on farmland in southeastern Ohio. It eats rodents and large insects in fields and pastures. Because of this, the black racer has earned the nickname "farmer's friend."

How would you know a black racer if you saw one? They are fairly thin and long. Black racer adults are usually 90–150 cm (36–60 in.) long. Sometimes they get to be more than 2 m (6 ft) long. Their back, sides, and belly are black. They usually have some white markings—on the chin and throat—and smooth scales.

Rodents are a major part of the black racer's diet.

The Blue Racer

The black racer is similar in appearance to its close relative the blue racer. The blue racer is a slightly greenish gray color. The blue racer lives mostly in the western part of Ohio. Black racers and blue racers sometimes live in the same area. They can breed with each other. Their offspring may have characteristics of both parents. Black racers, blue racers, or both are found in all 88 counties in Ohio.

The blue racer is closely related to the black racer.

More About Black Racers

In addition to farm fields, the black racer also lives in woodlands and on rocky ledges. Although it is called the "farmer's friend," the black racer is not very friendly. Black racers tend to be nervous and aggressive when people come close to them. They vibrate their tails like rattlesnakes when threatened. They may even strike and bite. While the bite of the black racer can be painful, the snakes are not venomous. Many snakes are dangerous when confronted, but when left alone, they are usually harmless. This is the case with the black racer.

Besides eating rodents and insects, black racers also eat small mammals, frogs, lizards, and other snakes. The scientific name of the black racer is *Coluber constrictor constrictor.* The name seems to indicate that the black racer is a constrictor, a type of snake that squeezes its prey to death. However, the black racer is not a constrictor.

The black racer can travel at 13–16 km/hr (8–10 mi/hr). It is diurnal, which means that it is active during the day rather than at night. It breeds in April and May and produces about 10–12 eggs a year. When they hatch, the snakes are 20–25 cm (8–10 in.) long.

The black racer snake is not only the farmer's friend, but also an important part of Ohio's natural environment.

The black racer is the farmer's friend.

Think and Do

I. SCIENCE AND TECHNOLOGY How do you think attempts to control rodents and insects with pesticides would affect the black racer? Explain how using chemical pesticides may produce other problems for local ecosystems and for humans. Write a paragraph to explain your ideas.

2. SCIENTIFIC THINKING Suppose you want to try to find a black racer to study. What hazards might you face? What precautions should you take? What should you do to ensure the safety of the snake? Write your answers as safety tips.

How Does a Wildflower Change Over Time?

Materials
- camera (optional)
- large notebook with blank pages
- ruler
- brick
- pencil
- colored pens or pencils
- stapler or tape

Procedure

1. Find a wildflower near the school. If there are no wildflowers to observe, find a flower in a garden.

2. Take a picture of the flower every day for a week. If you do not have a camera, do a sketch of the flower each day. If you cannot do this activity over a week, try to do it over one day, taking pictures every hour or two.

3. Put the brick on the ground next to the flower. Place the ruler on it and measure the height of the flower. The brick is used to get a consistent footing for the ruler. Record the height of the flower each day. If you use a camera, you can take a picture of the flower with the ruler each day.

4. Make as many observations as you can about the wildflower each day, and write them in your notebook. Print each photo and attach it to the page where you made your observations.

Draw Conclusions

1. How did the flower change over time?

2. Did the height of the flower change over the week?

3. Were there any surprises in the observations you made?

Survey of Ohio's Plants and Animals

Materials
- blank paper
- pencil
- ruler

Procedure

1. Various animals and plants are mentioned in the three articles. Do a small survey of Ohio's plants and animals by listing each species mentioned.
2. Draw a chart like the one below. List under the correct head each of the organisms you read about.

Organisms I Have Read About

Plants	Animals

Draw Conclusions

1. Do you think this survey is a good representation of plants and animals of Ohio? Why or why not?
2. Why are more plants listed than animals? Do you think this is true of all of Ohio?
3. Describe how you would do a complete survey of the plants and animals of Ohio.

Extend the Activity

Do a survey of the plants and animals around your school. Describe or draw each the best you can. If you cannot identify a plant or animal, use your written description or drawing to try to identify it in a nature book.

SI-1 Select and use appropriate tools; **SI-3** Communicate investigation results

Physical Sciences

The Chapters and features in this unit address these Grade Level Indicators from the Ohio Academic Content Standards for Science.

Chapter 6 Energy

PS-1 Define temperature as the measure of thermal energy and describe the way it is measured.

PS-2 Trace how thermal energy can transfer from one object to another by conduction.

Chapter 7 Electricity

PS-3 Describe that electrical current in a circuit can produce thermal energy, light, sound and/or magnetic forces.

PS-4 Trace how electrical current travels by creating a simple electric circuit that will light a bulb.

Chapter 8 Sound and Light

PS-5 Explore and summarize observations of the transmission, bending (refraction) and reflection of light.

PS-6 Describe and summarize observations of the transmission, reflection, and absorption of sound.

PS-7 Describe that changing the rate of vibration can vary the pitch of a sound.

Unit C Ohio Expeditions

The investigations and experiences in this unit also address many of the Grade Level Indicators for standards in Science and Technology, Scientific Inquiry, and Scientific Ways of Knowing.

OHIO

Marblehead Peninsula

Columbus

Ohio River

TO: nara@hspscience.com

FROM: Traveler@hspscience2.com

RE: Marblehead Lighthouse

Dear Nara,

Today I toured the Marblehead Lighthouse. It is the oldest lighthouse on the Great Lakes. It has been guiding ships into Sandusky Bay since 1822! The light itself has an amazing history. At first, it was made of thirteen oil lamps. Large metal mirrors were used to reflect the light from the lamps over the lake. In 1858, a new invention made it possible to use one lamp instead of thirteen. A curved lens, called a Fresnel lens, made the light much brighter. The Fresnel lens lasted until 1900. Then a new lens, with prisms, made the light brighter still. The lighthouse lamp did not have an electric bulb until 1923. In 1958, the light was automated. Now it shines through a 300 mm lens. The lens makes the light focus. It shines a green flash every six seconds that can be seen 11 miles out in the lake!

Brightly yours,

Argent

Experiment!

Good Musicians

Ohio musicians have been entertaining visitors for many years. A good musician can hear if an instrument is out of tune. How does a guitar player fix a guitar that is out of tune? How can a piano play so many different notes? Plan and conduct an experiment to find out.

Chapter 6 Energy

Vocabulary

energy	convection
kinetic energy	radiation
potential energy	reflection
energy transfer	fossil
solar energy	resource
light	nonrenewable resource
chemical energy	conservation
mechanical energy	renewable resource
electric energy	pollution
heat	
system	
conduction	

What do **YOU** wonder?

Ice sailing began in the Netherlands in the 1700s. When lakes and rivers froze, people used ice boats to travel and move cargo across waterways. What gives an ice boat the energy to move?

What Are Kinetic and Potential Energy?

Fast Fact

Bull's-Eye! The farther back an archer pulls the bow, the more energy the arrow has when it's released. Some Olympic archers can score a bull's-eye from 90 m (295 ft) away. The arrow must hit the target before it falls too far. In the Investigate, you'll explore factors that affect how objects fall.

Going Up!

Materials
- paper strip, 100 cm long
- tape measure
- tape
- colored pencils
- rubber ball

Procedure

1. Work with a partner. Tape the paper to the wall as shown. Using the tape measure, mark the paper strip at 10-cm intervals. Start with 0 cm at the floor, and end with 100 cm at the top.

2. Have your partner hold the ball next to the 50-cm mark. You should sit facing the paper, with your eyes at the level of the 50-cm mark.

3. Have your partner drop the ball while you observe how high it bounces. Record the height with a colored mark on the paper.

4. Repeat Steps 2 and 3 two more times. Record each height in a different color.

5. Switch roles with your partner. This time, drop the ball from the 100-cm mark. Repeat Step 4.

Draw Conclusions

1. How did your results change when you dropped the ball from 100 cm?

2. **Inquiry Skill** For this experiment, you dropped the ball from 50 cm and 100 cm. Draw conclusions about what was different when you dropped the ball from 100 cm.

Step 1

Step 3

Investigate Further

Write a hypothesis about how far the ball will bounce if you drop it from 200 cm. Then try it to check your hypothesis.

VOCABULARY
energy p. 198
kinetic energy p. 200
potential energy p. 200
energy transfer p. 202

SCIENCE CONCEPTS
► how kinetic energy differs from potential energy

READING FOCUS SKILL

COMPARE AND CONTRAST Look for similarities and differences between potential energy and kinetic energy.

| alike | different |

Energy

Sometimes a simple word can be hard to define. For example, how would you define the word *show*? You've probably used it often but haven't thought much about its meaning. A common word is often used in different ways.

Defining common words can be especially difficult in science. Some words are so ordinary that people use them without thinking. And the words used in science may have several everyday meanings. But scientists need specific definitions.

For example, think about the word *energy*. You might say after school that you don't have enough energy to do your chores. This personal feeling about energy is not based on the scientific definition. Scientists define **energy** as the ability to cause a change in matter.

The energy from this falling ice produces a big splash, a movement of the water.

One kind of change is movement, or a change in position. Does the glacier in the photograph have energy? Since part of it is moving, a scientist would say it has energy.

The race car in the photo is also moving, so it has energy. But where does its energy come from? A car can't just make the energy it needs. This is part of the *law of conservation of energy.* The law states that energy can never be made or destroyed, but it can change forms.

The race car's engine changes the energy stored in gasoline into movement. The car moves, or changes position, because one form of energy changes into another.

Now look at the volleyball player. He is giving energy to the ball, making it move. Where does the volleyball player get this energy? It comes from inside his body, from the food he eats. During a hard game, he may feel that he lacks energy because he is tired. In the scientific sense, however, he definitely has energy.

People use the energy stored in food to move, to talk, and even to sleep. Energy stored in food is used in the body for all life processes and also for making the body and objects move.

 COMPARE AND CONTRAST How is the everyday use of the word *energy* different from the way a scientist uses the word?

The volleyball player's muscles provide the energy for the ball to move. ▼

▲ The car's engine provides the energy to move the car forward on the track.

Kinetic and Potential Energy

There are many forms of energy and many ways to classify them. One way divides all forms into two groups: kinetic energy and potential energy.

Kinetic energy is the energy of motion. If something is moving, it has kinetic energy. The faster an object is moving, the more kinetic energy it has. An airplane flying through the air has more kinetic energy than a person riding a bicycle.

Potential energy is the energy an object has because of its condition or position. For example, the higher an object is, the more potential energy it has. So a ball on the roof of a building has more potential energy than a ball on your desk, because it can fall farther.

Think about a book on a shelf. It has the potential to move down if it falls off the shelf, so it has potential energy. If it did fall and hit the floor, it would no longer have the same amount of potential energy.

An object can have potential and kinetic energy at the same time. As the book falls from the shelf, it loses potential energy and gains kinetic energy.

As the roller coaster car in the photo moves to the top of a hill, it gains potential energy. The higher the car rises, the more potential energy it has. When the car moves down, it has kinetic energy. As it falls, its kinetic energy increases and its potential energy decreases.

The other photo shows a boy jumping up and down on a pogo stick. When he first jumps onto the pogo stick, he is moving down, so he has kinetic energy. As he moves down, the spring inside the pogo

Is the roller coaster car gaining potential energy or using kinetic energy?

stick compresses. This adds potential energy to the spring.

At the bottom of the jump, the boy is not moving, so he has no kinetic energy. But the spring's potential energy transfers to him. It moves him up, so he has kinetic energy again.

At the top of the jump, the boy stops moving. He has no kinetic energy, but he has potential energy. As he moves down, the potential energy changes back to kinetic energy.

Focus Skill **COMPARE AND CONTRAST** How is kinetic energy different from potential energy?

◀ As the boy goes up and down, sometimes he has potential energy, sometimes he has kinetic energy, and sometimes he has both.

Insta-Lab

Energy Release

Balance a ruler on top of a pencil. Place a small wad of paper on one end. Push the other end down quickly. When did you add potential energy? When did you see the effect of kinetic energy?

201

Energy Transfer

Energy can move between places or objects, as shown in this picture. In the picture, an acrobat is standing still on a teeterboard. He has no kinetic energy, and he doesn't have potential energy.

There is also a man flying through the air. He's moving, so now he has kinetic energy. What will happen when he lands on the teeterboard? His kinetic energy will be transferred to the other acrobat. When he drops, he will push his end of the teeterboard down. This will give potential energy to the first acrobat as the teeterboard raises up. He will also gain kinetic energy and be launched off the teeterboard.

Energy transfer is the movement of energy from one place or object to another. In the circus act, energy moved from the first acrobat to the second. Remember the boy on the pogo stick? His kinetic energy was transferred to the spring, where it changed into potential energy. As the spring expanded, that potential energy was transferred to the boy as kinetic energy, bouncing him into the air.

 COMPARE AND CONTRAST How is the circus teeterboard like the spring in the pogo stick?

What would happen if the acrobat dropped onto the side of the teeterboard that was on the ground? Would the teeterboard transfer any of the energy? ▼

1. COMPARE AND CONTRAST Draw and complete this graphic organizer.

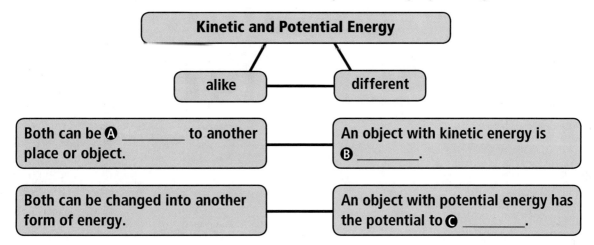

Kinetic and Potential Energy

alike — different

Both can be **A** _____ to another place or object.

An object with kinetic energy is **B** _____.

Both can be changed into another form of energy.

An object with potential energy has the potential to **C** _____.

2. SUMMARIZE Write three sentences that summarize this lesson.

3. DRAW CONCLUSIONS If you throw a baseball, where does the ball's kinetic energy come from?

4. VOCABULARY Write a dictionary entry for each vocabulary word.

Test Prep

5. Critical Thinking Why does a book on a high shelf have more potential energy than a book on a low shelf?

6. Which has potential energy?
   A. a bike lying on a driveway
   B. a rock at the top of a cliff
   C. a chair sitting on the floor
   D. a baseball lost in the weeds

Links

Writing

Expository Writing
Your class is making a science video about energy. One part will show a girl playing with a yo-yo. Write the **narration** for this scene, describing the potential and kinetic energy in the yo-yo at any time.

Math

Compare Numbers
When compressed fully and then released, Spring A sent a 10-kg mass 2 m into the air. Under the same conditions, Spring B sent the mass 8 m into the air. Which spring had more potential energy?

Language Arts

Definitions
Look up an everyday meaning of the word *potential.* Write a paragraph explaining that meaning and how it relates to potential energy.

For more links and activities, go to www.hspscience.com

What Are Some Forms of Energy?

Fast Fact

Cool Lights! Neon tubes give off light in bright colors, but unlike some light bulbs, they don't get hot. The reaction that takes place in these tubes releases light energy but not much heat. In the Investigate, you'll test another reaction to see if it releases heat.

Warmer or Cooler?

Materials
- measuring cup
- safety goggles
- water
- plastic cup
- thermometer
- plastic spoon
- calcium chloride

Procedure

1 Make a table like the one shown.

2 **CAUTION: Put on safety goggles. Do not touch the calcium chloride.** Measure 50 mL of water, and pour it into the plastic cup.

3 Using the thermometer, measure the temperature of the water. Then record the temperature in your table.

4 Add 2 spoonfuls of calcium chloride to the water, and stir until the calcium chloride is dissolved. Wait 30 seconds.

5 Measure the temperature of the water, and record it in your table.

6 Repeat Step 5 one minute and two minutes after the calcium chloride has dissolved.

Draw Conclusions

1. How did the temperature of the water change after you added the calcium chloride?

2. **Inquiry Skill** What energy change can you infer takes place when calcium chloride dissolves in water?

Step 4

Temperature Changes	
Time	Temperature
Before dissolving calcium chloride	
30 seconds after dissolving	
1 minute after dissolving	
2 minutes after dissolving	

Investigate Further

Write a hypothesis about what would happen if you used 100 mL of water. Then plan and conduct a simple investigation to test your hypothesis.

Reading in Science

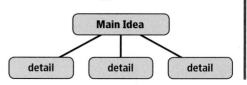

PS-3 Describe conversion of electricity into other energy; **PS-6** Describe sound

---

VOCABULARY
solar energy p. 206
light p. 206
chemical energy p. 208
mechanical energy p. 208
electric energy p. 210

SCIENCE CONCEPTS
▶ how to identify and describe different forms of energy
▶ how energy can be changed from one form to another

READING FOCUS SKILL

MAIN IDEA AND DETAILS Look for details about the different forms of energy.

Main Idea
detail · detail · detail

Solar Energy

You have read that all energy can be classified as potential energy or kinetic energy. Scientists also classify energy in other forms. However, the classification of energy you'll read about here isn't as simple as the main division into potential energy and kinetic energy. Sometimes two or more forms of energy overlap.

One form of energy is around you every day. Energy that comes from the sun is called **solar energy**. The word *solar* means "of the sun." People use solar energy in many ways. Do you have a calculator that doesn't need batteries? Many calculators have solar cells that change light energy from the sun into electricity. You'll learn more about electricity, or electric energy, later on.

Other forms of energy come from the sun directly. Energy from the sun travels as *radiation*. The sun produces several kinds of radiation. **Light** is radiation we see, and heat is radiation we feel. X rays and ultraviolet rays also come from the sun. The sun even produces radio waves, which we hear as static on radios.

On a warm, dry day you can feel radiation from the sun. You can also see the effects of radiation changing the temperature of the air.

◀ Most of the heat and hot water for this home comes from the sun's energy, collected by the solar panels on the roof.

Without solar energy, Earth would be just a ball of frozen rock with no life. Heat from the sun allows Earth to support life forms. Light from the sun helps plants make food and oxygen. In fact, the sun is the source of almost all energy on Earth. Its energy is stored in fossil fuels—the coal, oil, and natural gas that come from long-dead plants and animals. The sun's energy is also the source of weather. Uneven heating of the Earth's surface produces winds and the water cycle.

Solar energy is useful in other ways, too. You know that light from the sun can provide electricity for tools such as calculators. Solar cells can also provide electricity for places that are hard to reach with standard power lines. Solar collector panels are used to absorb the sun's energy to heat water. The heated water can then be used to heat swimming pools or to provide hot water for home use.

However, although solar energy is free, solar cells and collectors can be expensive.

Another problem is that many places don't have enough sunny days to make solar energy practical.

 MAIN IDEA AND DETAILS What forms of energy come directly from solar energy?

Insta-Lab

Solar Chips
Put a handful of chocolate chips on each of two plates. Place both plates in the sun. Then use a hand lens to focus sunlight on the chips on one of the plates. What happens? What do you think causes this?

Chemical energy in fuel is used to keep this remote-control model helicopter flying.

Chemical and Mechanical Energy

It takes a lot of energy to move something as heavy as a car. Where does that energy come from? In most cars, an engine burns gasoline, a fuel. Burning a fuel releases the energy stored in it.

The energy stored in fuel is **chemical energy**. This is energy that can be released by a chemical reaction, such as burning. When it is not being used, chemical energy is potential energy. A chemical reaction is needed to change this potential energy into kinetic energy.

Earlier, you read that your muscles get energy from the food you eat. The potential energy stored in food is chemical energy. When it's released, it gives you kinetic energy to move.

Have you ever used a heat pack to warm your hands or feet? The pack contains substances that have potential chemical energy. When you squeeze the pack, the substances mix, and a chemical reaction occurs. The heat from the reaction is what warms you.

Many substances release energy in chemical reactions. For example, wood releases heat when it is burned. A glow stick releases light when a chemical reaction occurs. In the Investigate, you observed the release of chemical energy stored in a substance called calcium chloride.

Another form of energy that includes both potential energy and kinetic energy is mechanical energy. **Mechanical energy** is the combination of all the potential and kinetic energy that something has. The windup toy in the photo has a key attached to a spring. When you turn the key, you wind up, or tighten, the spring, giving the toy potential energy. The tighter the spring is wound, the more potential energy the toy has.

When the toy is moving, it has kinetic energy. Since the spring is still partly wound up, the toy also has some potential energy. The toy's mechanical energy is the combination of its potential energy and its kinetic energy.

The remote-control helicopter is moving, so you know that it has kinetic energy. The fuel in its tank has chemical energy, which is potential energy. The helicopter's mechanical energy is the combination of its kinetic and its potential energy.

 MAIN IDEA AND DETAILS Is chemical energy potential or kinetic energy?

Chemical energy is stored in fireworks. ▶

▲ **A windup toy is operated by mechanical energy. Where does this toy get its kinetic energy?**

Electricity and Sound

Have you ever experienced a blackout? Candles can help you see during a blackout, but they don't provide enough light to read easily. Televisions and computers don't work. Kitchen appliances don't either, so cooking is difficult. In a blackout, you realize how much you depend on electricity. Electricity, or **electric energy**, is energy that comes from an electric current. An electric current results from the movement of electrons. Electrons are particles in atoms.

You can see some effects of electric energy when you use appliances. You may have even felt electric energy. Have you ever walked across a rug on a dry day and then touched a doorknob? You probably felt electric energy in the form of a small shock.

People have invented a great many devices that use electric energy to make life better. These include all the basic things you'd miss in a blackout. They also include modern, battery-operated devices such as portable games, cell phones, and music players.

Another useful form of energy is sound. *Sound* is energy in the form of vibrations that travel through matter.

Sound vibrations pass through the particles of matter in a kind of domino effect. When a vibration reaches a particle of matter, that particle starts to vibrate, too. If it's close enough to other particles,

This band uses a lot of electric energy and produces a lot of sound energy. ▼

A megaphone focuses sound in one direction. Without the megaphone, the energy would spread out in all directions.

▲ Electric energy makes sound louder with this bull horn.

they also start to vibrate. In this way, sound vibrations can spread out, not just in a straight line, but in all directions.

Like light energy, sound energy can travel through many objects. Sound vibrations travel easily through air, so people can hear sounds—even quiet ones—at a distance.

Deep inside the ear is a thin membrane called the eardrum. Hearing begins with the vibration of the eardrum. When sound vibrations in the air reach the eardrum, it vibrates. These vibrations are transmitted deeper into the ear, where they are changed into nerve messages that travel to the brain. If the sound you are listening to is too loud, its vibrations can damage your ears and affect your hearing.

People can also experience sound energy in other ways. If you place your hands on the radio or television, you can feel the sound vibrations. Some people with hearing disabilities have been able to become dancers by feeling the vibrations of the music through their feet.

Another time you might be able to feel sound is at a fireworks show. Many fireworks produce not only bright colors, but also loud whistles, pops, and bangs. You can often feel the energy of these sounds on your body.

 MAIN IDEA AND DETAILS List three things in your classroom that use electric energy.

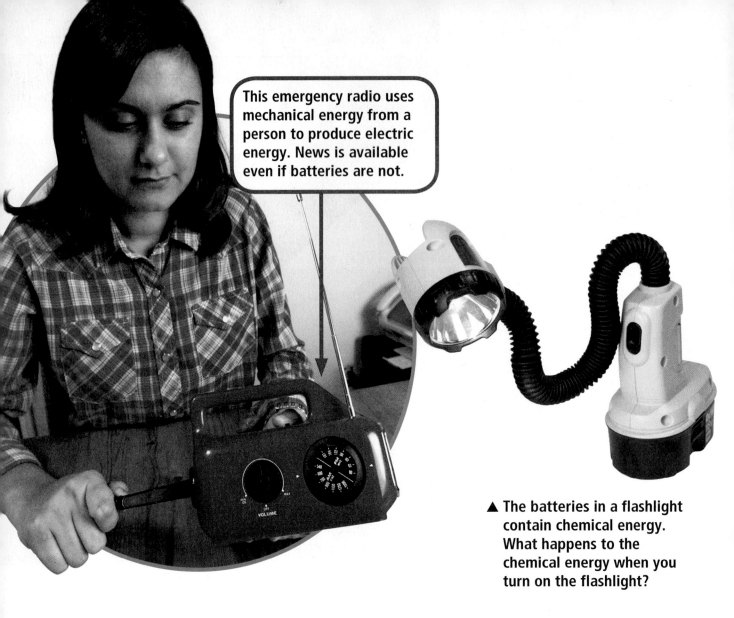

This emergency radio uses mechanical energy from a person to produce electric energy. News is available even if batteries are not.

▲ The batteries in a flashlight contain chemical energy. What happens to the chemical energy when you turn on the flashlight?

Changing Energy Forms

In this lesson, you've examined different energy forms and some of their uses. Often, one form of energy changes into another form.

The batteries in a flashlight contain chemical energy, but the flashlight bulb gives off light. Where does the light come from? The batteries' chemical energy changes into electric energy. Then the bulb in the flashlight changes the electric energy into light energy.

When you turn the crank of an emergency radio, you add potential energy to the radio. When you turn on the radio, sound energy is produced. The potential energy you added was changed into electric energy. Then the electric energy was changed into sound energy.

Look again at the photo of the concert stage. The microphones change sound energy into electric energy, which is amplified, or increased. Then the speakers change the electric energy back into sound. In this situation and many others, energy is constantly being changed from one form to another in order to make it more useful to us.

 MAIN IDEA AND DETAILS Why do people change energy from one form to another?

1. MAIN IDEA AND DETAILS Draw and complete this graphic organizer.

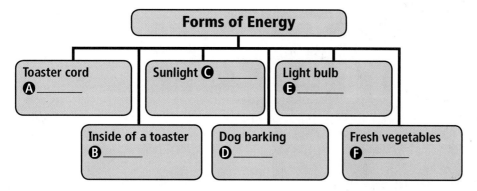

Forms of Energy

Toaster cord **A**_____

Sunlight **C**_____

Light bulb **E**_____

Inside of a toaster **B**_____

Dog barking **D**_____

Fresh vegetables **F**_____

2. SUMMARIZE Write a summary of this lesson by using each of the lesson vocabulary words in a sentence.

3. DRAW CONCLUSIONS A light bulb changes electric energy into two other forms of energy. What are they?

4. VOCABULARY Make a crossword puzzle, including clues, that contains all of this lesson's vocabulary words.

Test Prep

5. Critical Thinking Bess says that thunder produces sound energy. Her friend says kinetic energy comes from thunder. Who is correct? Explain.

6. Which of the following changes chemical energy directly into light energy?

A. a candle   **C.** a flashlight

B. a car key   **D.** a light switch

Links

Writing

Narrative Writing
Many forms of energy are around us and within us. Write two or three paragraphs **describing** some ways you use energy in a typical day.

Math

Compare Fractions
Battery A contains a full charge of chemical energy. Battery B has $\frac{2}{5}$ of a full charge, and Battery C has $\frac{2}{3}$ as much energy as Battery A. Which battery contains the least chemical energy?

Music

Composition
Write a one-minute song about energy. Include lyrics and, if possible, a melody.

For more links and activities, go to www.hspscience.com

How Is Heat Transferred?

Fast Fact

Where's the Heat? A thermogram shows
the heat patterns in a person's body. The
colors show the different levels of heat that
the body gives off. Red and yellow show the
warmest areas, and green and blue show
the coolest. In the Investigate, you'll observe
some other heat patterns.

214

Hot Buttered Knives

Materials
- cold butter
- metal knife
- large plastic foam cup
- hot water
- plastic knife

Procedure

1. Place two pats of butter on the blade of the metal knife—one in the middle and one near the tip. Place the knife, handle first, in the cup to check that both pats are above the rim. Remove the knife.

2. **CAUTION: Be careful when pouring the hot water.** Fill the cup with hot water. Carefully place the knife, handle first, back in the cup.

3. Observe the knife and the pats of butter for 10 minutes. Record your observations.

4. Repeat Steps 1–3, substituting the plastic knife for the metal one. Record your observations.

Step 1

Step 4

Draw Conclusions

1. On which knife did the butter melt faster? On that knife, which pat of butter melted faster?

2. **Inquiry Skill** Draw a conclusion about which material—metal or plastic—transfers heat faster.

Investigate Further

Write a hypothesis about which knife would *lose* heat faster. Then plan and conduct a simple investigation to check.

VOCABULARY

heat p. 216
system p. 217
conduction p. 218
convection p. 218
radiation p. 219
reflection p. 219

SCIENCE CONCEPTS

▶ how heat moves by means of conduction, convection, and radiation

READING FOCUS SKILL

MAIN IDEA AND DETAILS
Describe each of the main points about heat transfer.

```
        Main Idea
       /    |    \
  detail  detail  detail
```

Heat and Temperature

You probably know that the terms *heat* and *temperature* are related, but you may not know how. You also know that objects with a high temperature give off heat, but what exactly is heat?

Remember that all matter is made up of tiny particles that are always moving. Since they move, they have kinetic energy also that is called *thermal energy.* The faster the particles move, the more thermal energy the matter has.

When particles of one substance come in contact with particles of another substance that are moving at a different rate, thermal energy is transferred. **Heat** is the transfer of thermal energy between objects with different temperatures.

Thermal energy travels from a warmer object to a cooler object. Energy from the stove burner flows through the pot and into the water, causing it to get hot. Energy doesn't travel from the low-temperature water to the high-temperature burner.

But what is temperature? *Temperature* is the measurement of the average kinetic energy of all the particles in a substance. You can measure temperature with a

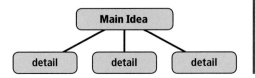
Thermal Energy Transfer

▲ The water in this pot is cool. Its particles don't have much kinetic energy, so its temperature is low.

▲ The particles of water in this pot have more kinetic energy than those in the first pot. This water's temperature is high.

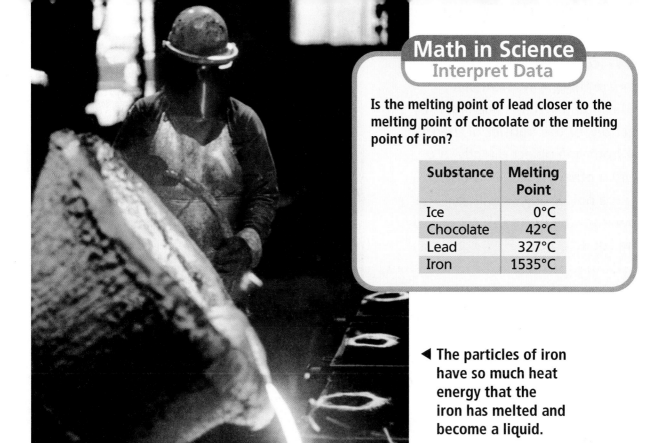

Math in Science
Interpret Data

Is the melting point of lead closer to the melting point of chocolate or the melting point of iron?

Substance	Melting Point
Ice	0°C
Chocolate	42°C
Lead	327°C
Iron	1535°C

◀ The particles of iron have so much heat energy that the iron has melted and become a liquid.

thermometer. The number shown on a thermometer is related to the amount of kinetic energy in a substance.

Some systems are very efficient at transferring thermal energy. A **system** is a set of parts acting together as a whole object. A burner, a pot, and water are a system through which thermal energy moves. The burner transfers thermal energy to the pot. The pot transfers thermal energy to the water. As the water receives more and more thermal energy, its particles move faster and faster.

The movement of particles helps explain changes in state. In ice, water particles are held together in a rigid pattern. They don't move around, but they vibrate in place. As thermal energy is added, they vibrate faster and faster. At a certain point, the particles have so much energy that they break out of the rigid pattern and flow easily around each other. The ice melts.

If you keep adding thermal energy, the water particles keep moving faster and faster. Finally, they have so much thermal energy they separate from each other and rise into the air. The water boils.

Some systems need more thermal energy than others to cause a change of state. For example, more energy is needed to make iron melt than to make chocolate melt. This is because it takes more energy to separate the particles in iron from each other than to separate the particles in chocolate.

 MAIN IDEA AND DETAILS How is temperature related to heat?

Thermal Energy Transfer

There are three ways heat can move through a system. The first is by **conduction**, or the transfer of thermal energy from one object directly into another. In other words, if an object is touching a hotter object, thermal energy will flow from the hotter object directly into the cooler object.

The pot in the burner-pot-water system is heated by conduction. The pot is in contact with the burner, so thermal energy from the burner flows directly into the pot. The water is in contact with the pot, so thermal energy from the pot flows into the water.

Of course, only the water at the bottom and the sides is actually in contact with the pot. The water in the middle is heated by a process called convection. **Convection** is the transfer of thermal energy through the movement of a gas or a liquid. As a gas or a liquid is heated, the heat causes it to move upward, carrying heat to the area above the heat source.

That's how the water in the middle gets warm. Thermal energy from the pot flows into the water at the bottom by conduction. Then the heated water moves upward by convection, bringing thermal energy to the water above it.

▲ Heat from the iron moves directly into the clothing by conduction.

Inside the balloon, heated air moves up, carrying thermal energy to the air above it by convection. ▶

218

The meerkat is warming itself under the lamp. Radiation carries thermal energy from the lamp to the meerkat.

The third way thermal energy can be transferred is by radiation. **Radiation** is the transfer of energy by waves that move through matter and space. Remember that solar energy travels as light, X-ray, radio, and ultraviolet waves. It also travels as infrared waves. Infrared waves carry thermal energy from the sun and from heat sources such as campfires and toasters.

Unlike conduction and convection, radiation doesn't need matter for the heat to travel through. Conduction requires that two objects be in contact. Convection requires a gas or a liquid. Radiation can transfer thermal energy from the sun across 150 million km (93 million mi) of space to Earth.

Not all of this radiation from the sun reaches Earth's surface. Some of it is reflected back into space by the atmosphere. **Reflection** occurs when heat or light bounces off an object.

 MAIN IDEA AND DETAILS What are the three ways by which thermal energy can be transferred?

Distance and Heat
Hold a thermometer 40 cm from a light bulb. (Don't use a fluorescent light.) After two minutes, record the temperature. Repeat the procedure, holding the thermometer 30, 20, and 10 cm from the bulb. How does distance affect the transfer of thermal energy?

Insulators and Conductors

On a hot beach, the drinks inside an ice chest stay cold. It seems as if heat doesn't move from the air into the drinks. In fact, the heat does move, but it moves very slowly because the cooler is an insulator. Anything that slows the movement of thermal energy is an *insulator*.

Heat always moves from something warmer to something cooler. However, certain factors affect the rate at which heat moves from one object to another.

Not all insulators keep things cool. Thick coats keep us warm by trapping heat close to our bodies on winter days. Coats prevent warm air from escaping.

There are also things that allow heat to move through them very easily. If you use a metal spoon to eat hot soup, the handle may get very hot, even though it never touches the soup. Heat moves from the soup to and through the spoon by conduction. Anything that allows thermal energy to move through it easily is called a *conductor*. Have you ever seen a pan with a copper bottom? Copper is a good conductor of heat, so food in the pan cooks quickly and evenly. Many metals are good conductors of heat.

 MAIN IDEA AND DETAILS What are insulators and conductors?

◀ The lunch bag prevents heat in the air from moving into the bag. This keeps the food in the bag cool.

The cookie sheet is a conductor. The oven mitt is an insulator.

1. MAIN IDEA AND DETAILS Draw and complete the graphic organizer.

Heat can be transferred in three ways.

In **Ⓐ** ____ , heat is transferred from one object to another.

In convection, heat causes a **Ⓑ** _____ or a **Ⓒ** _____ to move upward.

In **Ⓓ** _____ , waves of energy move through matter and space.

2. SUMMARIZE Use the graphic organizer to write a summary of this lesson.

3. DRAW CONCLUSIONS When you face a campfire, why does your front feel warmer than your back?

4. VOCABULARY Use each lesson vocabulary term in a sentence.

Test Prep

5. Critical Thinking If you put one thermometer 10 cm (4 in.) above a flame and another one 10 cm to the side of the flame, which would show the higher temperature? Explain.

6. If you want heat to move from a light bulb to an object by conduction, where should you place the object?

A. above the light bulb

B. next to the light bulb

C. below the light bulb

D. touching the light bulb

Links

Writing

Expository Writing
Suppose you're tutoring a younger student in science. Write an **explanation** of how heat can be transferred within a system. Be sure to keep your explanation as simple as possible.

Math

Solve Problems
A substance in a beaker has a temperature of 22°C. At 1:00, you begin to heat it. After 14 minutes, its temperature reaches 48°C, and you stop heating it. By 2:03, it has cooled back down to 22°C. How long did it take to cool?

Language Arts

Word Usage
Use a dictionary to find as many words as you can that are related to the word *conduction*. List and define the words.

 For more links and activities, go to **www.hspscience.com**

How Do People Use Energy Resources?

Fast Fact

Power Up The energy station at Hoover Dam, on the border between Arizona and Nevada, has 17 turbines that produce electricity. All the turbines are turned by the energy of falling water. In the Investigate, you will experiment to discover the effect distance has on the energy of falling water.

Water Power

Materials
- 2 plastic disks
- pencil
- string, 100 cm
- washers

- stapler
- masking tape
- 10-g mass (paper clip, weight)
- bottle of water

- scissors
- stopwatch
- meterstick
- basin

Procedure

1. **CAUTION: Be careful with the scissors.** Staple the disks together at their centers. Cut four 3-cm slits as shown. On the left side of each slit, fold the disks in opposite directions to form a vane.

2. Carefully pierce a small slit through the center of both disks. Insert the pencil.

3. Tape one end of the string to the pencil. Tie or tape the mass to the string.

4. Slide a washer onto each end of the pencil. Hold your water wheel by the washers so it can turn freely. Hold it horizontally over the basin, with the closed ends of the vanes away from you.

5. Have a partner slowly pour water from a height of 10 cm onto the vanes. Measure and record the time it takes for the mass to be wound up to the pencil. Repeat, pouring water from 15 cm and 20 cm.

Step 2

Step 5

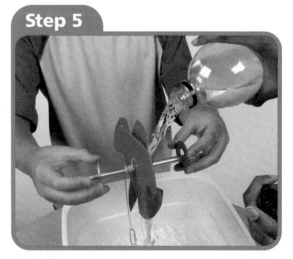

Draw Conclusions

1. What variable did you control? What variable did you change?

2. **Inquiry Skill** What can you conclude about the effect of the distance the water fell on the speed at which the water wheel turned?

Investigate Further

Write a **hypothesis** about how the rate of the water's flow affects the speed of the water wheel. Then plan and conduct an experiment to check it.

SCIENCE CONCEPTS

▶ why it is important to conserve energy resources

▶ how to conserve energy resources

 READING FOCUS SKILL

COMPARE AND CONTRAST Look for similarities and differences between renewable energy sources and nonrenewable energy sources.

alike	different

Nonrenewable Energy Resources

Think about the hot water you use at home. Where does the energy that heats the water in your home come from? If your water heater is electric, it gets its energy, as your home's other electric appliances do, from an electric energy station. Some energy stations, such as the one at Hoover Dam, produce electricity by using the energy of falling water. Electricity made in this way is known as *hydroelectric energy*.

Most energy stations burn coal, oil, or natural gas as sources of energy to produce electricity. Burning these fuels changes their chemical energy to thermal energy, which is used to change water to steam. The steam, like the falling water in dams, powers the machines that produce electricity.

Coal, oil, and natural gas are *fossil fuels*. A **fossil** is the remains or traces of past life, and it is found in sedimentary rock. Fossil fuels are fuels that formed from the remains of once-living things.

This energy station in Australia burns coal to produce electricity. The coal comes from the remains of plants that lived and died millions of years ago.

It takes millions of years for coal, oil, and natural gas to form. When supplies are used up, there will be no more. This is why coal, oil, and natural gas are called nonrenewable resources. A **resource** is any material that can be used to satisfy a need. A **nonrenewable resource** is a resource that, once used up, cannot be replaced within a reasonable amount of time.

Does this mean that we will use up our nonrenewable resources? This will happen in time, but there are things we can do to keep from using them up before we find other resources to use in their place.

One thing people can do is use less of these fuels. Using less of something to make the supply last longer is called **conservation**. For example, if everyone uses less hot water, less fossil fuel will be burned to make electricity to heat the water. That will help make the world's supply of fossil fuel last longer.

Another thing people can do to conserve nonrenewable resources is switch to using resources that won't run out. Scientists are working to develop new ways to do this.

 COMPARE AND CONTRAST What do coal, oil, and natural gas have in common?

Since there is a limited supply of oil, the more gasoline we use now the less we will have in the future for driving and manufacturing.

As oil resources are used up, it takes more work to get the oil that is left. This drilling platform pumps oil from under the ocean floor.

Renewable Energy Resources

Some resources are renewable. A **renewable resource** is a resource that can be replaced within a reasonable amount of time.

You may be wondering how an *energy* resource can be renewable. After all, once you burn a fuel, isn't it gone?

The key is that not all energy resources need to be burned in order to release energy. As you read at the beginning of this chapter, there are many different forms of energy.

One form of energy is solar energy, which can be changed directly into electric energy

by solar cells. Some highway signs use solar cells in the daytime to produce the electricity they need to light them at night. Since Earth gets sunlight every day, solar energy is a renewable energy resource.

Science Up Close

A Hybrid Car

A hybrid car runs on electricity at slow speeds and on gasoline at high speeds.

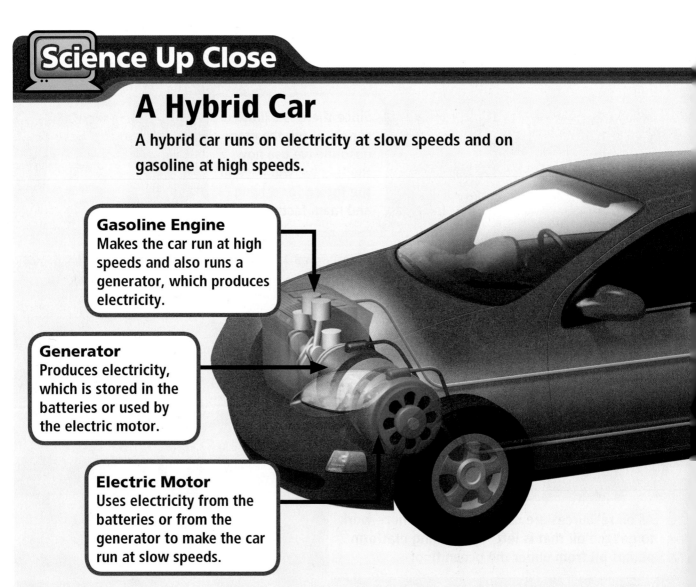

Gasoline Engine
Makes the car run at high speeds and also runs a generator, which produces electricity.

Generator
Produces electricity, which is stored in the batteries or used by the electric motor.

Electric Motor
Uses electricity from the batteries or from the generator to make the car run at slow speeds.

◄ One windmill can produce only a small amount of electricity. That's why energy companies build "wind farms" that have hundreds of windmills.

You have just read about energy stations that use the energy of falling water to produce electricity. Falling water is a renewable energy resource, too. Water is constantly recycled and is not used up as fossil fuels are.

Wind is another renewable energy resource. Moving air can power windmill turbines that produce electricity, just as falling water powers turbines in dams.

Today, we still need nonrenewable resources. We don't yet have the technology to get enough energy from renewable resources at a reasonable cost. However, scientists are working to find lower-cost ways of using renewable energy resources in the future. An example is the research being done on windmills. Research also continues on ways to conserve nonrenewable resources, such as by using hybrid cars.

 COMPARE AND CONTRAST How are renewable energy resources the same as nonrenewable energy resources? How are they different?

Gas Tank
Holds the fuel for the gasoline engine.

Batteries
Store chemical energy, which is changed into electrical energy.

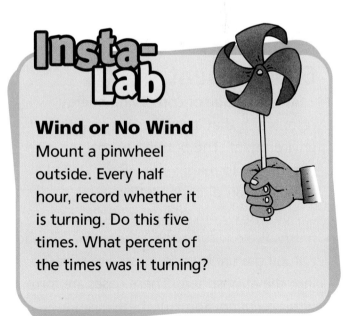

Insta-Lab

Wind or No Wind
Mount a pinwheel outside. Every half hour, record whether it is turning. Do this five times. What percent of the times was it turning?

For more links and activities, go to www.hspscience.com

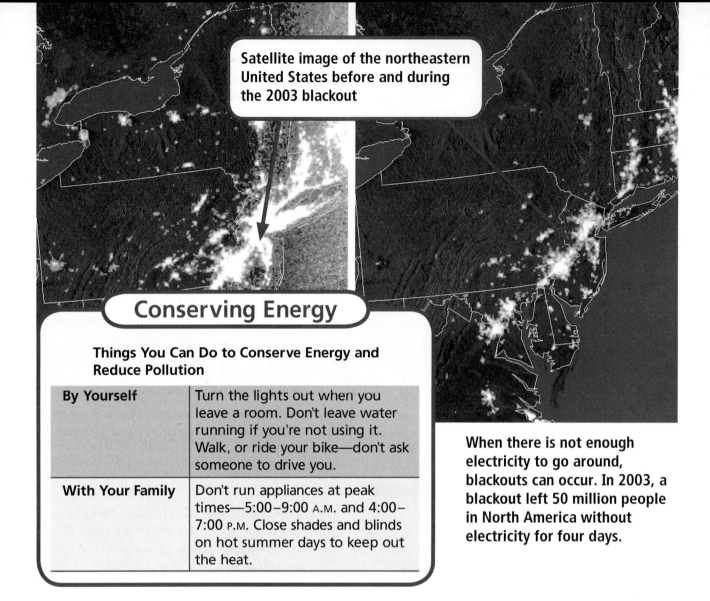

Satellite image of the northeastern United States before and during the 2003 blackout

Conserving Energy

Things You Can Do to Conserve Energy and Reduce Pollution

By Yourself	Turn the lights out when you leave a room. Don't leave water running if you're not using it. Walk, or ride your bike—don't ask someone to drive you.
With Your Family	Don't run appliances at peak times—5:00–9:00 A.M. and 4:00–7:00 P.M. Close shades and blinds on hot summer days to keep out the heat.

When there is not enough electricity to go around, blackouts can occur. In 2003, a blackout left 50 million people in North America without electricity for four days.

Conservation and the Environment

An advantage of conserving energy resources is that it reduces harm to the environment. The burning of coal, oil, and natural gas to release the energy stored in them also produces pollution.

Pollution is anything that dirties or harms the environment. When coal, oil, and natural gas are burned, gases are released into the atmosphere. These gases are forms of *air pollution*. Some of these gases are poisonous. Others combine with water in the air to form acid, which harms plants and animals.

The conservation methods and the inventions you have read about not only save energy resources, they also reduce pollution. For example, a hybrid car runs on gasoline just part of the time. This means that when it travels the same distance as a regular car, it burns less fossil fuel. Driving a hybrid car can help conserve fossil fuel.

There are many other things people can do to conserve energy resources. The table above lists some of them.

 COMPARE AND CONTRAST How does conserving energy resources also help the environment?

1. COMPARE AND CONTRAST Draw and complete this graphic organizer.

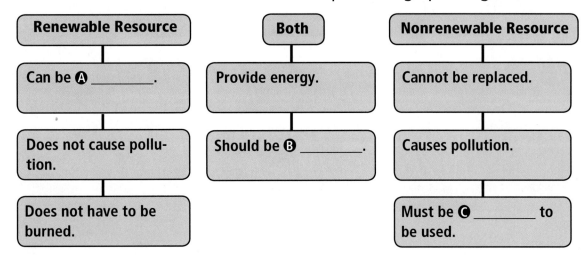

Renewable Resource	Both	Nonrenewable Resource
Can be **Ⓐ** _____.	Provide energy.	Cannot be replaced.
Does not cause pollution.	Should be **Ⓑ** _____.	Causes pollution.
Does not have to be burned.		Must be **Ⓒ** _____ to be used.

2. SUMMARIZE Write two sentences that tell what this lesson is mainly about.

3. DRAW CONCLUSIONS Solar panels on roofs produce electricity for homes. Why don't all homes have solar panels?

4. VOCABULARY Write a paragraph using all of the lesson vocabulary words.

Test Prep

5. Critical Thinking Suppose someone invented an inexpensive solar cell for producing electricity from sunlight. What drawback would the solar cell still have?

6. Which of the following is a renewable energy resource?
   A. coal   **C.** oil
   B. gasoline   **D.** wind

Links

Writing

Expository Writing
"Reduce, reuse, recycle" is a motto about protecting the environment. Find out what each of these words means. Then write a brief **definition** of each one.

Math

Find Area
An array of solar cells covers a rectangle that measures 450 m on two sides and 200 m on the other two sides. What is the area of the array?

Social Studies

Hydropower
Find out how long people have been using water power and what technologies they have used to capture it. Summarize your findings in a brief report with diagrams.

 For more links and activities, go to www.hspscience.com

Dream Machines

Welcome to the car showroom of the future. Step right up and take a look at some of our new models. If going fast is your thing, climb into this superfast car that can zip along at 405 km (252 miles) per hour! Say goodbye to smog with these cars. The AUTOnomy runs on clean-burning hydrogen instead of gasoline. The Hypercar runs on gasoline and hydrogen.

Zoom, Zoom, Zoom

A European car maker recently unveiled its 1001-horsepower, ultrafast supercar, which can reach a top speed of 405 km (252 miles) per hour. The car is made of lightweight materials. It also has specially made tires that won't melt when the car hits high rates of speed.

Engineers also designed the bottom of the car to create the venturi effect. The venturi effect is a downward pull that helps keep the car on the road.

H Is for Hydrogen Power

Can engineers design a car that doesn't cause pollution? An American carmaker thinks it can. The carmaker is working to build cars that operate on hydrogen-powered fuel cells.

Fuel cells, like batteries, store energy. But unlike batteries, fuel cells never lose power or need to be recharged as long as there is enough hydrogen fuel. Fuel cells create energy through the combination of hydrogen and oxygen. That energy can power an electric car motor.

The new AUTOnomy car runs on a series of hydrogen fuel cells. Instead of producing pollution, the AUTOnomy produces water vapor. Scientists expect AUTOnomy's hydrogen-powered system to get the equivalent of 161 km (100 miles) per gallon of gasoline.

Another type of hydrogen-powered car is the Hypercar, which will run on a gasoline- and hydrogen-powered fuel system. Scientists say the vehicle will be able to travel 482 km (300 miles) on a gallon of gas.

The design of the Hypercar is environmentally friendly too. The vehicle is made from lightweight materials called composites—two or more substances that strengthen the individual properties of each material. The Hypercar is not as heavy as a typical vehicle, so it needs less energy to accelerate.

Think About It

1. How might cars powered by fuel cells help prevent pollution?
2. How might using lighter materials to build a car help with fuel efficiency?

Drive, He Said

The cars of the future are already here as prototypes and might be available by the time you get your driver's license.

Find out more! Log on to
www.hspscience.com

Fill'er Up With Grease

Everyone knows that French fries are lip-smacking good. But did you know that the grease from French fries can power a car?

Three students from Green Bay, Wisconsin, Michael Lindsley, Brittanie Curtis, and Leah Erickson, found a way to turn the grease from fast food into a clean burning fuel mixture used in diesel-powered cars and trucks.

The students made the new fuel, biodiesel, by combining 80 percent restaurant grease with 20 percent ethanol, an alcohol-based fuel made from fermented corn, fruits, and vegetables.

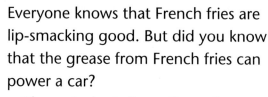

You Can Do It!

Materials
- rubber ball
- spring scale
- tape measure
- tape

Quick and Easy Project

Where Does a Ball Get Its Bounce?

Procedure

1. Work with a partner. You will need two tables or shelves of different heights.
2. Tape the ball to the end of the spring scale. Lift the ball from the floor to the lower shelf. Record how much force you use and how far you lift the ball.
3. Repeat, using the higher table or shelf.

Draw Conclusions
Did the ball have more potential energy in Step 2 or in Step 3? Could you have predicted that from earlier findings? If so, how?

Design Your Own Investigation

Follow the Bouncing Ball

You learned that a pogo stick has potential energy at the bottom of its bounce. You can see that a spinning yo-yo has kinetic energy at the bottom of its downward motion. Plan and conduct a simple investigation to see if a ball has any energy at the bottom of its bounce and, if so, which kind of energy.

Review and Test Preparation

Vocabulary Review

Use the terms below to complete the sentences. The page numbers tell you where to look in the chapter if you need help.

energy p. 198   conduction p. 218
kinetic energy p. 200   convection p. 218
potential energy p. 200 radiation p. 219
solar energy p. 206   conservation p. 225
chemical energy p. 208 renewable
                        resource p. 226

1. Saving something so it doesn't get used up is _____.

2. Energy that comes from the sun as heat and light is _____.

3. The transfer of thermal energy between touching objects is _____.

4. The transfer of thermal energy within a hot-air balloon is _____.

5. Hydroelectric energy is an example of using a _____.

6. Energy released through a chemical reaction is _____.

7. The ability to cause changes in matter is _____.

8. The energy of an object because of its condition or position is _____.

9. The energy of motion is _____.

10. The transfer of energy in waves through matter and space is _____.

Check Understanding

Write the letter of the best choice.

11. **MAIN IDEA AND DETAILS** Which is a nonrenewable resource?

    A. natural gas   **C.** water
    B. sunlight   **D.** wind

Use the diagram to answer questions 12 and 13.

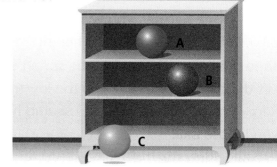

12. **COMPARE AND CONTRAST** Which statement is correct?

    F. Ball A has more potential energy than Ball B or C.
    G. Ball B has more potential energy than Ball A or C.
    H. Ball C has more potential energy than Ball A or B.
    J. All the balls have the same amount of potential energy.

13. Which ball has the most kinetic energy?
   A. Ball A
   B. Ball B
   C. Ball C
   D. They all have the same amount.

14. Which type of heat transfer does an oven mitt prevent?

   F. conduction
   G. convection
   H. radiation
   J. all of the above

15. Which kind of energy is stored in a battery?
   A. kinetic energy
   B. solar energy
   C. chemical energy
   D. light energy

16. Which change in form of energy occurs in a stereo speaker?
   F. sound energy to electric energy
   G. chemical energy to sound energy
   H. potential energy to kinetic energy
   J. electric energy to sound energy

Inquiry Skills

17. The Jenkinses' car can go 12 miles on a gallon of gasoline. The Guerreros' car can go 14 miles on a gallon of gasoline. The Watanabes' car can go 56 miles on a gallon of gasoline. What can you **infer** about the Watanabes' car?

18. If you leave a solar-powered flashlight in the sun for 8 hours, it will be able to stay lit for 3 hours. **Hypothesize** what would happen if you placed the flashlight under a bright light bulb for 8 hours.

Critical Thinking

19. A car is rolling down a hill. What determines how much potential energy and how much kinetic energy it has?

20. Energy changes form in many modern devices.
   Part A In a movie projector, how does energy change, and what forms of energy result?
   Part B Do the same changes happen in a TV set? Explain.

Chapter

7 Electricity

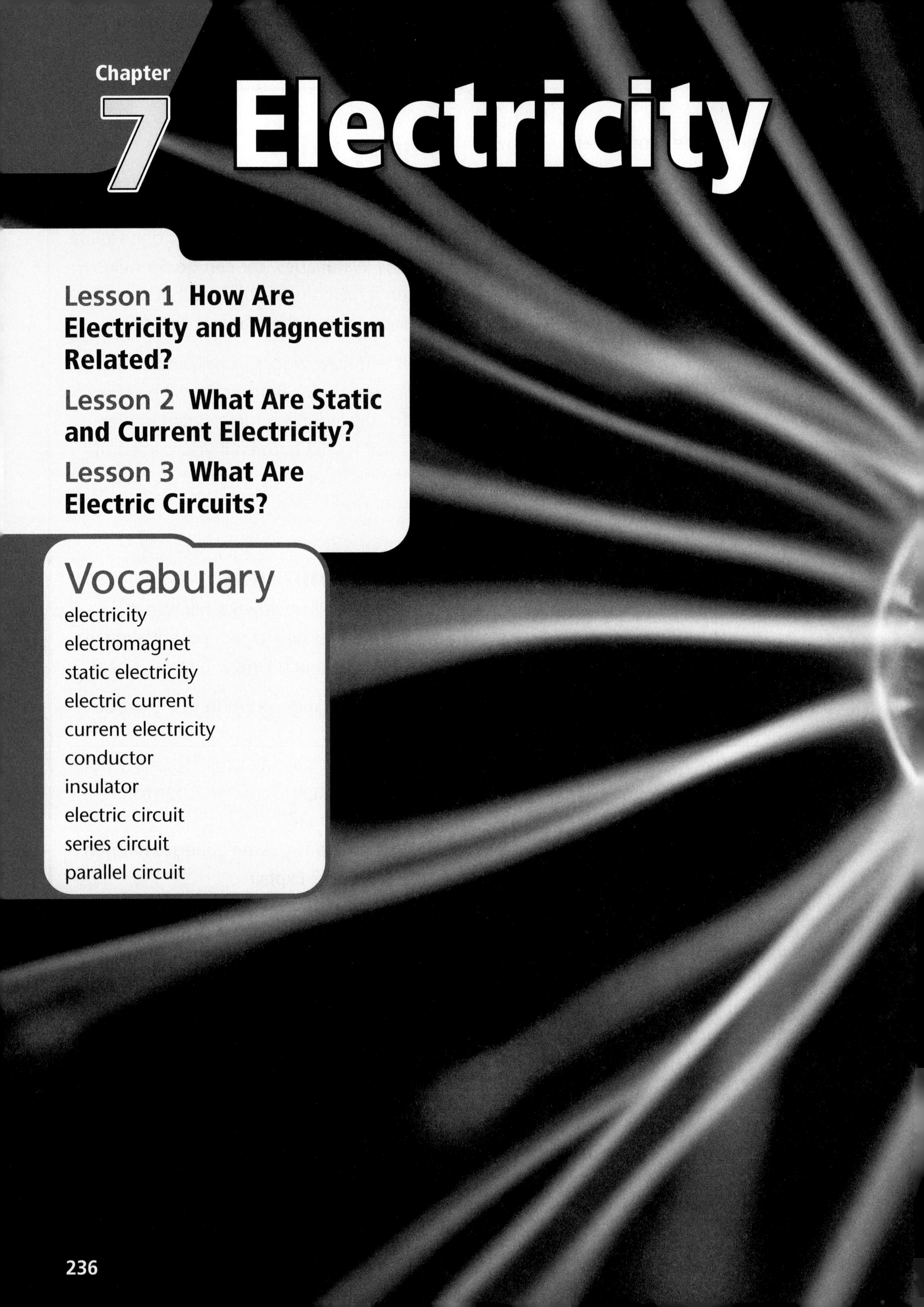

Vocabulary

electricity
electromagnet
static electricity
electric current
current electricity
conductor
insulator
electric circuit
series circuit
parallel circuit

What do YOU wonder?

A plasma ball is electricity in action! Electrons move from the small ball in the center toward an outer glass surface. As the electrons collide with gas atoms inside the outer ball, the gas atoms give off light. Where have you seen similar displays of electricity?

How Are Electricity and Magnetism Related?

Fast Fact

The Northern Lights Electrically charged particles from the sun follow Earth's magnetic field as they travel toward the North Pole. As they speed through the atmosphere, the particles collide with gas atoms, causing the atoms to give off light. This produces the *aurora borealis*, or northern lights, often seen in parts of Alaska and Canada. In the Investigate, you'll discover another way in which electricity and magnetism are related.

Build an Electromagnet

Materials
- 3 m of insulated copper wire
- iron nail, 15 cm long
- battery holder for D-cell
- paper clips
- D-cell
- sheet of paper

Procedure

1. Wrap the wire in a tight coil around the nail. Leave about 20 cm of wire free at each end.

2. Connect the ends of the wire to the battery holder.

3. Put a small pile of paper clips on your desk. Hold the nail above the pile, and lower it toward the clips. Observe what happens.

4. Turn on your electromagnet by putting the D-cell into the battery holder.

5. Hold the nail above the pile of paper clips, and lower it slowly. Observe what happens.

6. While you hold the nail and paper clips above a sheet of paper, have your partner remove the cell from the battery holder. Observe what happens. Count and record the number of paper clips your electromagnet picked up.

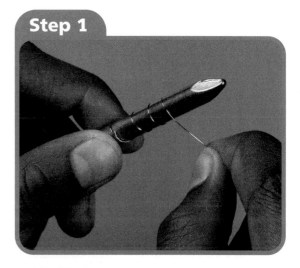
Step 1

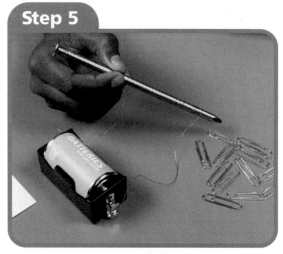
Step 5

Draw Conclusions

1. How did the nail change when the battery was connected?

2. **Inquiry Skill** Electromagnets are used on construction cranes to pick up steel. Compare a construction crane's electromagnet with yours.

Investigate Further

What would happen if you added another cell to your electromagnet? Plan and conduct a simple experiment **to find out.**

VOCABULARY
electricity p. 241
electromagnet p. 242

SCIENCE CONCEPTS
▶ how electricity produces magnetism
▶ that electricity can be changed to other forms of energy

READING FOCUS SKILL

MAIN IDEA AND DETAILS Look for examples of how electricity and magnetism are related.

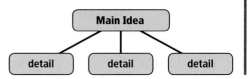

Electricity

Have you used electricity in the past hour? Did you turn on a lamp? Did you watch TV? Did you get something cold to drink from the refrigerator? If you did any of these things, you used electricity.

You use electricity every day, but do you know what it is? To understand electricity, you have to think about atoms. Recall that atoms contain charged particles. A proton has a positive charge. An electron has a negative charge.

An atom can have more electrons than protons. This gives the atom a negative charge. An atom with more protons than electrons has a positive charge. Atoms with opposite charges attract each other.

In an atom, electrons move around outside the nucleus. In some elements, electrons can also move from one atom to another. Protons don't move in this way.

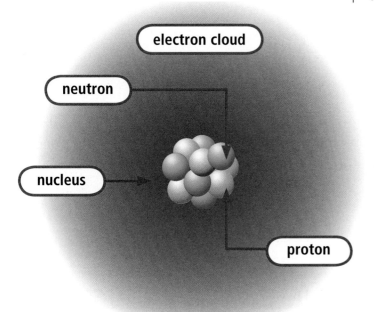

▲ In a neutral atom, the number of protons equals the number of electrons. If the number of protons and the number of electrons are not equal, the atom has a charge.

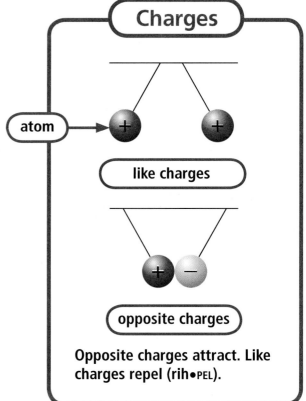

Opposite charges attract. Like charges repel (rih•PEL).

The lights on this fountain and in the buildings around it all use electricity. Electricity is changed to motion as water is pumped through the fountain, and it is changed to light in the buildings.

This movement of electrons produces electricity. **Electricity**, or electric energy, is a form of energy produced by moving electrons.

Electricity can be changed to other forms of energy. People use electricity to run lights in homes, schools, and offices. Electricity also runs street lights and traffic lights. Lamps change electricity into light energy.

Look at the fountain shown on this page. The lights use electricity. The fountain also uses electricity in another way. Electric motors pump the water through the fountain and push it up into the air. Here, electricity changes to motion, or mechanical energy.

Electric motors can be small enough to power a model train. They can be large enough to drive a huge freight train or a ship loaded with cargo. Electric motors even run some cars.

▲ Electricity can also be changed to heat. For example, people can use a small electric heater to warm a room.

Electricity can also change to heat energy. Toasters and electric ovens produce heat from electricity. So do hair dryers. Many homes are heated by electricity.

What do a doorbell and a radio have in common? They both use electricity to produce sound energy. Radios use the electricity from batteries or outlets to produce sound.

 MAIN IDEA AND DETAILS What are four kinds of energy that electricity can be changed into?

Electricity and Magnetism

In the Investigate, you used electricity to make a magnet. But your magnet worked only when the wire was connected to the battery. The battery was a source of electricity.

You wrapped the wire around a nail. When electricity flowed through the wire, the nail became a kind of magnet. An **electromagnet** is a magnet made by coiling a wire around a piece of iron and running electricity through the wire.

While electricity was flowing through the wire, the wire had a magnetic field around it. A single wire doesn't have a very strong magnetic field. Winding the wire into a coil makes the magnetic field stronger. Each extra turn of the wire makes the field even stronger.

Electromagnets are useful because they can be turned on and off. In some buildings, they are used to hold heavy fire doors open. In an emergency, the electricity can be turned off. Because the magnet no longer works, the doors close, blocking the spread of a fire.

Electromagnets are used on cranes in steel recycling centers. The magnets can lift heavy iron or steel objects, such as old cars. Electromagnets can also be used to lift metal objects on and off ships.

Electromagnets are used in recycling centers and junkyards to move cars and other iron or steel objects. ▶

electromagnet

An electromagnet causes a cone inside the speaker to vibrate, producing sound. ▼

cone

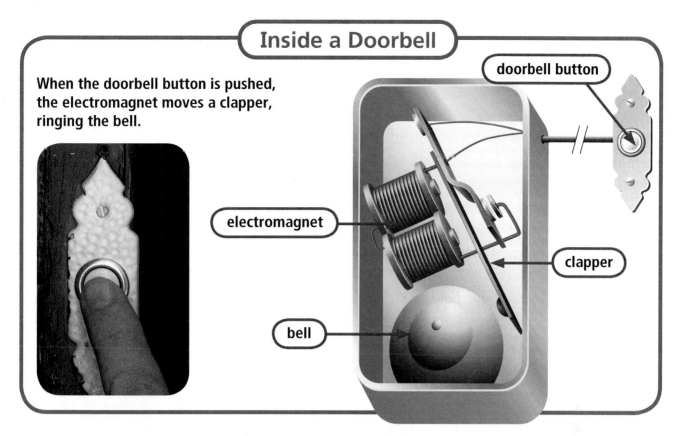

Inside a Doorbell

When the doorbell button is pushed, the electromagnet moves a clapper, ringing the bell.

doorbell button

electromagnet

clapper

bell

Scientists and engineers are working to develop a shipping dock that uses electromagnets. Today, a tugboat must pull a ship to a dock. The new magnetic dock will pull the steel ship toward it. The magnets will be strong enough to hold the ship in place without any ropes.

A much smaller electromagnet is used in a doorbell. When you press the button, electricity flows through the electromagnet, which pulls a steel spring toward it. The spring moves a clapper that hits the bell.

A speaker in a stereo system is similar to a doorbell. An electromagnet makes parts inside the speaker vibrate. You hear the vibrations as sound.

You have seen that electricity can produce magnetism. This also works the other way around—a magnet can produce electricity. That's how an energy station works.

In an energy station, a coil of wire turns inside the magnetic field of a huge magnet. When the wires cut across the magnetic field, electricity flows through the wires. Electricity travels from the station over a series of wires to schools, homes, and offices. Magnets produce the electricity we use every day.

 MAIN IDEA AND DETAILS What are some ways in which electromagnets are used?

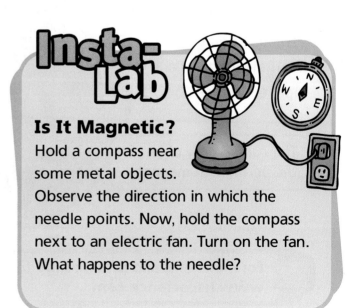

Insta-Lab

Is It Magnetic?
Hold a compass near some metal objects. Observe the direction in which the needle points. Now, hold the compass next to an electric fan. Turn on the fan. What happens to the needle?

Electric Motors

You know that electricity can be changed to mechanical energy. Have you ever made a fruit drink in a blender or cooled off with an electric fan? If you have, you have seen motion produced by electricity. The motion of an electric device is produced by an electric motor. The electric motor is the opposite of a generator that produces electricity in an energy station.

A motor contains a coil of wire that can spin inside the magnetic field of a permanent magnet. When the motor is switched on, electricity produces a magnetic field in the coil of wire. The coil becomes an electromagnet. The poles of this electromagnet are attracted and repelled by the poles of the permanent magnet. This causes the electromagnet to spin. The motion of the spinning coil can turn the blades of the blender or the fan.

 MAIN IDEA AND DETAILS What are the two main parts of a motor?

Science Up Close

How an Electric Motor Works

The electric motor inside a fan contains a coil of wire and a permanent magnet. When the fan is turned on, the coil becomes an electromagnet. The poles of the electromagnet are attracted to the opposite poles of the permanent magnet, so the coil turns. To keep the coil moving, the direction of the electricity keeps changing. This causes the coil and the permanent magnet to alternately attract and repel each other.

Inside the Motor

The wires are a part of the turning coil.

The curved gray object is the permanent magnet.

For more links and activities, go to www.hspscience.com

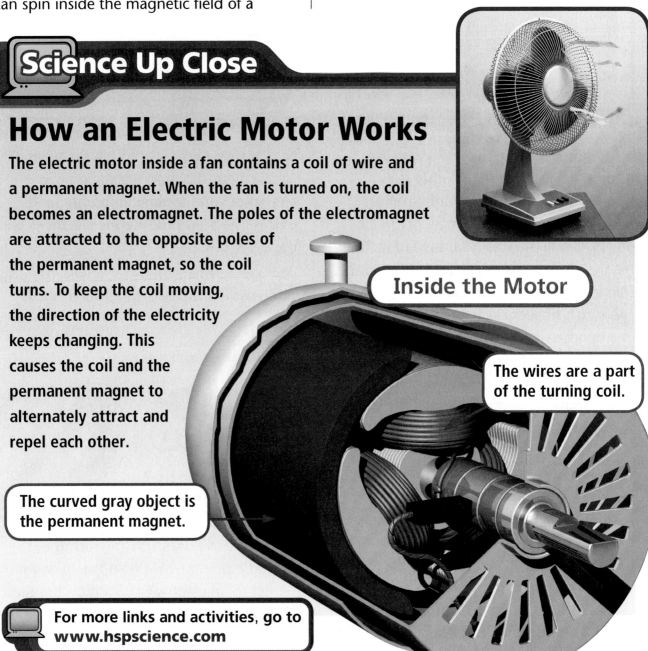

1. MAIN IDEA AND DETAILS Copy and complete this graphic organizer.

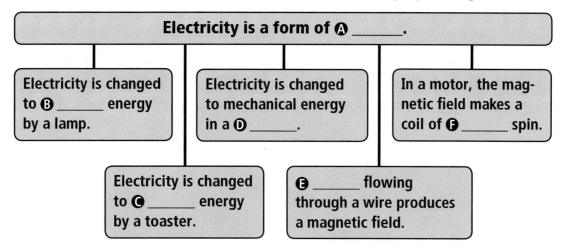

Electricity is a form of **A** _____.

Electricity is changed to **B** _____ energy by a lamp.

Electricity is changed to mechanical energy in a **D** _____.

In a motor, the magnetic field makes a coil of **F** _____ spin.

Electricity is changed to **C** _____ energy by a toaster.

E _____ flowing through a wire produces a magnetic field.

2. SUMMARIZE Write two sentences to summarize what this lesson is about.

3. DRAW CONCLUSIONS Why is electricity sometimes described as a flow of electrons?

4. VOCABULARY Show how the vocabulary words are related by using them together in a sentence.

Test Prep

5. Critical Thinking How do neutrons affect electric charge?

6. How can you make an electromagnet stronger?

A. Keep it turned on longer.

B. Add more turns of wire to the nail.

C. Use a smaller nail.

D. Shorten the wire.

Links

Writing

Expository Writing

Many household devices, such as TVs, radios, speakers, and refrigerators, use electromagnets. Research one of these devices, and write a **how-to paragraph** explaining how it works.

Math

Solve Problems

An iron nail electromagnet with 10 coils of wire picks up 6 paper clips. With 20 coils of wire, it picks up 12 paper clips. How many paper clips would it pick up with 30 coils of wire?

Health

Pacemakers

Some people wear pacemakers, devices that use electricity to keep the heart beating regularly. Research pacemakers. Draw and label a diagram that shows how they work.

 For more links and activities, go to www.hspscience.com

What Are Static and Current Electricity?

Fast Fact

Super-Size Sparks! The Van de Graaff generator was invented in 1929 by the physicist Robert Van de Graaff. This machine produces huge electrical charges that jump between objects the way lightning does. Machines such as this can produce electrical discharges of millions of volts of electricity. In the Investigate, you'll see how charges that are much smaller affect matter.

Make an Electroscope

Materials
- steel paper clip
- cardboard, 10 cm by 10 cm
- wool cloth
- aluminum foil
- wide-mouth glass jar
- tape
- plastic comb

Procedure

1. Straighten one end of the paper clip to form a J-shaped hook.

2. Push the paper clip's straight end through the middle of the piece of cardboard. Tape it in place so that 2 or 3 cm of the straight end extend above the cardboard.

3. Cut two strips of foil, 1 cm wide and 4 cm long. Push the hook through one end of the foil strips so that they hang together from it.

4. Set the cardboard on the jar, with the hook inside, and tape it in place. You have completed your electroscope.

5. Hold the comb near the end of the paper clip. Observe what happens.

6. Rub the comb with the cloth. Repeat Step 5. Observe what happens as you move the comb away from and toward the paper clip.

Step 3

Step 4

Draw Conclusions

1. What happened as you moved the rubbed comb toward or away from the electroscope?

2. **Inquiry Skill** Scientists often predict what will happen in a certain situation. Predict what you think will happen to the foil if you rub the comb with the cloth and hold the cloth near the electroscope. Explain your prediction. Then test it. Was it correct?

Investigate Further

What do you think will happen if you touch the comb, the cloth, or your finger to the paper clip? Plan and conduct a simple experiment to test your ideas.

VOCABULARY
static electricity p. 248
electric current p. 250
current electricity p. 250
conductor p. 252
insulator p. 252

SCIENCE CONCEPTS
▶ what causes static electricity
▶ what causes electricity to flow

READING FOCUS SKILL
CAUSE AND EFFECT Look for conditions that cause electricity to build up or flow.

cause ⟶ effect

Static Electricity

Have you ever heard crackling noises or felt small shocks when you pulled a sweater over your head? If the room was dark, you might have seen tiny flashes of light. These effects are caused by electricity.

Most objects have no charge. The atoms making up the matter are neutral. They have equal numbers of protons and electrons. But when one object rubs against another, electrons move from atoms of one object to atoms of the other object. The numbers of protons and electrons in the atoms are no longer equal. The objects become either positively or negatively charged. The buildup of charges on an object is called **static electricity**.

When you took off your sweater, it rubbed against your other clothing, your skin, and your hair. You and the sweater

A large buildup of static electricity can cause spectacular lightning bolts.

Static electricity on the wires of this device, called a tesla coil, is discharged in a spark.

All the cat's hairs are charged alike, so they repel one another. The balloon carries the opposite charge, so the hairs are attracted to it.

both became electrically charged. After you pulled the sweater over your head, did your hair stand out from your head? If it did, the strands of hair all had the same charge, so they repelled one another.

Opposite charges attract each other. Charged objects can also attract neutral objects. When items of clothing rub together in a dryer, they can pick up a static charge. Because some items are positive and some are negative, they stick together.

When objects with opposite charges get close, electrons sometimes jump from the negative object to the positive object. This evens out the charges, and the objects become neutral. The shocks you felt when

you pulled off the sweater were sparks caused by electrons moving to balance the charges. These sparks are called *static discharge.* The crackling noises you heard were the sounds of the sparks.

Lightning is also a static discharge. Where does the charge come from? Scientists hypothesize that collisions between water droplets in a cloud cause the drops to become charged. Negative charges collect at the bottom of the cloud. Positive charges collect at the top of the cloud. When electrons jump from one cloud to another, or from a cloud to the ground, you see lightning. The lightning heats the air, causing it to expand. As cooler air rushes in to fill the empty space, you hear thunder.

Earth can absorb lightning's powerful stream of electrons without being damaged. But lightning that strikes a tree or a house can start a fire. If lightning strikes a beach, it can melt grains of sand into pieces of glass!

 CAUSE AND EFFECT What causes an object to build up a static charge?

Insta-Lab

Static Cereal
Place some puffed rice cereal on a sheet of paper. Hold a plastic comb above the cereal, and observe what happens. Rub the comb with a piece of wool cloth. Hold the comb over the cereal again. What happens?

Current Electricity

Static electricity is a kind of potential energy. Energy is stored when electrons move from one object to another and a static charge builds up. The potential energy can change to kinetic energy. This is what happens when electrons move in a static discharge.

The kinetic energy of a static discharge can change to other forms of energy. For example, the electric energy of lightning changes into heat, light, and sound.

Because a static discharge is a short burst of kinetic energy, it isn't very useful as an energy source. For electricity to be a useful source of energy, it must be a steady flow of electrons. If electrons have a path to follow,

they will move in a steady flow instead of building up a static charge. This flow of electrons is called an **electric current**. Electricity that flows in this way is a kind of kinetic energy called **current electricity**.

To keep the current flowing, a constant supply of electrons is needed. Batteries supply electrons to flashlights and other small devices. Energy stations produce a much larger flow of electrons to supply electric current to whole cities. An energy station's electrical system can include homes, businesses, and factories. When you plug in a lamp, you are connecting to such an electrical system.

You can compare using current electricity to watering a garden. When you water a

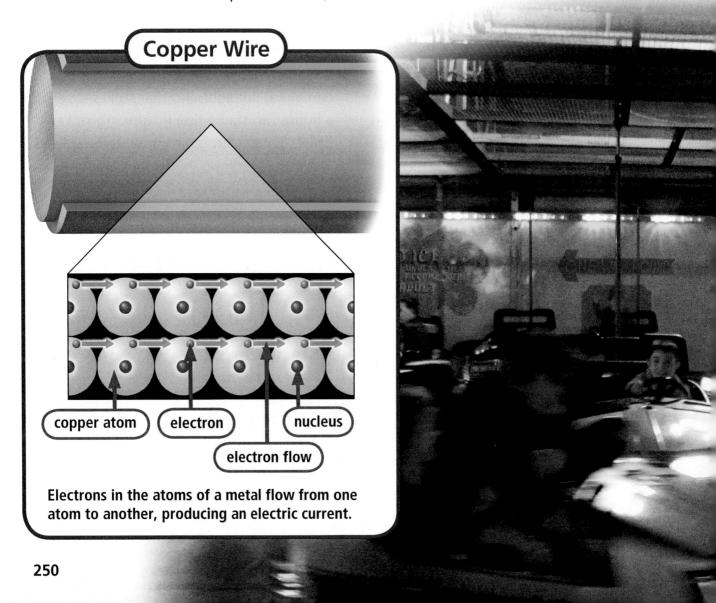

Copper Wire

copper atom   electron   nucleus

electron flow

Electrons in the atoms of a metal flow from one atom to another, producing an electric current.

garden, you connect a hose to a pipe and turn on the water. Water pressure pushes water through the hose.

To use current electricity to light a lamp, you connect the lamp to the wires in your home. Then you switch on the lamp. Electrical pressure forces current through the wires, giving the electrons energy. This electrical pressure is measured in *volts.* Batteries have labels that show the number of volts they supply. One lightning strike can have more than 1 billion volts of electricity!

The rate at which electric current flows is measured in *amps.* There are many more amps in power lines than you need to operate the appliances in your home.

The combination of volts and amps can be dangerous, which is why many objects that use electricity have warning labels.

The electric devices you use all change electricity into some other form of energy. But not all of them use the same amount of electricity. The amount of electric energy a device uses each second is measured in *watts.* A label on a hair dryer, light bulb, or clock shows how many watts it uses.

Electric energy companies bill people for the amount of electricity they use. A watt is a very small unit, so electrical use is measured in kilowatts. One kilowatt is equal to 1000 watts.

 CAUSE AND EFFECT What causes an electric current to keep moving?

The current electricity that powers a bumper car flows from the ceiling, down the pole, and into the motor that makes the car move.

Math in Science
Interpret Data

Using Electricity
Some devices use more electric energy than others. For example, a 100-watt light bulb uses four times the amount of energy that a 25-watt bulb uses. How many 100-watt light bulbs use the same amount of energy as a toaster?

Device	Energy Use
Hair dryer	1600 watts
Microwave oven	1000 watts
Computer and monitor	270 watts
Clothes washer	400 watts
DVD player	25 watts
TV	110 watts
Toaster	900 watts

Conductors and Insulators

Electricity moves more easily through some kinds of matter than others. A material through which electricity moves well is a **conductor**. Most metals are conductors. The electrons of metals are held loosely by the atoms. This makes it easy for the electrons to move between atoms, causing current to flow.

Copper is a very good conductor. It's used for most electrical wiring in homes. The inside of the cord you use to plug in a lamp is made of copper wire.

If you look at a lamp cord, you won't see the copper wire. The copper is covered with a layer of plastic. Plastic doesn't conduct electricity well. Its electrons are not free to move between atoms. A material that conducts electricity poorly is an **insulator**. Wood, glass, and rubber are also insulators.

Insulators are important because they protect you from the electric current in the wire. If the layer of plastic on a wire peels off or cracks, the wire should be replaced. If you touch a bare wire that is conducting current, the current will flow through you and could hurt you. Also, wires get warm when they carry electricity. A bare wire that touches paper or cloth could start a fire.

 CAUSE AND EFFECT What causes a metal to be a good conductor?

Electric wiring is made of a conductor, such as copper wire, covered with an insulator, such as plastic or rubber. ▼

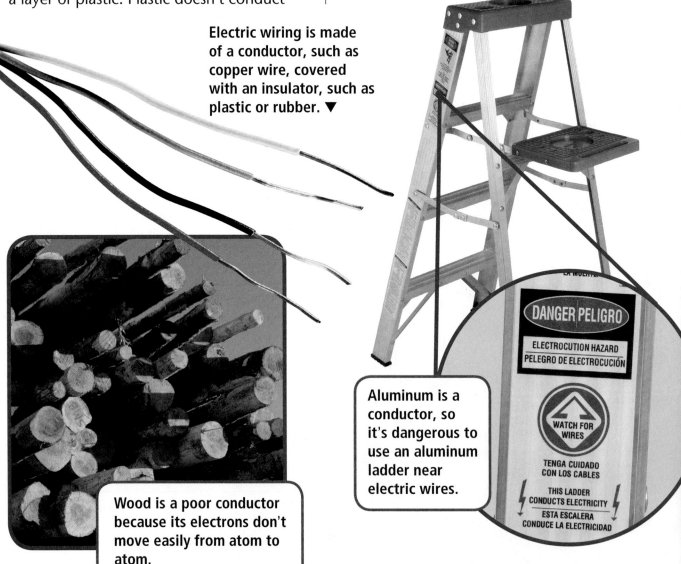

Wood is a poor conductor because its electrons don't move easily from atom to atom.

Aluminum is a conductor, so it's dangerous to use an aluminum ladder near electric wires.

DANGER PELIGRO

ELECTROCUTION HAZARD
PELIGRO DE ELECTROCUCIÓN

WATCH FOR WIRES

TENGA CUIDADO CON LOS CABLES

THIS LADDER CONDUCTS ELECTRICITY
ESTA ESCALERA CONDUCE LA ELECTRICIDAD

1. CAUSE AND EFFECT Copy and complete these graphic organizers.

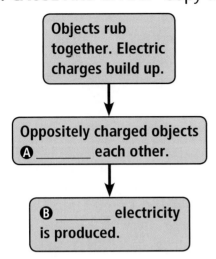

Objects rub together. Electric charges build up.

↓

Oppositely charged objects **Ⓐ** _____ each other.

↓

Ⓑ _____ electricity is produced.

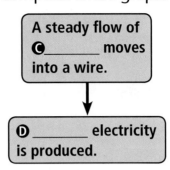

A steady flow of **Ⓒ** _____ moves into a wire.

↓

Ⓓ _____ electricity is produced.

2. SUMMARIZE Use your completed graphic organizer to write a summary of the lesson.

3. DRAW CONCLUSIONS What kind of electricity does a TV use? What kinds of energy does the TV produce from this electricity?

4. VOCABULARY Use the vocabulary terms to make a crossword puzzle.

Test Prep

5. Critical Thinking Some air filters have metal plates that build up a static charge. How can this clean the air?

6. What is the volt used to measure?
   A. electrical pressure
   B. speed of an electric current
   C. amount of electrical energy used
   D. how well an insulator works

Links

Writing

Expository Writing
Write a **business letter** to your local power company, asking for information on how the company generates electricity.

Math

Compare Numbers
A 100-watt light bulb costs $1. It lasts about 1000 hours. A 15-watt fluorescent bulb provides the same amount of light. It costs $6 and lasts about 10,000 hours. Which bulb is the better buy? Why?

Social Studies

Scientists in History
Scientific units are often named after early scientists in the field. Research and report on Alessandro Volta, James Watt, or André-Marie Ampère.

For more links and activities, go to **www.hspscience.com**

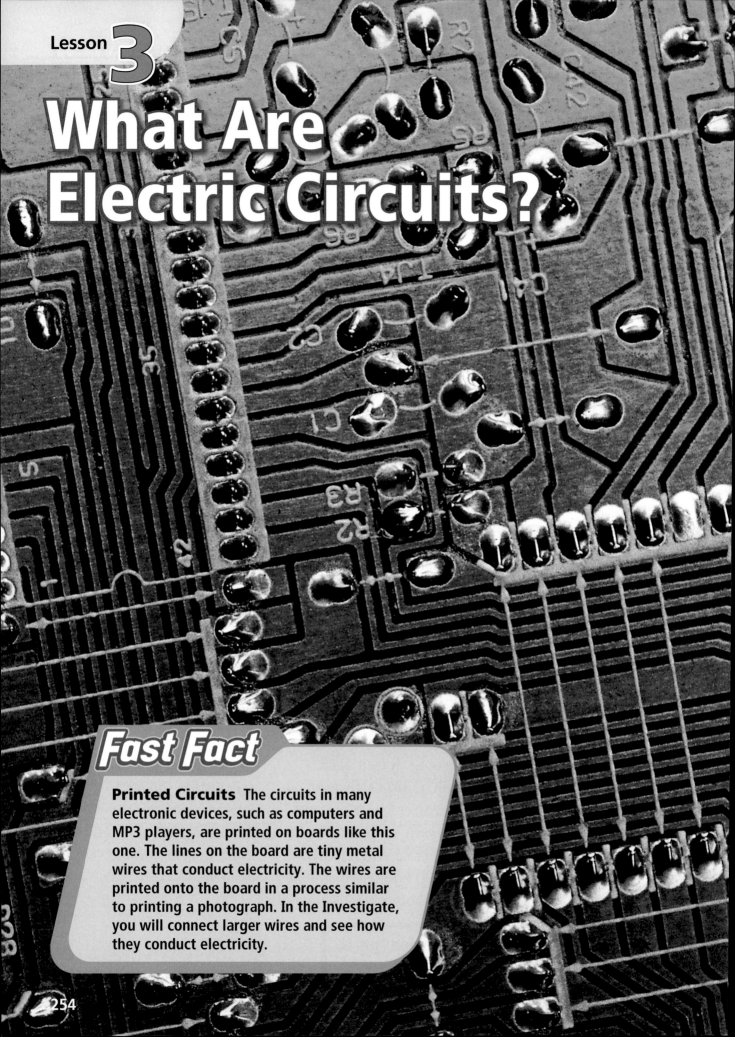

What Are Electric Circuits?

Fast Fact

Printed Circuits The circuits in many electronic devices, such as computers and MP3 players, are printed on boards like this one. The lines on the board are tiny metal wires that conduct electricity. The wires are printed onto the board in a process similar to printing a photograph. In the Investigate, you will connect larger wires and see how they conduct electricity.

Build an Electric Circuit

Materials
- 3 lengths of insulated wire with bare ends
- 2 light-bulb holders
- battery holder
- 2 light bulbs
- D-cell

Procedure

1. Use the wire to connect the light-bulb holders and the battery holder as shown in the diagram. Have your teacher check to make sure you have assembled the parts correctly.

2. Screw the light bulbs firmly into the holders.

3. Insert the D-cells into the battery holder. Observe and record what happens.

4. Remove the D-cells from the battery holder. Observe and record what happens.

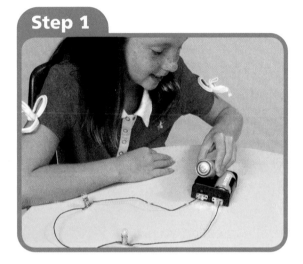

Step 1

Draw Conclusions

1. What happened when you put the cells into the battery holder?

2. What happened when you took the cells out of the battery holder?

3. Think about the path you made for the electric current. How did putting the cells into the holder affect this path?

4. **Inquiry Skill** Draw a diagram of the path you made for the electric current. Make a model of how the current in one room of your home might move through various appliances, such as lamps or the TV. Draw a diagram of your model.

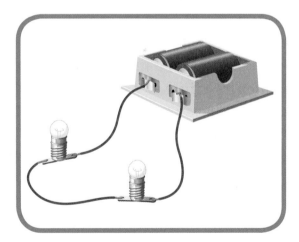

Investigate Further

Is there another way to connect two light bulbs and cells? Plan and conduct a simple experiment to find out.

VOCABULARY
electric circuit p. 256
series circuit p. 257
parallel circuit p. 258

SCIENCE CONCEPTS
▶ what parts make up an electric circuit
▶ how series and parallel circuits compare

READING FOCUS SKILL

MAIN IDEA AND DETAILS Look for details about the difference between series and parallel circuits.

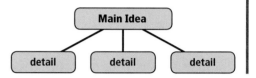

Series Circuits

If the toaster doesn't toast your bread, the first thing you do is check to see that it's plugged in. You know that the toaster won't work unless it's connected to the wires in your home. The wires give the electricity a path to follow. The path an electric current follows is called an **electric circuit**.

An electric circuit needs two things for current to flow. First, it needs a source of current, or electrons. Plugging the cord into the wall gives the toaster a source of current. Second, the circuit has to be complete. If there is a break in the circuit, the current won't flow. In the Investigate,

Old signs like this one were wired with series circuits.

the batteries were the source of current. The batteries, wires, and light bulbs formed a complete circuit.

A switch controls the flow of current by opening and closing the circuit. When the switch is on, the circuit is complete. The light comes on. When you turn the switch off, a piece of metal inside the switch moves. This breaks the flow of current, and the light goes out.

Lights Out!
Use the circuit you built in the Investigate. Insert the batteries, and make sure the lights come on. Remove one of the lights from its socket. What do you observe? Explain your observations.

The kind of circuit you built in the Investigate is called a series circuit. In a **series circuit**, the current has only one path to follow. The parts are connected one after the other in a single loop. Removing any part of the circuit breaks the circuit, and current stops flowing.

Series circuits aren't used for most wiring in buildings. The only way for current to flow in a series circuit is to have everything connected at the same time. What would that be like in a home? All electric devices would have to be switched on all the time. If you unplugged a radio, all the lights in your home would go out!

Series circuits were once used in lighted signs and scoreboards that had only a few lights. If one light burned out, the whole sign went out. Series circuits were also used in strings of decorative lights. If one light didn't work, none of the others worked, either. People didn't know which bulb had burned out, so they had to check them all. It was easy to check and replace a small number of lights. But for anything with a lot of bulbs, keeping a series circuit working took a lot of time.

 MAIN IDEA AND DETAILS What two things are needed in order for current to flow in a circuit?

Strings of decorative lights used to be wired in series. If one light burned out, they all went out. Imagine having to climb a tree to find and replace the burned-out bulb!

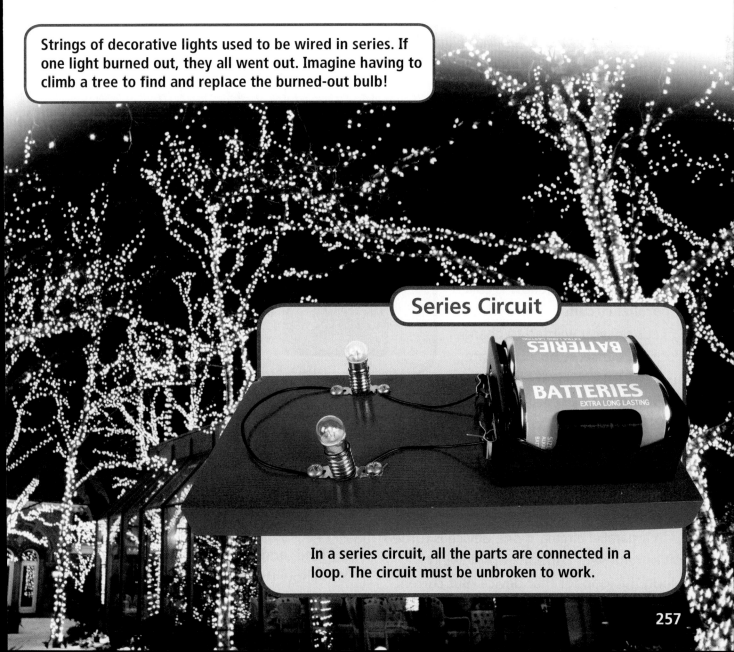

Series Circuit

In a series circuit, all the parts are connected in a loop. The circuit must be unbroken to work.

Parallel Circuit

A parallel circuit has more than one path that current can follow. Use your finger to trace the different paths shown here.

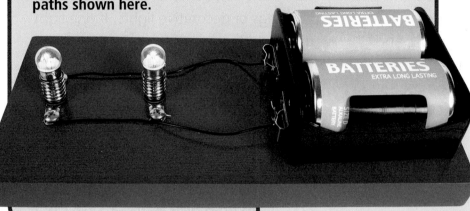

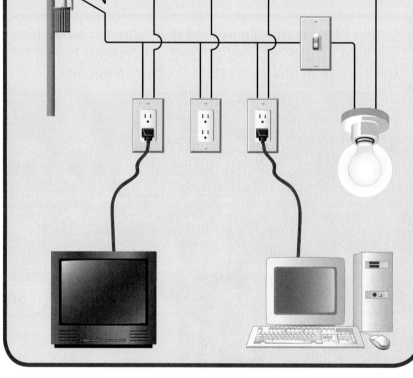

This circuit diagram shows how several devices can be connected in a parallel circuit.

Parallel Circuits

You have seen why a series circuit isn't very convenient to use. Luckily, there's a better way to connect the parts of a circuit. Instead of giving the current only one path, you can make a path for each device in the circuit. A circuit that has more than one path for current to follow is called a **parallel circuit**.

Let's say you wanted to change your circuit from the Investigate to a parallel circuit. You would use extra wire to give each bulb its own loop branching off from the battery. The current for each bulb would have a separate path. If one path was broken, current could still flow through another path. The second bulb would stay lit.

In a parallel circuit, if one device is turned off or removed, current stops flowing along the loop for that device. But current

continues to flow through the rest of the circuit. The other devices don't stop working. This makes a parallel circuit more practical to use than a series circuit.

Think of a parallel circuit as a path that branches and comes together again. Suppose you are walking in the woods with a friend, and the path splits into two paths. You know that each path has a bridge

258

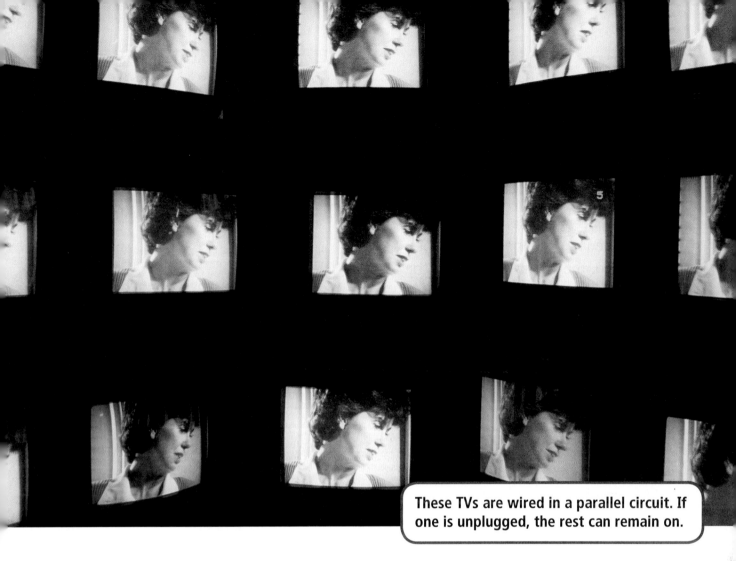

These TVs are wired in a parallel circuit. If one is unplugged, the rest can remain on.

across a nearby river. You take one path, and your friend takes the other. After you each cross a different bridge, you meet where the paths join.

What happens if you get to the river and see that the bridge on your path has washed away? You can go back and take the other path. This time, you use the same bridge that your friend used.

Homes, schools, and businesses are wired with parallel circuits. Each loop of a parallel circuit may have a switch in it. The switch controls only that one loop. For example, a ceiling light is usually controlled by a switch in the wall. You can turn the light on and off without having to reach the ceiling. But the switch doesn't affect other loops of the circuit. If you turn off a ceiling light, the

clock, the TV, and other devices in the room stay turned on.

Remember the sign with light bulbs connected in a series circuit? If the bulbs were connected in a parallel circuit, one bulb could burn out and the other lights would remain on.

A parallel circuit has another advantage over a series circuit. You can connect more devices in a parallel circuit. If you connect too many light bulbs in a series circuit, they all become dimmer. That's why old signs wired in series circuits didn't have many bulbs. But in a parallel circuit, adding more bulbs doesn't change how bright they are.

MAIN IDEA AND DETAILS What are two advantages that parallel circuits have over series circuits?

Drawing Circuits

You have learned that devices that use electricity have circuits inside them. Engineers design these circuits. Some circuits, such as those in a blender or a lamp, are simple. Some, such as those in a car or an airplane, are more complicated.

When engineers work on a new design, they don't begin by connecting a lot of wires. Instead, they draw diagrams of the circuits they will use. Circuit diagrams use symbols to show the parts of a circuit. Each part of a circuit has a different symbol.

A diagram of the series circuit you built in the Investigate would have symbols for the batteries, the wires, and the two lights. These symbols would be connected in a single loop.

A circuit diagram of a washing machine includes symbols for wires, switches, a motor, and a pump. A parallel circuit

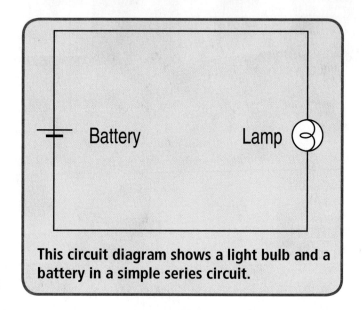

This circuit diagram shows a light bulb and a battery in a simple series circuit.

diagram of the washer and a dryer would have many different loops.

A jet airliner has more than 56 km (35 mi) of wire in it. Just imagine how complicated that circuit diagram would be!

MAIN IDEA AND DETAILS What do you see on a circuit diagram?

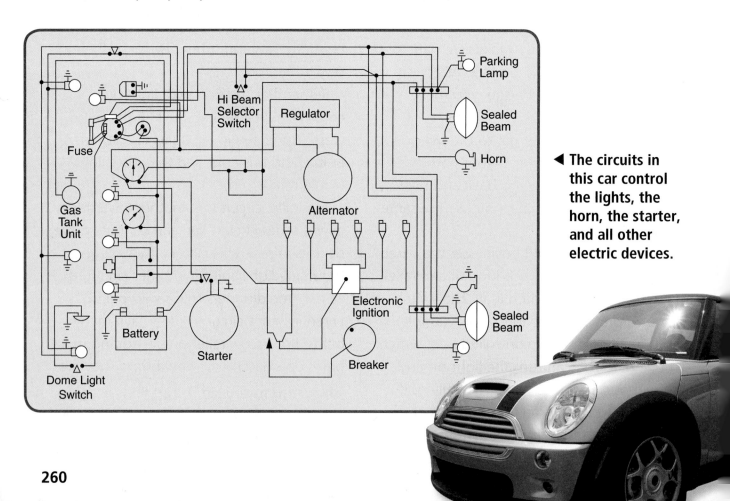

◀ The circuits in this car control the lights, the horn, the starter, and all other electric devices.

Focus Skill

1. MAIN IDEA AND DETAILS Copy and complete this graphic organizer.

Electric Circuits

In a **Ⓐ**_____ circuit, there is only one path for the current to take.

In a **Ⓑ**_____ circuit, there is more than one path for the current to take.

Circuit **Ⓒ**_____ show how the parts of a circuit are connected.

2. SUMMARIZE Write three sentences that tell the most important information in this lesson.

3. DRAW CONCLUSIONS Why do many appliances include circuit diagrams in their instructions?

4. VOCABULARY Look up *series*, and tell why this word is a good choice to name a type of circuit.

Test Prep

5. Critical Thinking If you want a switch to turn a light on and off, should you connect them in series or in parallel? Explain.

6. What two things are needed for current to flow in a circuit?

   A. wires and a switch

   B. a current source and a light bulb

   C. a current source and a path

   D. extra paths for the current

Links

Writing

Narrative Writing

Write a **short story** that tells about the journey of an electron as it flows through the circuit you built in the Investigate.

Math

Make a Bar Graph

Keep a log of the ways you use electricity at school. For example, keep track of the number of hours a day the lights are on and the number of hours you use the TV. Make a bar graph to show your use of each device.

Art

Wire Art

Draw a circuit diagram for a recreation room you would like to have. Attach pictures cut from magazines to show the devices in the circuit.

 For more links and activities, go to www.hspscience.com

RACING WITH THE SUN

Recently, dozens of cars entered the American Solar Challenge. They sped silently along Route 66 from Chicago to Claremont, California. The cars did not have to make any pit stops to refuel, however. Their power came from changing energy from the sun into electricity. Because the cars used rays from the sun for power, race organizers called the race a sun "rayce."

What's a Solar Cell?

The secret behind the solar-powered cars is the solar cell. Solar cells collect sunlight and turn it into electricity. Each car carries about 1000 solar cells. Combined, the cells provide about 1000 watts of power. A watt is a measurement of electrical power.

A solar cell has a positive pole and a negative pole, just like a battery. The negative pole is called the *cathode*. The positive pole is the *anode*. When sunlight strikes the anode, electrons are released. The electrons move toward the cathode. The moving electrons make electricity.

This new car uses both gasoline and electricity.

After a solar cell changes solar energy into electricity, most of that power runs the car. Some electricity is stored in batteries. When the car needs extra power, it draws it from the battery and the solar cells.

Of course the amount of sunlight changes with the time of day and amount of cloud cover. On a sunny day, however, a solar-powered car can reach speeds up to 80 miles per hour.

Lots of Potential

One of the purposes of the American Solar Challenge is to teach people about renewable energy sources, such as solar power. Renewable energy does not rely on fossil fuels, such as oil or coal, and does not create pollution. Other types of renewable energy are hydropower and wind power.

Commenting on the race, a U.S. energy official said, "This accomplishment. . . demonstrates the significant potential renewable energy holds for our nation's future."

THINK ABOUT IT

1. In what other ways could solar cells be used?
2. What do you think are the limits to a solar-powered car?

Find out more! Log on to
www.hspscience.com

ST-1 Investigate technology impact;
ST-2 Revise an existing design

263

The Birth of Batteries

The next time you have to replace the batteries in a toy or electronic instrument, you might want to say "Thanks, Count Volta!" Count Alessandro Volta, who studied electricity in Italy in the late 1700s, invented the first battery.

Volta called his device the "Voltaic Pile," which he made by stacking disks of zinc and silver in an alternating pattern. Between every two disks, he placed a small piece of paper that had been soaked in salt water. Wires were attached to the disks at each end of the pile and the result was a low current of electricity.

If you have any portable devices, you know that batteries play an important role in most people's lives. That's because rather than relying on the electric current in a home or business, batteries produce a similar current of electricity, but without the power cord.

Career   Electrical Line Installer

Electrical line installers have to like working outdoors in any weather. That's because an installer's job is to run miles of cable from energy sources to customers. They may also check connections for proper voltage readings and install circuit breakers, switches, fuses, and other equipment to control and direct the electrical current.

You Can Do It!

Quick and Easy Project

Build a Switch

Materials
- battery and holder
- wires
- light bulb and holder
- scissors
- plastic-covered paper clip

Procedure

1. Assemble a simple circuit as you did for the Lesson 3 Investigate. But use just one bulb, and don't put the battery in the battery holder.

2. Cut one of the wires in half. Put the battery in the battery holder, and observe the bulb to see if it lights.

3. With your teacher's help, remove some of the insulation from the cut ends of the wire.

4. Straighten a paper clip. Remove the plastic covering from the ends of the paper clip.

5. Place the paper clip across the space between the cut ends of the wire so that the bare ends of the paper clip touch the bare ends of the wire. Observe what happens.

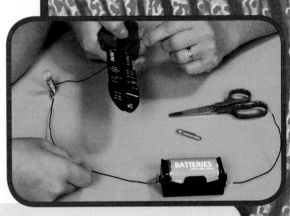

Draw Conclusions

How does the paper clip act as a switch? Why did you have to remove some of the plastic covering from the paper clip before using it as a switch?

Design Your Own Investigation

Observe a Magnetic Field

When current passes through a wire, it produces a magnetic field around the wire. Use a compass and a simple circuit to study the magnetic field around a wire that is conducting current. Then turn the battery around in the holder. Does this have an effect on the magnetic field? Why do you think this happens?

Review and Test Preparation

Vocabulary Review

Use the terms below to complete the sentences. The page numbers tell you where to look in the chapter if you need help.

electricity p. 241   **conductor** p. 252

electromagnet p. 242   **insulator** p. 252

static electricity p. 248 **series circuit** p. 257

current   **parallel**
  electricity p. 250   **circuit** p. 258

1. The buildup of charges on an object is _____.

2. Electricity that flows along a path is _____.

3. An electric circuit in which current has only one path to follow is a _____.

4. A material that doesn't allow electricity to flow easily through it is an _____.

5. The form of energy produced by moving electrons is _____.

6. A material that allows electricity to flow easily through it is a _____.

7. An electric circuit in which current has more than one path to follow is a _____.

8. A device that acts like a magnet when electricity is flowing through it is an _____.

Check Understanding

Write the letter of the best choice.

9. Which of these is a conductor?
   A. copper
   B. glass
   C. plastic
   D. wood

10. **CAUSE AND EFFECT** What causes the behavior of the balloons in this picture?
    F. Neither balloon has a charge.
    G. The red balloon is positive and the blue balloon is negative.
    H. The red balloon is positive and the blue balloon is neutral.
    J. Both balloons have the same charge.

11. What is the path that electric current follows called?
    A. an insulator
    B. an electric circuit
    C. potential energy
    D. kinetic energy

12. Tai walked across a carpet and felt a shock when she touched a doorknob. What caused this?

    F. The knob was an electromagnet.

    G. The knob was an insulator.

    H. Tai developed a static charge.

    J. The carpet was a conductor.

13. What device is used to start and stop the flow of electric current in a circuit?

    A. a battery

    B. an electromagnet

    C. a motor

    D. a switch

14. **MAIN IDEA AND DETAILS** Jamal built the circuit shown here. Use the diagram to infer what happens when he takes the bulb out of holder 2.

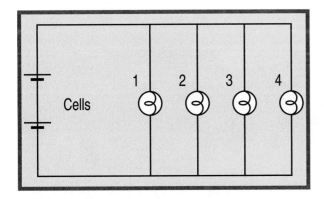

    F. Only bulbs 1 and 2 go out.

    G. Only bulbs 3 and 4 go out.

    H. All the other bulbs go out.

    J. All the other bulbs stay on.

15. When a microwave oven's timer beeps, to what kind of energy is electricity being changed?

    A. heat

    B. light

    C. motion

    D. sound

16. Which appliance costs the most to use for a half hour?

    F. a 1200-watt hair dryer

    G. a 110-watt TV

    H. a 1000-watt vacuum cleaner

    J. a 75-watt window fan

Inquiry Skills

17. **Predict** what will happen to the brightness of the bulbs if you add two more bulbs to the circuit shown here.

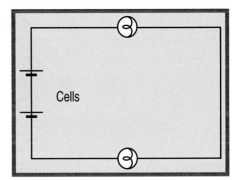

18. How would you **plan an experiment** to test whether a substance is a conductor?

Critical Thinking

19. Why is the electron the part of the atom that moves when an electric current flows?

20. For a party, you are about to hang a string of tiny lights wired in a parallel circuit. You test the string, and the bulbs all light. Your friend is worried because you have no spare bulbs to replace any that burn out.

    Part A What will happen if a bulb burns out?

    Part B How can you explain your answer to your friend?

Chapter

Sound and Light

Lesson 1 **What Is Sound?**

Lesson 2 **What Is Light?**

Vocabulary

vibration
volume
pitch
frequency
reflection
opaque
translucent
transparent
refraction
concave lens
convex lens

Wrigley Field, in Chicago, Illinois, is right in the middle of a crowded neighborhood. The people who live nearby can hear the roar of the crowd. At night, the stadium lights up the sky. How do sound and light travel from the baseball stadium to the area that surrounds it?

What Is Sound?

Fast Fact

Pipe Organ A pipe organ makes sounds by blowing air through pipes. This large organ in Salt Lake City, Utah, has 11,623 pipes. The longest pipe is about 10 m (32 ft) high. The smallest pipe is about the size of a drinking straw. In the Investigate, you'll find out how the length of part of a musical instrument can affect the sound that's made.

Making Sound

Materials   • 2 pieces of string, 100 cm long   • 2 metal spoons   • meterstick

Procedure

1. Tie one end of each piece of string to one of the spoons.

2. Wrap the other end of each piece of string around your index fingers. Each finger should be wrapped with one string. Gently place those fingers in your ears.

3. Let the spoon hang freely. Have a partner measure the string lengths between your fingers and the spoon. Wrap more string around your fingers until the lengths are 75 cm each.

4. Have your partner gently tap the spoon with the other spoon. Record your observations.

5. Repeat Steps 2, 3, and 4, but shorten the string lengths to 50 cm.

6. Repeat Steps 2, 3, and 4, but shorten the string lengths to 25 cm.

Draw Conclusions

1. What did you hear in Step 4 of the activity?

2. Did the sound change when you shortened the strings? If so, how?

3. **Inquiry Skill** Before scientists conduct experiments, they must identify the variables to be tested. What variable did you test in this activity?

Step 1

Step 4

Investigate Further

Plan and conduct a simple experiment **to find out if the sound changes with plastic objects instead of metal spoons.**

VOCABULARY

vibration p. 272
volume p. 273
pitch p. 274
frequency p. 274

SCIENCE CONCEPTS

▶ what makes sounds vary

▶ how sounds travel

READING FOCUS SKILL

MAIN IDEA AND DETAILS Look for the characteristics of sound.

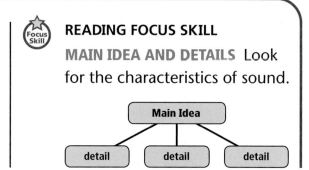

Sound Energy

Have you ever been to a Native American powwow? People dance and celebrate to the rhythm of a drum. The drum may be big—about 1 m (3 ft) in diameter. Eight or more people play the drum and sing. The sound gets very loud and can be heard far away.

Sound is a form of energy that travels through the air. Sound is made when something vibrates. A **vibration** is a back-and-forth movement of matter. When a drummer hits a drum's head, or covering, the head moves back and forth very quickly. These movements are vibrations. They cause the air nearby to vibrate, making the sound energy that you hear.

The head of a drum—a thin covering—is flexible and tight, so it vibrates when it is hit. ▶

Math in Science
Interpret Data

How Loud Are Some Sounds?

Sound	Decibel Level
Whisper	20 dB
Quiet radio	40 dB
Conversation	60 dB
Dishwasher	80 dB
Jackhammer	100 dB
Thunderclap	120 dB

Why do factory workers and jack-hammer operators wear ear protection?

◀ These representatives at the United Nations are wearing headsets so they can listen to speeches in their own languages. Each person can adjust the volume of the sound for comfort and clarity.

Musical instruments make sounds in various ways. Some, like drums, vibrate when they're hit. A stringed instrument, like a violin, vibrates when the player plucks the strings or draws a bow across them. A woodwind instrument, like a clarinet, has a thin wooden reed attached to it. When the player blows into the instrument, the reed vibrates.

Some sounds are louder than others. If the drummers at the powwow hit the drum gently, the sound is soft. If they hit the drum harder, the sound gets stronger and louder. The loudness of a sound is called the **volume**. Can you think of a sound with a low volume and a sound with a high volume?

When a drummer hits a drum harder, more energy is transferred to the drum and to the sound. The more energy a sound has, the greater its volume is.

The volume of a sound is measured in units called *decibels* (DES•uh•buhlz), abbreviated *dB*. The softest sound a human can hear is 0 dB. A high-decibel sound is loud and has a lot of energy. Have you ever heard a sound that made your ears ring? Sounds above 100 dB can cause pain and can damage a person's ears. That's why people who work around loud sounds wear ear plugs or other ear protection.

MAIN IDEA AND DETAILS Describe the ways in which three types of musical instruments make sound.

273

Sound Waves

Sound travels through the air as waves. When a jackhammer strikes the sidewalk, the sidewalk vibrates and pushes on the air directly above it. Molecules of air are *compressed,* or squeezed together. The compressed air pushes on the air next to it. This passes the compression along, like a wave at the beach.

You already know that some sounds are higher than others. If you've ever listened to a brass band, for example, you know that a trumpet makes a higher sound than a tuba does. The **pitch** of a sound is how high or how low it is. In the Investigate, you found that changing the length of the strings altered the pitch of the sound you heard. That's because the length of the strings affected how fast they vibrated. A shorter string vibrates faster. There are more vibrations per second. The number of vibrations per second is the **frequency** of a sound.

A sound with a high frequency has a high pitch. A sound with a low frequency has a low pitch. Small objects often vibrate at higher frequencies than large objects do. In the Investigate, shortening the strings made them vibrate at a higher frequency. A trumpet is smaller than a tuba, so the trumpet makes sound waves with higher frequencies.

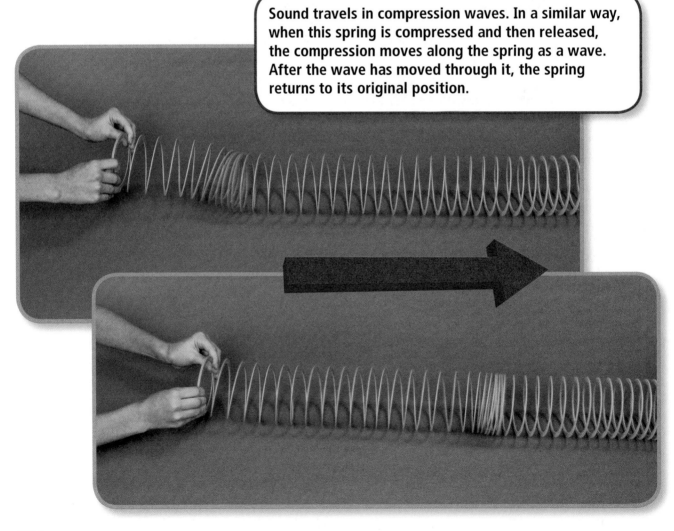

Sound travels in compression waves. In a similar way, when this spring is compressed and then released, the compression moves along the spring as a wave. After the wave has moved through it, the spring returns to its original position.

▲ If you shout toward a hard surface, such as a cliff, you may hear an echo of your voice. The echo isn't as loud as the original sound because the surface absorbs some of the energy.

Sound waves move out in all directions from an object that makes a sound. When a sound wave hits something, some or all of the energy is absorbed. Soft surfaces absorb more sound energy than hard surfaces. A sound that hits a hard surface bounces back—not much of it is absorbed. A sound that bounces off a surface is called an *echo.* If you stand at the foot of a cliff and shout, you may hear an echo of your voice. Some caves and canyons are famous for the echoes they produce.

 MAIN IDEA AND DETAILS How do sounds travel?

Playing the Glasses
You can make a sound by tapping on a drinking glass. If you put water in the glass, the pitch of the sound changes. Use water and several glasses to make different notes. How does adding water to the glasses affect the pitch of the sounds you make?

Sound Transmission

Have you ever set up a line of dominoes and then knocked them down? The first domino pushes over the second and so on. The wave of energy moves down the line, but the individual dominoes do not. Sound has energy just like the dominoes. Waves can carry energy a long distance. The energy travels from place to place, but the matter that carries the energy stays where it is.

In a similar way, sound waves move through air because particles in the air vibrate right where they are.

When you talk to a friend, vibrations move from you to your friend through the air. But the air doesn't have to move to your friend. If it did, a breeze blowing in your face would prevent your friend from hearing your words because they'd be blown back to you!

How Sound Reaches You

Molecules of air carry sound waves from the source to the listeners.

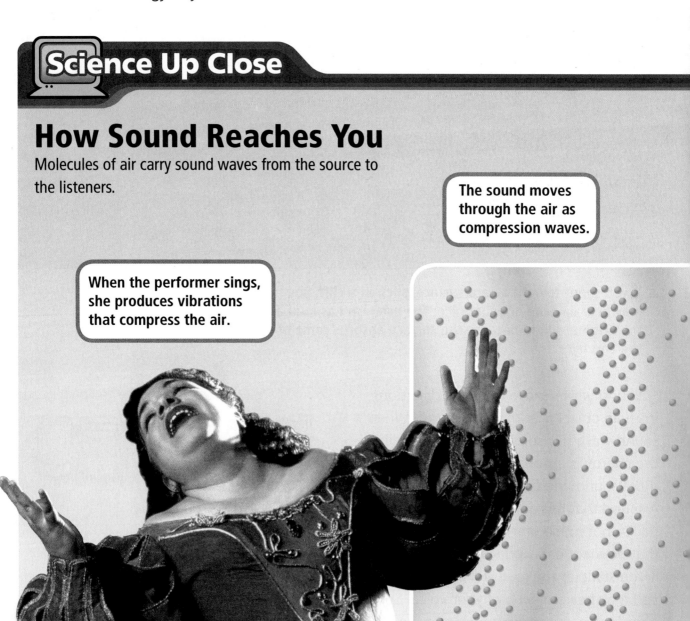

The sound moves through the air as compression waves.

When the performer sings, she produces vibrations that compress the air.

Air is not the only matter that can carry sound waves. Any kind of matter can be made to vibrate and carry sound. Matter that carries sound waves is called a *medium.* Sound waves can't travel without a medium. That's why there's no sound in space, which has no air or other suitable medium.

The speed of sound depends on the medium through which it's moving. The speed doesn't depend on how loud or soft the volume is or how high or low the pitch is. All sounds travel through a certain kind of medium at the same speed.

If the medium changes, the speed of sound changes. Sound moves faster in warm air than in cold air. It travels faster in solids and liquids than it does in gases.

MAIN IDEA AND DETAILS In reference to sound traveling, what is a medium?

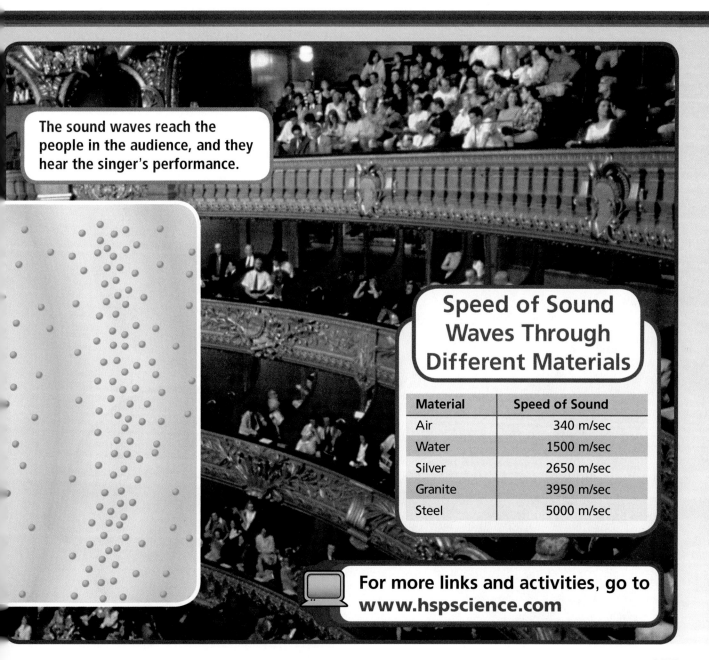

The sound waves reach the people in the audience, and they hear the singer's performance.

Speed of Sound Waves Through Different Materials

Material	Speed of Sound
Air	340 m/sec
Water	1500 m/sec
Silver	2650 m/sec
Granite	3950 m/sec
Steel	5000 m/sec

For more links and activities, go to www.hspscience.com

Animals and Sound

People can hear sounds over a wide range of frequencies. The highest sounds that people can hear have frequencies of about 20,000 vibrations per second.

Many animals can hear sounds that are outside the range of human hearing. Dogs can hear sounds with higher frequencies than people can hear—frequencies of 25,000 vibrations per second.

Bats have better hearing than most other animals. They can hear sounds with frequencies as high as 100,000 vibrations per second. Bats can also produce sounds with that frequency.

As a bat flies, it produces many short, high-frequency sounds. These bounce off objects in the bat's path, and the bat hears the echoes. The echoes help the bat fly at night by giving it information about its surroundings. They also help the bat hunt. Echoes that bounce from insects give information to the bat about where to find its next meal.

People, dogs, and bats have parts of their ears on the outside of their bodies. But this isn't true for all animals. Snakes and birds have no outside ear parts.

Grasshoppers pick up vibrations in several ways. A membrane near the leg picks up vibrations in the air. Hairlike structures on the body pick up vibrations in the ground.

MAIN IDEA AND DETAILS What are two ways animals sense vibrations?

A grasshopper picks up vibrations through structures near its hind legs.

A bat uses echoes to find its prey in the dark.

A snake uses its lower jaw to sense vibrations from the ground.

1. MAIN IDEA AND DETAILS Draw and complete this graphic organizer.

Two Characteristics of Sound

Frequency

A sound with a high frequency has a high **Ⓐ** _____.

A sound with a low frequency has a **Ⓑ** _____ pitch.

Volume

A sound with a high volume is **Ⓒ** _____.

A sound with a low volume is **Ⓓ** _____.

2. SUMMARIZE Write two sentences that tell what this lesson is mainly about.

3. DRAW CONCLUSIONS A guitar player changes the vibrating length of the strings by holding them down against the frets, which are ridges on the guitar. What does changing the length in this way do to the sound?

4. VOCABULARY Write a paragraph that uses the terms in this lesson.

Test Prep

5. Critical Thinking Why does carpet make a room seem quiet?

6. What happens to a sound if the frequency of the vibrations increases?

A. The volume decreases.
B. The pitch increases.
C. The sound echoes.
D. The sound gets louder.

Links

Writing

Narrative Writing
Write a **story** about how a bat hunts for insects. Write your story from the bat's point of view.

Math

Construct a Graph
Research the speed sound travels through different materials. Make a bar graph to show your data. Be sure to include the materials listed in Science Up Close.

Social Studies

The Sound Barrier
A vehicle that travels faster than the speed of sound is said to break the sound barrier. Find out what kinds of vehicles have broken the sound barrier. Make a time line to show your findings.

 For more links and activities, go to www.hspscience.com

2
What Is Light?

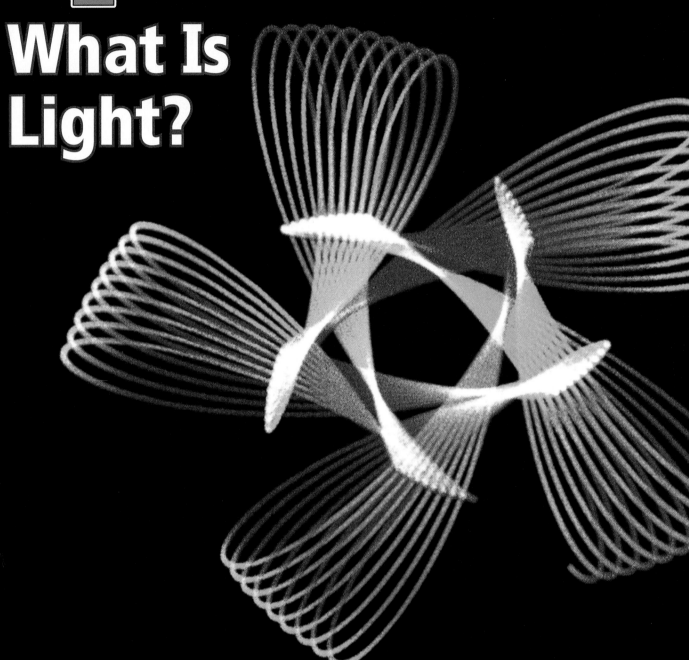

Fast Fact

Laser Shows Dozens of lasers are used to make a display like this. The color of each laser beam depends on the kind of material contained in the laser. Each laser also contains a pair of mirrors that reflect energy from the material inside. In the Investigate, you'll observe and record the path of reflected light.

The Path of Reflected Light

Materials
- piece of corrugated cardboard, 10 cm x 10 cm
- ruler
- 3 pushpins of different colors
- masking tape
- small mirror
- protractor

Procedure

1. Lay the cardboard flat, and use tape to stand the mirror vertically at one end of the cardboard. Push two of the pins into the cardboard, about 5 cm in front of the mirror.

Step 1

2. Position yourself so your eyes are level with the pins. Align yourself so that your view of one pin lines up with the reflection of the other pin. Push a third pin into the cardboard, at the edge of the mirror, right in front of where you see the reflection. The first pin, the third pin, and the reflection of the second pin should appear to be in a straight line.

3. Draw lines on the cardboard to connect the third pin with the others. These lines show how the light from the second pin traveled to your eye.

Step 3

4. Draw a line along the front of the mirror, and remove the mirror from the cardboard. Using the protractor, measure the angle between each line and the edge of the mirror. Record your results.

Draw Conclusions

1. Compare the two angles you measured.

2. **Inquiry Skill** Suppose you know the angle at which light hits a mirror. Predict the angle at which the light will reflect.

Investigate Further

Predict **how light will be reflected by a mirror that isn't flat. Then** plan and conduct an experiment **to test your prediction.**

VOCABULARY
reflection p. 286
opaque p. 286
translucent p. 287
transparent p. 287
refraction p. 287
concave lens p. 288
convex lens p. 288

SCIENCE CONCEPTS
► what kinds of light waves there are
► how matter affects light

READING FOCUS SKILL
MAIN IDEA AND DETAILS Look for ways that light can be changed.

Light Energy

Have you ever taken pictures with a camera? Did you know that light is what allows an image to form on the film? Light, like sound, is a form of energy that travels in waves. However, unlike sound, light can travel through empty space. All waves carry energy. When the waves reach an object, some of the energy can be absorbed by that object. You often see the results. For example, light energy that strikes film in a camera causes a chemical change, enabling a picture to be made.

Light is one small part of a range of energy known as the *electromagnetic spectrum*. The waves that make up the

Electromagnetic Spectrum

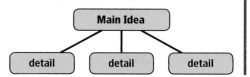

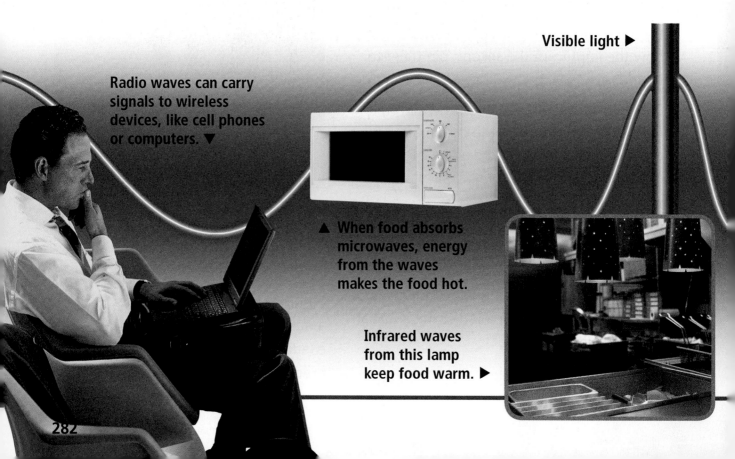

Visible light ►

Radio waves can carry signals to wireless devices, like cell phones or computers. ▼

▲ When food absorbs microwaves, energy from the waves makes the food hot.

Infrared waves from this lamp keep food warm. ►

electromagnetic spectrum differ in their frequencies. The part of the spectrum that humans can see is called *visible light*. Radio waves have lower frequencies than visible light waves. X rays have higher frequencies.

Waves with high frequencies carry more energy than waves with lower frequencies. High-energy waves pass through matter more easily. You know that light doesn't pass through your body. But other forms of waves, such as X rays, do, at least partially. Has a dentist ever taken an X-ray image of your teeth? You hold a piece of film in your mouth, and the dentist points an X-ray machine at your jaw. X rays go from the machine, through your jaw, and to the film.

Did you notice that your teeth are white on the X ray, but everything else is dark? When X rays pass through your jaw, your teeth absorb more of the X-ray energy than the rest of your mouth does. The result is that different amounts of energy reach the film in different places.

On the film, the X-ray energy causes changes that can be seen. The different amounts of energy in different places make a picture of your teeth on the film.

 MAIN IDEA AND DETAILS **What types of waves are found in the electromagnetic spectrum?**

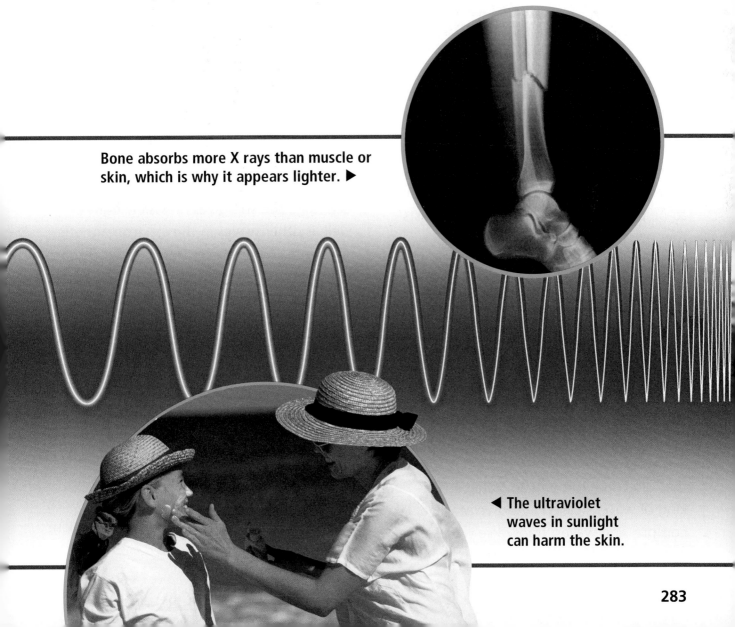

Bone absorbs more X rays than muscle or skin, which is why it appears lighter. ▶

◀ **The ultraviolet waves in sunlight can harm the skin.**

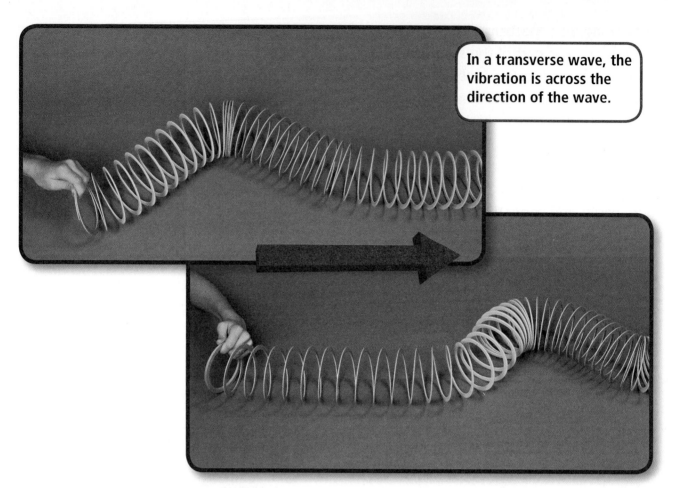

In a transverse wave, the vibration is across the direction of the wave.

Light Waves

Light is unlike anything else in the universe! Scientists have been studying light for centuries, but there is a great deal yet to be discovered about it. Many scientists theorize that light travels in waves.

Light waves are different from sound waves. Sound waves travel as compressions in matter. Light does not compress matter.

Have you watched waves at the ocean or on a lake? While the water moves up and down, it does not move forward or backward. Light moves like ocean waves.

If you hold one end of a rope and shake it up and down, you make a wave that moves along the rope. But the vibration is across that direction, forming an S shape. This kind of wave is called a *transverse* wave. Like compression waves, transverse waves carry only energy. After the wave has passed, the rope is still in your hand, even though the energy has traveled away from you.

Since light waves do not need matter, light can travel through empty space. For example, the sun gives off visible light as well as other waves in the electromagnetic spectrum. These waves travel through space and reach Earth.

Light travels very fast. Scientists have not found anything faster. Even the slowest light waves move thousands of times faster than sound waves. Light is so fast that sunlight takes only about 8 minutes to travel the distance to Earth—about 150 million km (93 million mi).

You feel the energy in light when you stand in sunlight. Your body absorbs the energy, and you feel it as heat. If you absorb too much of that energy, it harms your skin, and you get a sunburn.

The light from a light bulb doesn't have as much energy as sunlight. You can't get a sunburn from standing under an ordinary lamp. A light bulb gives off heat because an electric current heats up the filament, or wire, inside the bulb. This makes the filament give off light.

The sun and a light bulb give off light in all directions. A laser, though, gives off light in a narrow beam. Inside a laser, light waves line up, like the members of a band marching in step in one direction. When the waves come out of the laser, they stay together and don't spread out. The concentrated light is very powerful. It is also dangerous. You should never look into a source of laser light.

 MAIN IDEA AND DETAILS What characteristics do light waves have?

Laser

The light energy from lasers is so concentrated that factories use lasers to cut steel. ▶

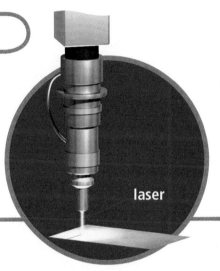

laser

Light Bulb

The light from an ordinary light bulb spreads out in all directions. The energy you get from the bulb decreases as you move away. ▶

Absorption, Reflection, and Refraction

Have you ever seen frosted glass? Its surface is rough, not smooth. Some light passes through, but you can't see objects clearly through the glass.

When light hits an object, the object affects the path of the light. An object can absorb light, make it bounce back, or let it pass through.

Some of the light energy that hits an object is absorbed. Objects of different colors absorb different amounts of light. Dark-colored objects absorb the most light.

Objects don't absorb all the light that hits them. Some of the light bounces off. **Reflection** is the bouncing of light from a surface. Usually, light scatters as it is reflected. The reflected light that reaches your eyes from an object enables you to see the object.

A smooth surface reflects light in a predictable way. The light isn't scattered. Instead, it reflects in a pattern that you see as an image in the surface. This is what happens when you see the sky reflected by the smooth windows of a building or when you see yourself in a mirror.

Whether the surfaces are smooth or rough, most objects absorb some light and reflect the rest. They don't allow light to pass through them. Materials that do not allow light to pass through are **opaque** (oh•PAYK). Most of the objects around you—books, chairs, walls, floors—are opaque. You can't see through them.

The glass used in this building is coated with chemicals that reflect light like a giant mirror. ▶

▲ A prism refracts white light into a rainbow of colors. Refraction of light as it leaves the water makes the pelican's belly and legs look separated from its body.

Materials that allow only some amount of light to pass through are **translucent** (trans•LOO•suhnt). Wax paper and bubble wrap are translucent. So are some kinds of window shades.

With the shades up, though, you can look through glass windows to see what's outside. You can see through glass because light passes through it. A material that allows light to pass through is **transparent**. Most glass, water, and plastic wrap are transparent. Transparent objects don't scatter light like translucent objects can.

You may think that light doesn't change as it passes through transparent materials. But when light moves into a different material, it bends. This bending of light as it moves from one material to another is called **refraction**. Refraction changes the angle at which you see things. When you look at an object through two different materials, the bent light can make a solid object look as if it's in two parts.

 MAIN IDEA AND DETAILS Give one example each of transparent, translucent, and opaque materials.

Dark objects absorb more light energy than light-colored objects do. That's why it's good to wear light colors on a bright summer day. ▶

Lenses

Use a hand lens to look at this page. A hand lens magnifies objects, or makes them look larger. Most hand lenses contain one glass or plastic lens. A lens is a curved transparent object that bends light. The shape of the curve affects how the light bends.

There are two basic kinds of lenses. A **concave lens** is thicker at the edges than it is at the center. It spreads light waves apart. The viewfinder of a camera has a concave lens. The lens makes objects look smaller. That way, you can look in the viewfinder and see what the whole picture will look like.

A **convex lens** is thicker at the center than it is at the edges. It bends light waves to make them come together. A convex lens can be used as a magnifier or to make an image on a screen. The lens of a camera is a convex lens, too. It brings light waves together on the film, producing an image.

 MAIN IDEA AND DETAILS What are the two basic types of lenses?

Insta-Lab

Water Lens
Fill a test tube completely with water. Hold the test tube over a sink or pan to catch spills as you close the test tube with a stopper. Make sure the stopper is tight. Then hold the test tube over some writing, and look through it. How does your water lens change what you see? What kind of lens is it?

Camera Lenses

A concave lens spreads light waves apart. ▶

What kinds of lenses are in this camera? ▼

▲ A convex lens brings light waves together.

1. MAIN IDEA AND DETAILS Draw and complete this graphic organizer.

Light Waves Change When They Hit Objects

> **Opaque objects Ⓐ_____ some light and reflect the rest.**

> **Transparent objects let light pass through, although they make the light Ⓑ_____, or refract.**

> **Smooth surfaces Ⓒ_____ a lot of light.**

2. SUMMARIZE Write a summary of this lesson by using the lesson's vocabulary terms.

3. DRAW CONCLUSIONS Is the glass in a stained-glass window transparent, translucent, or opaque? Explain your answer.

4. VOCABULARY Use the vocabulary terms in this lesson to make a crossword puzzle.

Test Prep

5. Critical Thinking Which has more energy—microwaves or X rays? Explain your answer.

6. Which is true of a concave lens?
- **A.** Its center is thicker than its edges.
- **B.** It projects an image on a screen.
- **C.** It spreads light rays apart.
- **D.** It is used in a camera lens.

Links

Writing

Expository Writing
Suppose you are standing at the rim of a canyon, holding a telescope and a camera. Write a **paragraph** describing what you see through each device.

Math

Estimating
Light travels at about 300 million m/sec through empty space or through air. Sound travels at about 340 m/sec through air. About how many times as fast does light travel compared to sound?

Health

Sunscreens
Find out how sunscreens work and what the SPF ratings mean. Summarize your findings in a brief report.

For more links and activities, go to www.hspscience.com

A SOUND IDEA

For six years, Joanne Peterson lived in a silent world. Because she was deaf, Peterson could see her son play the piano, but she could not hear him. Thanks to a recently developed bionic ear, Peterson can hear again.

Electrical Impulses

Peterson was one of the first Americans to use the device. Unlike traditional hearing aids, which amplify sounds, the bionic ear changes sounds into electrical impulses. The bionic ear is also called a *cochlear implant*.

The first step is to surgically implant part of the bionic ear into the back of a patient's head. The doctors actually attach an electrode and tiny wires that connect to nerves. Those nerves are connected to the part of the brain that controls hearing.

The user wears a microphone that captures speech and sounds. The microphone is attached to a computer processor. The processor converts the sound into electrical impulses. Those impulses are sent to the surgical implant inside the user's head.

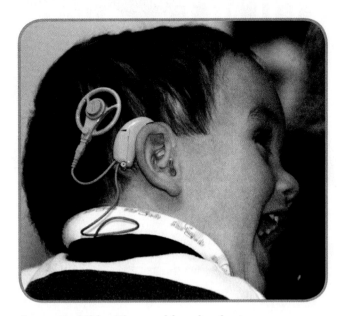

A young child with a cochlear implant.

She Longed to Hear Music

"He played Beethoven," Peterson said after listening to her son play the piano. "I thought that was so pretty to sit and listen to."

The implant then delivers the electrical impulses, through the tiny wires, to the nerves that are connected to the part of the brain that controls hearing. The brain is able to translate the impulses into sounds, allowing the user to hear.

Hearing Again

Doctors say the people who benefit the most from the bionic ear are those whose hearing is so bad that they cannot hear a telephone ring.

"I adore [the bionic ear]. At first it was a major shock to the system, to my head," said Cassie Bunker, who also regained hearing with the bionic ear. She thought, "I'm hearing things."

THINK ABOUT IT

1. Other than helping people hear, what else do nerves do in the body?
2. How is the bionic ear different from traditional hearing aids?

Find out more! Log on to
www.hspscience.com

Music to Their Ears

You probably listen to music on the radio or watch music videos on TV. Do you ever stop to think that music is made up of different sounds? That's what Nancy Li and other kids who take part in the Little Kids Rock program are learning.

Little Kids Rock is a program that teaches kids in school about music and about the sounds different instruments make. For example, the guitar that Nancy plays makes a lower pitch sound than that made by a piccolo. That's because the molecules of air are pushed together less frequently by the guitar than they are pushed together by the piccolo.

Materials
- plastic soda bottle
- scissors
- plastic wrap
- rubber band
- shallow container
- water

Quick and Easy Project

Watching Sound Waves

Procedure

1. **CAUTION** Be careful when using scissors! Use the scissors to cut off the bottom of the soda bottle.
2. Stretch a piece of plastic wrap over the open end of the bottle. Secure the wrap with the rubber band.
3. Add water to the shallow container to a depth of about 3 cm.
4. Hold the bottle so that its open neck is about 3 cm away from the surface of the water. Lightly tap on the plastic wrap. Observe what happens.

Draw Conclusions

1. Describe how the surface of the water looked when you tapped on the plastic wrap.
2. How can you explain your observations?

Design Your Own Investigation

Seeing Colors

Collect a group of colored items, such as crayons, jars of colorful paints, or sheets of colored construction paper. Design an experiment in which you determine how much light is required to identify the color of each item. How does the amount of light determine what colors you can see?

Review and Test Preparation

Vocabulary Review

Use the terms below to complete the sentences. The page numbers tell you where to look in the chapter if you need help.

volume p. 273	**transparent** p. 287
pitch p. 274	**refraction** p. 287
opaque p. 286	**concave lens** p. 288
translucent p. 287	**convex lens** p. 288

1. A sound with a high frequency has a high _____.

2. A material that does not allow any light to pass through is _____.

3. Light rays are bent and brought together by a _____.

4. The loudness of a sound is also known as _____.

5. Water and plastic wrap are materials that are _____.

6. A lens that is thicker at the edges than at the middle is a _____.

7. The bending of light as it moves from one material to another is _____.

8. Wax paper is _____.

Check Understanding

Write the letter of the best choice.

9. **MAIN IDEA AND DETAILS** Which of the following is a characteristic of sound waves?

   A. A medium is necessary for the waves to travel.

   B. The waves are transverse.

   C. Different types can be compared on the electromagnetic spectrum.

   D. They travel faster than other waves.

10. In the picture, Tod is using a microscope to examine a slide.

Which type of lens makes it possible for Tod to identify what is on the slide?

   F. concave   H. opaque

   G. convex   J. transparent

11. **MAIN IDEA AND DETAILS** What must happen in order for a sound wave to form?

   A. An electric current must flow.

   B. A certain frequency must be reached.

   C. Matter must vibrate.

   D. Volume must be absorbed.

12. Which of the following surfaces would bounce back almost all the light waves that hit it?

  F. a white wall
  G. a piece of plastic wrap
  H. a stained-glass window
  J. a mirror

13. Which of the following musical instruments makes sounds with the lowest frequencies?

A.

B.

Note: instruments not to scale

C.

D.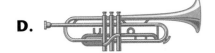

14. When we see a colored object, what are we really seeing?

  F. light that has been absorbed
  G. light that has not been absorbed
  H. light that has been refracted
  J. light that has not been refracted

15. What is the result of someone hitting a drum harder than before?

  A. The number of decibels increases.
  B. Pitch decreases.
  C. Frequency increases.
  D. The number of vibrations decreases.

16. What kind of image does this lens produce?

  F. a distorted image
  G. a larger image
  H. a reflected image
  J. a smaller image

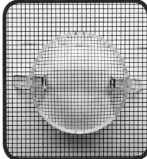

Inquiry Skills

17. Stephen is making sound waves by using strings of 12 different lengths. **Identify the variable** in Stephen's experiment.

18. **Predict** whether light and sound would be observed by somebody watching an explosion that occurs in space. Explain.

Critical Thinking

19. Elephants can detect sources of underground water by using their feet. Use what you know about sound waves to explain how this is possible.

20. Shakira is watching an approaching thunderstorm from her house. She can see and hear the lightning and thunder in the distance.
  Part A Would Shakira see the lightning first or hear the thunder first? Explain.
  Part B How will Shakira's observations of the lightning and thunder change as the thunderstorm gets closer?

Sandusky

OHIO

✪ Columbus

Ohio River

Monster Roller Coasters

You know the feeling. You wait with anticipation while your car slowly climbs the hill. With every click and clack, you get closer to the top. Then suddenly, you're falling! All around you people are yelling and laughing. And you? Maybe you feel as if you left your stomach back at the top of the hill. You're riding a roller coaster! If you love the thrill of riding roller coasters, check out Cedar Point.

Cedar Point is an amusement park near Sandusky. The first roller coaster was built there in 1892. Today, the park is home to 16 roller coasters. People come from all over the country to ride the roller coasters at Cedar Point. The power and speed obtained by some of these coasters may surprise you.

Millennium Force

The Millennium Force was built in the year 2000. It broke several world records when it was built. It was the tallest roller coaster, at 95 m (310 ft). It was the fastest, at 150 km/hr (93 mi/hr). And it had the longest drop of any roller coaster, at 90 m (300 ft). The Millennium Force covers almost 2 km (1.25 mi) of track, winding through the center of the park.

Top Thrill Dragster

Cedar Point's newest roller coaster is the Top Thrill Dragster. Built in 2003, it is 130 m (420 ft) tall. This is the same height as a 42-story skyscraper!

The thrill of a roller-coaster ride is hard to match.

The ride features a vertical drop of 120 m (400 ft). It reaches a top speed of 190 km/hr (120 mi/hr). This is more than twice the speed limit on some highways.

Roller Coasters and Physics

A roller coaster has no engine. It is called a "coaster" because its cars coast through most of the ride. So how does a roller coaster go so fast and climb so high? The answer involves basic laws of motion.

A motor and cable system tows the cars to the top of the first hill. The roller coaster at the top of the hill has a lot of potential energy. What happens when the roller coaster starts down the hill? The force of gravity converts potential energy into kinetic energy. Kinetic energy is the energy of motion. Once the roller coaster "falls" down that first hill, it has momentum. Momentum is mass (the roller coaster) with velocity (speed and direction). Momentum allows the roller coaster to climb the next hill. The coaster gains potential energy as it climbs. When it reaches the top, it begins to "fall" down the next hill.

The steeper the drop on a hill, the greater the effect of gravity will be on the roller coaster. The greater the effect of gravity, the faster the roller coaster will go.

So gravity is the answer to how a roller coaster goes so fast. And momentum allows it to climb so high. When a roller coaster is built, engineers figure out how gravity and momentum will affect the ride. Next time you ride a coaster, think about how these forces work before you go over the next hill.

The Top Thrill Dragster is the highest and fastest roller coaster at Cedar Point.

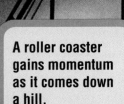

A roller coaster gains momentum as it comes down a hill.

Think and Do

1. **SCIENCE AND TECHNOLOGY** At first, roller coasters were built of wood, with steel rails. About 45 years ago, steel began replacing the wood framework. Research roller coasters to find out why steel was considered an improvement. Write a paragraph explaining your findings.

2. **SCIENTIFIC THINKING** Draw a design for your own roller coaster. At the top of each hill on the drawing, write the height. At the bottom, write how steep the hill is (very steep, kind of steep, not steep). Try to make a working model to see if momentum will carry a car all the way through.

Great American Ball Park

OHIO
Cincinnati
Columbus
Ohio River

The home of the Cincinnati Reds

Another Reds home run!

Nothing is more a part of American life than baseball. Ohio has many baseball teams. Fans in Canton, Toledo, and Dayton can root for their local minor league teams. If you live in northeast Ohio, you might cheer for the Cleveland Indians. And if you live anywhere near Cincinnati, you're probably a Reds fan.

The Reds are the oldest of all major league teams. The team was started more than 120 years ago. The Reds have played in several stadiums. They moved into Redland Field in 1912. When Powel Crosley bought the team in 1934, he changed the name to Crosley Field.

In 1970, the Reds moved to Riverfront Stadium. Since 2003, their home has been the Great American Ball Park. The new park has been very popular with fans. It preserves traditions of the past while providing a great place to watch the game today.

Outside Great American Ball Park is an area called Crosley Terrace. It features statues of famous Reds players. Inside, in left field, the park has one of the largest scoreboards in baseball. Right field features a model of a riverboat. It has two smokestacks and a paddle wheel. When a Reds player hits a home run, it shoots fireworks! The electricity of the scoreboard is converted into light energy. And the light energy is converted into fan energy!

The Physics of Baseball

One way to understand what happens in baseball is with physics. Baseball is about force and motion. Think about the following the next time you watch your local team play.

The action in baseball begins with the pitch. When the pitcher throws the ball, he or she applies a force. The force gives the ball motion. The baseball then has speed and direction. The combination of speed and direction is velocity.

Other forces also affect the velocity of the thrown ball. Gravity pulls it toward the ground. And just traveling through the air slows the ball down a little. This force is called drag or friction.

A Hit!

When the baseball crosses the plate, it can be affected by another force. The batter is trying to hit the ball. The bat has mass. As the batter swings the bat, the bat gains momentum. When the bat hits the ball, that momentum transfers to the ball. This gives the ball a new velocity.

Remember that velocity is speed and direction. Because the ball has been hit, it starts to move in a new direction. The amount of momentum that is transferred depends on two things. The first is how fast (or hard) the batter swings the bat. The second is how much of the bat hits the ball. If the batter makes good contact with a strong swing, a lot of force is transferred to the ball. As a result, the ball travels far and fast.

The forces that slow the ball down are the same as the ones that affect a pitch. Gravity pulls the ball toward the ground. Drag and friction slow the hit ball down a little bit.

The pitcher applies a force to the baseball.

The momentum of the bat changes the baseball's velocity.

Think and Do

I. SCIENCE AND TECHNOLOGY Suppose your summer league baseball coach asks for your help in selecting new bats. She wants to know whether the team should use wood or aluminum bats. Write a plan to help you determine which type of bat to use.

2. SCIENTIFIC THINKING Sandy Koufax became one of the greatest pitchers in history. But he struggled for many years to control his pitches. He learned to slow his pitches down. Review what you've read about baseball physics. Write a paragraph to explain why slowing his pitches might have made Sandy Koufax a better pitcher.

Cleveland Rocks

Cleveland

OHIO

Columbus

Ohio River

Rock and roll is all about the music. But if you are interested in its history, there is a place you have to visit. That place is in Cleveland—The Rock and Roll Hall of Fame and Museum.

The Rock and Roll Hall of Fame and Museum is one of Ohio's great attractions. The building is on the shore of Lake Erie. It was designed by world-famous architect I. M. Pei. He wanted the building to show the energy of rock and roll. It features a 50-m (165-ft) tower. The tower is surrounded by bold geometric forms.

The Museum

So what kinds of things can you see at the museum? There are hands-on exhibits, videos, and many artifacts. The artifacts include guitars and clothing that belonged to famous performers.

The museum sponsors concerts and special events throughout the year. The goal of the Rock and Roll Hall of Fame and Museum is to explore the past, present, and future of rock music and culture.

The museum is loaded with artifacts of every major rocker.

The dramatic building captures the energy of rock music.

Good Vibrations

Rock and roll is all about the music. So what is music? Music is sound, and sound can be studied scientifically. Sound begins with vibrations.

Think of the lead guitar player in front of a big crowd. She strums several strings as she plays the first chord. What is happening? The guitar strings vibrate. Those vibrations are amplified through electronic speakers. The amplified vibrations cause a disturbance of the surrounding air. That disturbance is a sound wave.

The sound wave pushes molecules of air as it travels. When those air molecules contact your ear, parts of your ear vibrate. You perceive the vibrations as sound. Musical sounds are different from noises. Noises are irregular. Music is often made of regular, uniform vibrations.

Two important qualities of musical sounds are pitch and volume. Pitch is how high or low a tone sounds. The greater the frequency of the vibration, the higher the tone will be. A lead guitar string vibrates with more frequency than a bass guitar string. Volume is how loud the music sounds. The greater the size of the sound wave, the louder the music. The size of a sound wave is called amplitude.

A rock guitarist controls the frequency and amplitude of sound waves. If done with enough art and skill, he or she may end up in the Rock and Roll Hall of Fame!

Think and Do

I. SCIENCE AND TECHNOLOGY Let's say you invent a device that will make a guitar string vibrate faster than strumming by hand. You publish your discovery in a scientific journal. Other sound engineers are critical of your idea. They say that the human ear will not be able to hear the tones your device generates. What should you do with your research now? Write a paragraph to explain your ideas.

2. SCIENTIFIC THINKING Some people don't like rock music because it is so loud. What do you think? Try listening to one of your favorite songs at soft, medium, loud, and very loud settings. (First, make sure it's okay with the adults in your home!) Make a chart to track your response to the volume of the song. In the first column, indicate how loud the song was. In the second column, write whether you liked the song at that volume. In the third column, list a reason why.

SK-2 Explain/support conclusions; SK-3 Explain why experiments are repeated; PS-6 Describe sound; PS-7 Describe how to change pitch

301

Does String Length Affect Pitch?

Materials
- looseleaf notebook
- ruler
- 1 extra-long rubber band

Be Safe safety goggles

Procedure
1. Wear safety goggles.
2. Stretch the rubber band around the short side of the notebook.
3. Open the notebook about 5 cm. Strum the rubber band. Record your observations of the sound. Describe the pitch as high, low, or somewhere in between.
4. Open the notebook about 8 cm and repeat step 3.
5. Repeat this procedure, always opening the notebook a different amount until you have 8 to 10 observations. Record your data.

Draw Conclusions
1. How does the length of a string affect pitch?
2. What other variables might affect the pitch in this experiment? How could you test your ideas?

Roller Coasters of the Future

Materials
- calculator
- pencil

Procedure
1. The first two lines on the chart show data from roller coasters that exists today. The data that follows is from roller coasters that might exist in the future.
2. Fill in the remainder of the chart, giving your best estimate of the speed that the future roller coasters might achieve.

High Drop (feet)	High Speed (miles per hour)
300	93
400	120
500	
600	
700	
800	
900	

Draw Conclusions
1. How does the height of the drop of a roller coaster affect its speed?
2. What are some possible technological problems that would need to be overcome in building these future roller coasters?
3. Do you think there are limits to how high a roller coaster can be built or how fast it can go? Are there limits to what humans can endure on a roller coaster? Explain.

SK-1 Explain how new information changes conclusions; **SI-3** Communicate investigation results; **SI-4** Identify variables

References

Contents

Health Handbook

Reading in Science Handbook

Math in Science Handbook   R28

Your Skin

Your skin is your body's largest organ. It provides your body with a tough protective covering. It produces sweat to help control your body temperature. It protects you from disease. Your skin also provides your sense of touch that allows you to feel pressure, textures, temperature, and pain.

When you play hard or exercise, your body produces sweat, which cools you as it evaporates. The sweat from your skin also helps your body eliminate excess salts and other wastes.

The skin is the body's largest organ. ▼

Epidermis
Many layers of dead skin cells form the top of the epidermis. Cells in the lower part of the epidermis are always making new cells.

Dermis
The dermis is much thicker than the epidermis. It is made up of tough, flexible fibers.

Hair Follicle
Each hair follicle has a muscle that can contract and make the hair "stand on end."

Pore
These tiny holes on the surface of your skin lead to your dermis.

Oil Gland
Oil glands produce oil that keeps your skin soft and smooth.

Sweat Gland
Sweat glands produce sweat, which contains water, salt, and various wastes.

Fatty Tissue
This tissue layer beneath the dermis stores food, provides warmth, and attaches your skin to underlying bone and muscle.

Caring for Your Skin

- To protect your skin and to keep it healthy, you should wash your body, including your hair and your nails, every day. This helps remove germs, excess oils and sweat, and dead cells from the epidermis, the outer layer of your skin. Because you touch many things during the day, you should wash your hands with soap and water frequently.

- If you get a cut or scratch, you should wash it right away and cover it with a sterile bandage to prevent infection and promote healing.

- Protect your skin from cuts and scrapes by wearing proper safety equipment when you play sports or skate, or when you're riding your bike or scooter.

- Always protect your skin from sunburn by wearing protective clothing and sunscreen when you are outdoors in bright sun.

Your Senses

Eyes

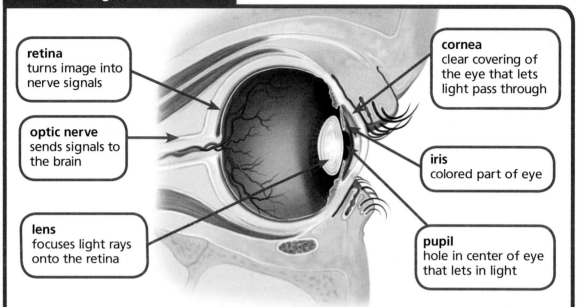

retina
turns image into
nerve signals

optic nerve
sends signals to
the brain

lens
focuses light rays
onto the retina

cornea
clear covering of
the eye that lets
light pass through

iris
colored part of eye

pupil
hole in center of eye
that lets in light

Light rays bounce off objects and enter the eye through the pupil. A lens inside
the eye focuses the light rays, and the image of the object is projected onto
the retina at the back of the eye. In the retina the image is turned into nerve
signals. Your brain analyzes these signals to "tell" you what you're seeing.

Ears

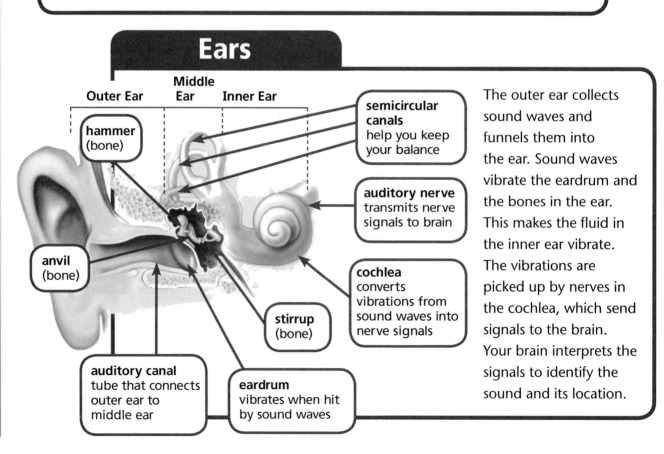

Middle
Outer Ear Ear Inner Ear

hammer
(bone)

anvil
(bone)

auditory canal
tube that connects
outer ear to
middle ear

stirrup
(bone)

eardrum
vibrates when hit
by sound waves

**semicircular
canals**
help you keep
your balance

auditory nerve
transmits nerve
signals to brain

cochlea
converts
vibrations from
sound waves into
nerve signals

The outer ear collects
sound waves and
funnels them into
the ear. Sound waves
vibrate the eardrum and
the bones in the ear.
This makes the fluid in
the inner ear vibrate.
The vibrations are
picked up by nerves in
the cochlea, which send
signals to the brain.
Your brain interprets the
signals to identify the
sound and its location.

Nose

When you breathe in, air is swept upward to nerve cells in the nasal cavity. The nasal cavity is the upper part of the nose, inside the skull. Different nerve cells respond to different chemicals in the air and send signals to your brain.

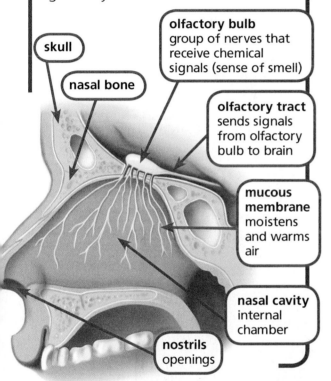

skull

nasal bone

olfactory bulb
group of nerves that receive chemical signals (sense of smell)

olfactory tract
sends signals from olfactory bulb to brain

mucous membrane
moistens and warms air

nasal cavity
internal chamber

nostrils
openings

Skin

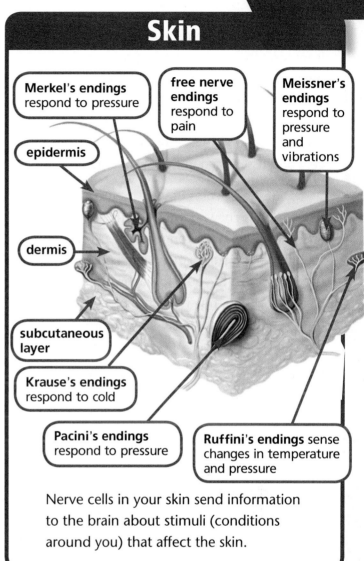

Merkel's endings
respond to pressure

free nerve endings
respond to pain

Meissner's endings
respond to pressure and vibrations

epidermis

dermis

subcutaneous layer

Krause's endings
respond to cold

Pacini's endings
respond to pressure

Ruffini's endings sense changes in temperature and pressure

Nerve cells in your skin send information to the brain about stimuli (conditions around you) that affect the skin.

Caring for Your Senses

• Injuries to these organs can affect your senses.

• Protect your skin and eyes by wearing sunscreen and sunglasses. Protect your ears from loud sounds. Protect your nose from harsh chemicals and your tongue from hot foods and drinks.

Tongue

The tongue is covered with about 10,000 tiny nerve cells, or taste buds, that detect basic tastes in things you eat and drink. Different taste buds respond to different chemicals, and send signals to your brain.

taste buds

Your Digestive System

Your body systems need nutrients from food for energy and for proper cell function. Your digestive system breaks down the food you eat into tiny particles that can be absorbed by your blood and carried throughout your body, so various cells and tissues can use the nutrients.

Digestion begins in your mouth when food is chewed, mixed with saliva, and swallowed. Your tongue pushes the food into your esophagus, which pushes the food down to your stomach with a muscular action, much like the one you use to squeeze toothpaste from a tube.

Your stomach produces gastric juices and mixes them with your food to begin breaking down proteins. Partially digested food leaves your stomach and moves to your small intestine.

Most of the digestive process occurs in your small intestine, where partially digested food is mixed with bile from your liver. This helps break down fats. Your pancreas also produces digestive juices that continue the process of digesting fats and proteins in the small intestine. Your pancreas also produces a special substance called insulin, which helps your body move sugar from your blood into your cells.

As food moves through your small intestine, nutrients are absorbed by the villi and pass into your blood.

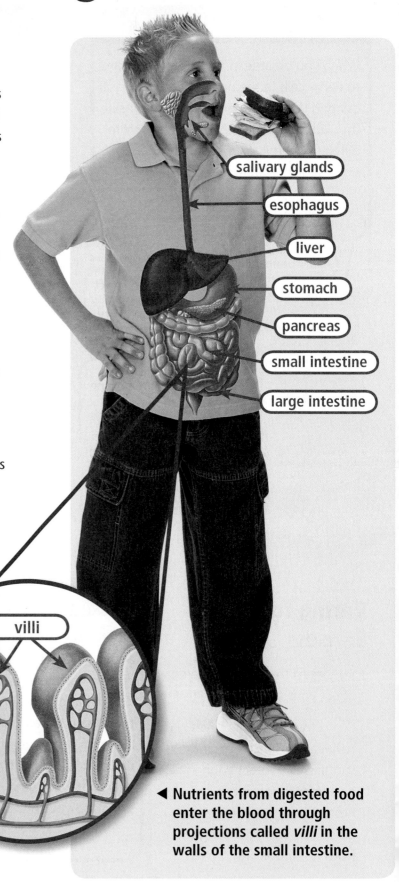

salivary glands

esophagus

liver

stomach

pancreas

small intestine

large intestine

villi

◀ Nutrients from digested food enter the blood through projections called *villi* in the walls of the small intestine.

Specialized Digestive Organs

Your liver produces a fluid called bile that helps break down fats. Bile is stored in your gallbladder. During digestion, the stored bile flows through the bile duct into your small intestine, to help with the digestive process.

Material that is not absorbed by your small intestine passes into your large intestine. This organ absorbs water and vitamins from the undigested materials. The remaining solid wastes are stored by your large intestine until it leaves your body.

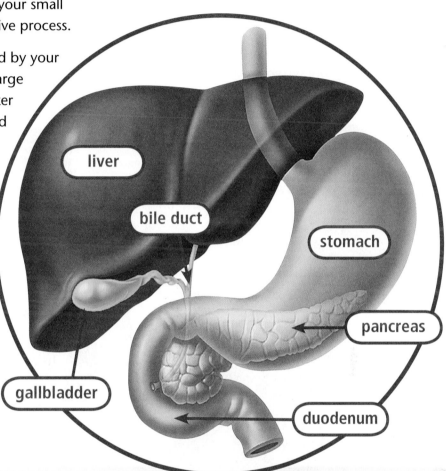

liver

bile duct

stomach

pancreas

gallbladder

duodenum

Caring for Your Digestive System

- Drink plenty of water every day. Water helps move food through your digestive system and helps your body replenish saliva, gastric juices, and bile consumed during digestion.

- Eat a variety of foods, choose a well-balanced diet, and maintain a healthy weight.

- Eat plenty of fruits and vegetables. These foods contain essential nutrients and help your digestive system function effectively.

- Chew your food thoroughly before swallowing.

Your Circulatory System

Your body relies on your circulatory system to deliver essential nutrients and oxygen to your organs, tissues, and cells. These materials are carried by your blood. As it circulates, your blood also removes wastes from your tissues. Your circulatory system includes your heart, arteries that carry oxygen and nutrient rich blood away from your heart, tiny capillaries that exchange gases and nutrients between your blood and your body's tissues, and veins that carry blood and wastes back to your heart. Your veins have a system of one-way valves that maintains the direction of blood flow within your circulatory system and helps maintain an even distribution of oxygen and nutrients to all parts of your body.

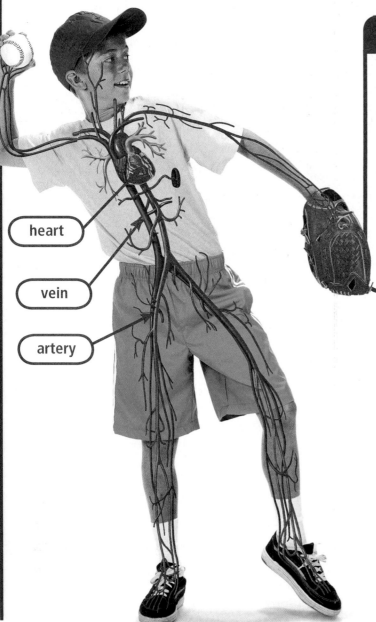

heart

vein

artery

Your Heart

Your heart is a strong, muscular organ that contracts rhythmically to pump blood throughout your circulatory system. When you exercise or work your muscles hard, your heart beats faster to deliver more oxygen and nutrient rich blood to your muscles. When you rest, your heartbeat slows. Regular exercise helps keep your heart muscle and the rest of your circulatory system strong.

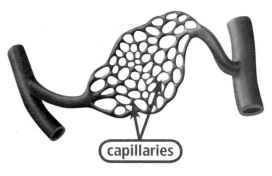

capillaries

▲ Oxygen and nutrients pass from the blood, through capillary walls, and into the cells. Cell wastes pass through capillary walls and into the blood.

Blood Flow and Your Excretory System

Your veins carry blood from your tissues back to your lungs where carbon dioxide and other waste gases are removed from your red blood cells and expelled when you exhale. Your blood also travels through your kidneys where small structures called nephrons remove salts and liquid wastes. Urine formed in your kidneys is held in your bladder until it is eliminated. Your liver removes other wastes from your blood, including blood cells. Red blood cells are living tissue, and they live for only 120 days. Specialized cells in your spleen and liver destroy damaged or dead red blood cells.

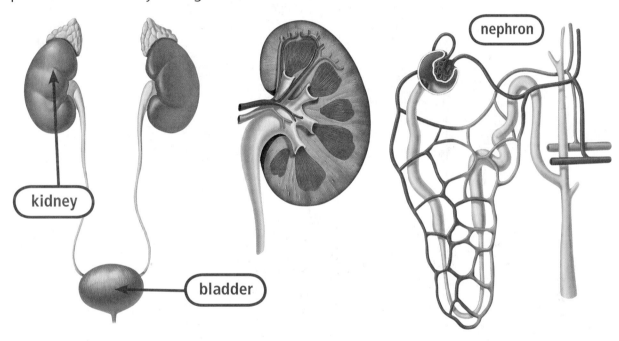

kidney

bladder

nephron

Caring for Your Circulatory System

• Eat foods that are low in fat and high in fiber. Fiber helps take away substances that can lead to fatty buildup in your blood vessels. Eat foods high in iron to help your red blood cells carry oxygen.

• Drink plenty of water to help your body replenish your blood fluid.

• Avoid contact with another person's blood.

• Exercise regularly to keep your heart and blood vessels strong.

• Never smoke or use tobacco. It can strain your heart and damage your blood vessels.

• Don't use illegal drugs or alcohol. They can damage your liver and your heart.

• Follow directions for all medicines carefully. Misuse of medicine can damage your blood's ability to clot after a cut, and can damage your liver and heart.

Your Immune System

A pathogen is an organism or virus that causes illness. An infection is the growth of pathogens in the body. Some pathogens weaken or kill body cells. A disease is an illness that damages or weakens the body, so you are not able to do the things you normally do. You may have a sore throat, or you may feel achy or tired, or you may have an unusually high body temperature, or fever. These are signs that your body is fighting an infection.

Infectious diseases have different symptoms because they are caused by different pathogens. There are four main types of pathogens: viruses, bacteria, fungi, and protozoa.

Diseases Caused by Pathogens

Pathogen	Characteristics	Diseases
Viruses	The smallest pathogens; the ones that cause most infectious diseases	Colds, chicken pox, HIV, infectious hepatitis, influenza (flu), measles, mumps, polio, rabies, rubella (German measles)
Bacteria	One-celled organisms that can—but do not always—cause disease; they make people ill by producing harmful wastes	Strep throat, pertussis (whooping cough), some kinds of pneumonia, Salmonella food poisoning, tetanus, tuberculosis (TB), Lyme disease
Fungi	Small, simple organisms like yeasts and molds; they most often invade the skin or respiratory system	Ringworm, athlete's foot, allergies
Protozoa	One-celled organisms somewhat larger than bacteria; they can cause serious diseases	Ameobic dysentery, giardiasis, malaria

There are pathogens all around you. You don't become ill often because your body has a complex system of defenses that prevents most pathogens from entering your body and destroys the ones that get through.

Sometimes pathogens do manage to overcome your body's defenses. When they do, your body's next line of defense is in your blood. Your blood contains white blood cells, which have their own role to play in fighting infection.

Some white blood cells manufacture substances called antibodies. Each antibody is designed to fight a specific kind of pathogen. The antibodies attach themselves to the pathogen and either kill it or mark it to be killed by another kind of white blood cell. When a pathogen enters your body, your immune system produces antibodies to fight it. This process may take several days, during which you may have a fever and feel some other symptoms of the disease. When you have recovered from an illness, your white blood cells remember how to make the antibody needed to fight the pathogen that made you ill. The ability to recognize pathogens and remember how to make antibodies to fight disease is called *immunity*.

You can also develop immunity to certain diseases by getting vaccinations from your doctor that prevent the diseases. A vaccine is usually a killed or weakened form of the pathogen that causes a particular disease.

Your Body's Defenses

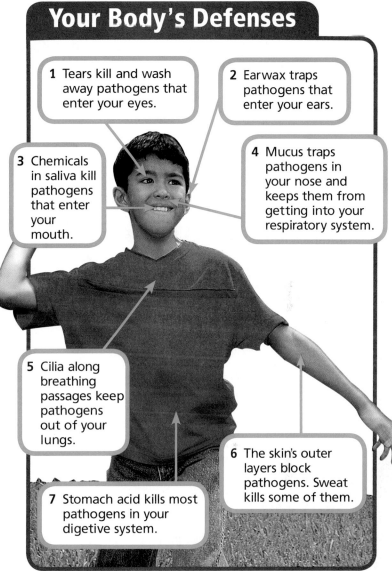

1 Tears kill and wash away pathogens that enter your eyes.

2 Earwax traps pathogens that enter your ears.

3 Chemicals in saliva kill pathogens that enter your mouth.

4 Mucus traps pathogens in your nose and keeps them from getting into your respiratory system.

5 Cilia along breathing passages keep pathogens out of your lungs.

6 The skin's outer layers block pathogens. Sweat kills some of them.

7 Stomach acid kills most pathogens in your digetive system.

Caring for Your Immune System

- Exercise regularly and get plenty of rest. This helps your body rebuild damaged tissues and cells.

- Eat a healthful, balanced diet. Good nutrition keeps your immune system strong.

- Avoid illegal drugs, tobacco, and alcohol, which can weaken your immune system.

- Wash your hands frequently and avoid touching your eyes, nose, and mouth.

Your Skeletal System

All of the bones in your body form your skeletal system. Your bones protect many vital organs and support the soft tissues of your body. Your skeletal system includes more than two hundred bones that fit together and attach to muscles at joints.

Types of Bones

Your skeleton includes four basic types of bones: long, short, flat, and irregular. Long bones, like the ones in your arms and legs, are narrow and have large ends. These bones support weight. Short bones, found in your wrists and ankles, are chunky and wide. They allow maximum movement around a joint. Flat bones, like the ones in your skull and ribs, protect your body. Irregular bones, like your vertebrae, have unique shapes and fall outside of the other categories.

Types of Joints

Each of the three types of joints is designed to do a certain job.

Ball and Socket Joints like your hips and shoulders allow rotation and movement in many directions.

Hinge Joints like your elbow and knees only move back and forth.

Gliding Joints like the vertebrae in your spine or the bones in your wrists and feet allow side-to-side and back-and-forth movement.

Some joints, like the ones in your skull do not allow any movement. These flat bones fit tightly together to protect your brain.

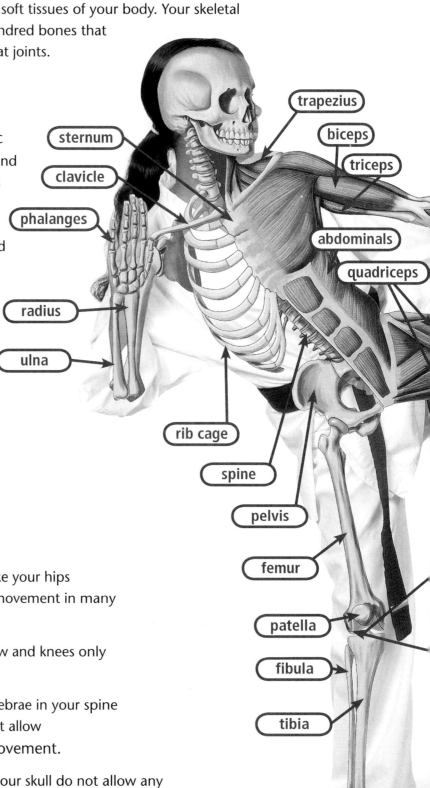

trapezius
sternum
biceps
clavicle
triceps
phalanges
abdominals
quadriceps
radius
ulna
rib cage
spine
pelvis
femur
patella
fibula
tibia

Parts of a Joint

Your bones attach to your muscles and to each other at joints. Your muscles and bones work together to allow your body to move. Joints are made up of ligaments and cartilage. Ligaments are tough, elastic tissues that attach one bone to another. Cartilage is a soft cushioning material at the ends of bones that helps bones move smoothly and absorbs some of the impact when you move. Tendons are dense, cordlike material that joins muscles to bones.

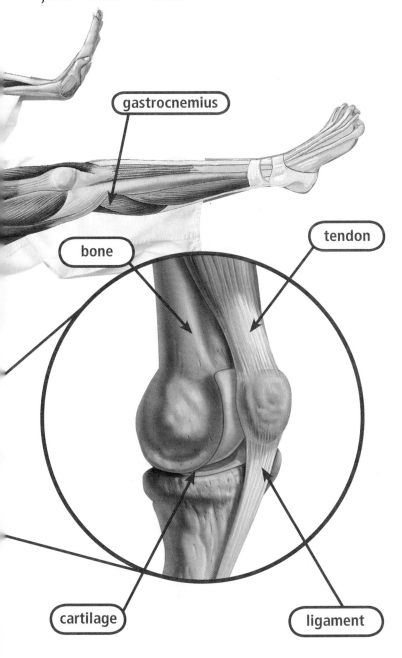

gastrocnemius

bone

tendon

cartilage

ligament

Caring for Your Skeletal System

- Always wear a helmet and proper safety gear when you play sports, skate, or ride a bike or a scooter.
- Your bones are mostly made of calcium and other minerals. To keep your skeletal system strong and to help it grow you should eat foods that are high in calcium like milk, cheese, and yogurt. Dark green, leafy vegetables like broccoli, spinach, and collard greens are also good sources of calcium.
- Exercise to help your bones stay strong and healthy.
- Always warm up before you exercise.
- Get plenty of rest to help your bones grow.
- Stand and sit with good posture. Sitting slumped over puts strain on your muscles and on your bones.

Your Muscular System

A muscle is a body part that produces movement by contracting and relaxing. All of the muscles in your body make up the muscular system.

Types of Muscle

Your muscular system is made up of three types of muscle. The muscles that make your body move are attached to the bones of your skeletal system. These muscles are called skeletal muscles. A skeletal muscle has a bulging middle and narrow tendons at each end. Tendons are strong flat bands of tissue that attach muscles to bones near your joints. Skeletal muscles are usually under your control, so they are also called voluntary muscles.

Your muscular system includes two other types of muscle. The first of these is called smooth muscle. This specialized muscle lines most of your digestive organs. As these muscles contract and relax, they move food through your digestive system.

Your heart is made of another specialized muscle called cardiac muscle. Your heart's muscle tissue squeezes and relaxes every second of every day to pump blood through your circulatory system. Smooth muscle and cardiac muscle operate automatically. Their contraction is not under your control, so they are also called involuntary muscles.

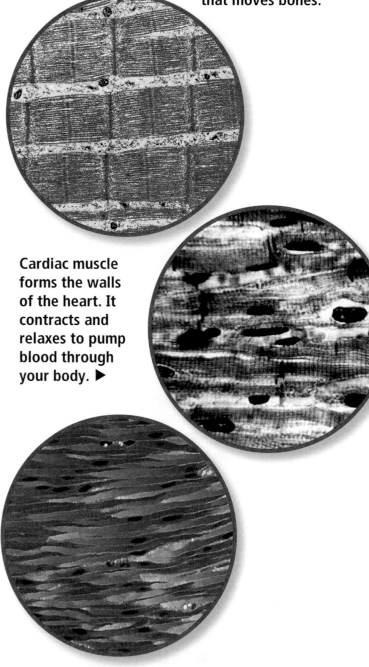

▼ Skeletal muscle appears striped. It is the kind of muscle that moves bones.

Cardiac muscle forms the walls of the heart. It contracts and relaxes to pump blood through your body. ▶

▲ Smooth muscle lines the walls of blood vessels and of organs such as your esophagus and stomach.

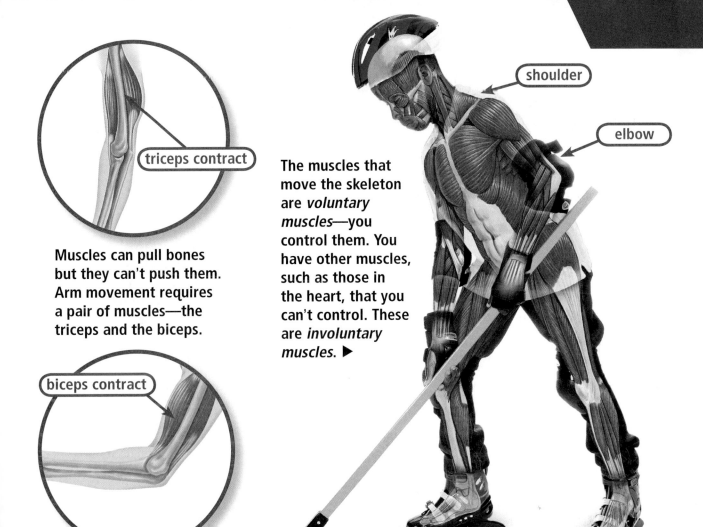

triceps contract

Muscles can pull bones but they can't push them. Arm movement requires a pair of muscles—the triceps and the biceps.

biceps contract

The muscles that move the skeleton are *voluntary muscles*—you control them. You have other muscles, such as those in the heart, that you can't control. These are *involuntary muscles*. ▶

shoulder

elbow

Caring for Your Muscular System

- Always stretch and warm your muscles up before exercising or playing sports. Do this by jogging slowly or walking for at least ten minutes. This brings fresh blood and oxygen to your muscles, and helps prevent injury or pain.

- Eat a balanced diet of foods to be sure your muscles have the nutrients they need to grow and remain strong.

- Drink plenty of water when you exercise or play sports. This helps your blood remove wastes from your muscles and helps you build endurance.

- Always cool down after you exercise. Walk or jog slowly for five or ten minutes to let your heartbeat slow and your breathing return to normal. This helps you avoid pain and stiffness after your muscles work hard.

- Stop exercising if your feel pain in your muscles.

- Get plenty or rest before and after you work your muscles hard. They need time to repair themselves and to recover from working hard.

Your Nervous System

Your body consists of a number of different systems. Each of your body's systems plays a different role. The different systems of your body work together to keep you alive and healthy.

Just as a leader directs the work of a group, your nervous system controls your body's activities. Some activities, like the beating of your heart or breathing, are controlled automatically by your nervous system.

Your nervous system allows you to move and to see, hear, taste, touch, and smell the world around you. Your brain also allows you to learn, remember, and feel emotions.

Your nervous system is made up of your brain, your spinal cord, and your nerves.

Your spinal cord is a thick bundle of nerves inside the column of bone formed by your vertebrae. Your nerves are bundles of specialized cells branching from your spinal cord. They send messages about your environment to your brain and send signals to your muscles.

A nerve cell is called a neuron. Signals travel to and from your brain along branching fibers of one neuron to branching fibers of other neurons.

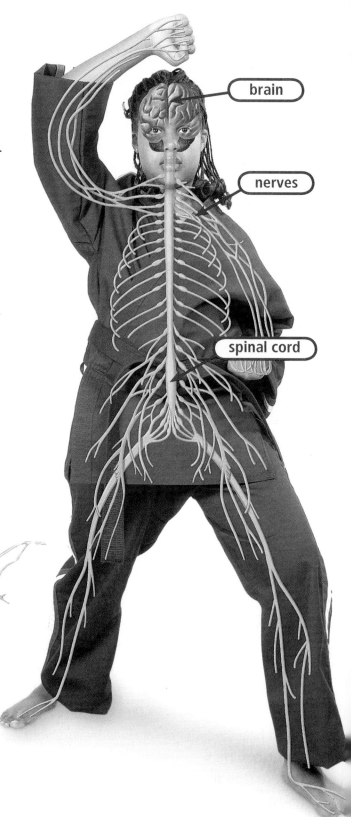

brain

nerves

spinal cord

Your brain contains about 100 billion neurons.
Different areas of your brain control different activities.

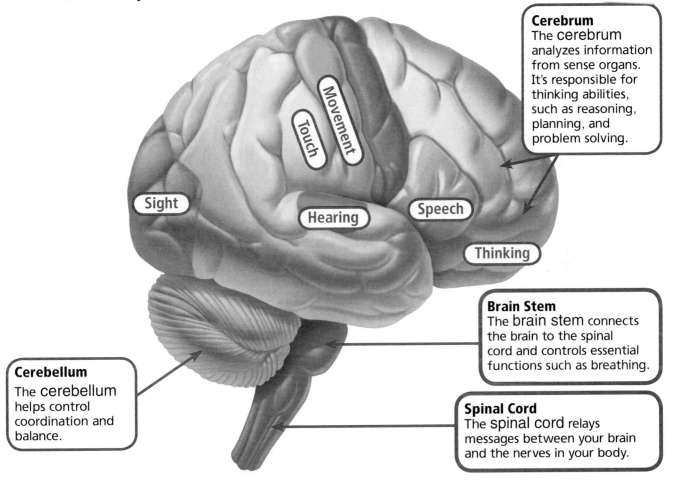

Cerebrum
The cerebrum analyzes information from sense organs. It's responsible for thinking abilities, such as reasoning, planning, and problem solving.

Movement

Touch

Sight

Hearing

Speech

Thinking

Brain Stem
The brain stem connects the brain to the spinal cord and controls essential functions such as breathing.

Cerebellum
The cerebellum helps control coordination and balance.

Spinal Cord
The spinal cord relays messages between your brain and the nerves in your body.

Caring for Your Nervous System

• Don't take illegal drugs and avoid alcohol. These substances can impair your judgment, which may cause you to react slowly or improperly to danger. They can also damage your nervous system.

• When your doctor prescribes medicines, follow the instructions your doctor gives you. Too much medicine can affect your nervous system. Never take medicine prescribed for someone else.

• Eat a well-balanced diet to be sure your nervous system receives the nutrients it needs.

• Protect your brain and spine from injury by wearing proper safety equipment when you play sports or ride a bike or scooter, or when you skate.

• Get plenty of rest. Sleep helps keep your mind sharp. Like all of your body's systems, your nervous system requires rest to stay healthy.

Identify the Main Idea and Details

Many of the lessons in this science book are written so that you can understand main ideas and the details that support them. You can use a graphic organizer like this one to show a main idea and details.

Main Idea: The most important idea of a selection

Detail:	Detail:	Detail:
Information that tells more about the main idea	Information that tells more about the main idea	Information that tells more about the main idea

Tips for Identifying the Main Idea and Details

- To find the main idea, ask—*What is this mostly about?*

- Remember that the main idea is not always stated in the first sentence.

- Be sure to look for details that help you answer questions such as *Who?, What?, Where?, When?, Why?* and *How?*

- Use pictures as clues to help you figure out the main idea.

Here is an example.

Main Idea

All living things are made up of one or more cells. Cells that work together to perform a specific function form tissues. Tissues that work together make up an organ. Each organ in an animal's body is made up of several kinds of tissues. Organs working together form a body system.

Detail

You could record this in the graphic organizer.

Main Idea: All living things are made up of one or more cells.

Detail:	Detail:	Detail:
Cells that work together form tissues.	Tissues that work together make up an organ.	Organs that work together form a body system.

More About Main Idea and Details

Sometimes the main idea of a passage is at the end instead of the beginning. The main idea may not be stated. However, it can be understood from the details. Look at the following graphic organizer. What do you think the main idea is?

Main Idea:

Detail: Bones make up the skeletal system.

Detail: The muscular system is made up of voluntary muscles, smooth muscles, and cardiac muscles.

Detail: Muscles are controlled by the central nervous system.

A passage can contain details of different types. In the following paragraph, identify each detail as a reason, an example, a fact, a step, or a description.

Digestion begins as you chew food. When you swallow, food passes through the esophagus. Gastric juice breaks down proteins. After several hours in the stomach, partly digested food moves into the small intestine. Digestion of food into nutrients is completed in the small intestine. From the small intestine, undigested food passes into the large intestine. In the large intestine, water and minerals pass into the blood and wastes are removed from the body.

Skill Practice

Read the following paragraph. Use the Tips for Identifying Main Idea and Details to answer the questions.

The circulatory, respiratory, digestive, and excretory systems work together to keep the body alive. The circulatory system transports oxygen, nutrients, and wastes through the body. In the respiratory system, oxygen diffuses into the blood and carbon dioxide diffuses out of the blood. The digestive system provides the nutrients your cells need to produce energy. The excretory system removes cell wastes from the blood.

1. What is the main idea of the paragraph?

2. What supporting details give more information?

3. What details answer any of the questions *Who?, What?, Where?, When?, Why?* and *How?*

★ Focus Skill — Compare and Contrast

Some lessons are written to help you see how things are alike or different. You can use a graphic organizer like this one to compare and contrast.

> **Topic:** Name the topic—the two things you are comparing and contrasting.

> **Alike**
> List ways the things are alike.

> **Different**
> List ways the things are different.

Tips for Comparing and Contrasting

- To compare, ask—*How are people, places, objects, ideas, or events alike?*

- To contrast, ask—*How are people, places, objects, ideas, or events different?*

- When you compare, look for signal words and phrases such as *similar, both, too,* and *also.*

- When you contrast, look for signal words and phrases such as *unlike, however, yet,* and *but.*

Here is an example.

Compare

> The two basic kinds of energy are kinetic energy and potential energy. Kinetic energy is the energy of motion. Any matter in motion has kinetic energy. However, potential energy is the energy of position or condition. Transformation of energy is the change between kinetic energy and potential energy. The total amount of energy does not change when energy is transformed.

Contrast

Here is what you could record in the graphic organizer.

> **Topic:** Kinetic and Potential Energy

> **Alike**
> Both are basic kinds of energy.
> The total amount of energy stays the same when it changes forms.

> **Different**
> Kinetic energy is the energy of motion.
> Potential energy is the energy of position or condition.

More About Comparing and Contrasting

Identifying how things are alike and how they're different can help you understand new information. Use a graphic organizer to sort the following information about kinetic energy and potential energy.

| kinetic energy | electric energy | thermal energy | mechanical energy | light energy |

| potential energy | elastic potential energy | gravitational potential energy | chemical energy |

Sometimes a paragraph compares and contrasts more than one topic. In the following paragraph, one topic of comparison is underlined. Find a second topic for comparison or contrast.

> Material that conducts electrons easily is called a conductor. An insulator is a material that does not carry electrons. An electric circuit is any path along which electrons can flow. Some circuits are series circuits. They have only one path for the electrons. Other circuits are parallel circuits, where each device is on a separate path.

Skill Practice

Read the following paragraph. Use the Tips for Comparing and Contrasting to answer the questions.

> Within an atom, electrons have a negative charge and protons have a positive charge. Most objects have equal numbers of protons and electrons. Both protons and electrons attract each other. Sometimes, however, electrons are attracted to the protons of another object and rub off. These objects become negatively charged.

1. What are two ways protons and electrons are alike?

2. Explain a difference between protons and electrons.

3. Name two signal words that helped you identify likenesses or differences in this paragraph.

Cause and Effect

Some of the lessons in this science book are written to help you understand why things happen. You can use a graphic organizer like this one to show cause and effect.

Cause:	Effect:
A cause is an action or event that makes something happen.	An effect is what happens as a result of an action or event.

Tips for Identifying Cause and Effect

- To find an effect, ask—*What happened?*

- To find a cause, ask—*Why did this happen?*

- Remember that events can have more than one cause or effect.

- Look for signal words and phrases, such as *because* and *as a result* to help you identify causes and effects.

Here is an example.

> Earth's surface is made up of many plates. Plates are rigid blocks of crust and upper mantle rock. Earth's plates fit together like the pieces of a puzzle. Plate movement is very slow. As plates move around, they cause great changes in Earth's landforms. Where plates collide, energy is released, and new landforms are produced. On land, mountains rise and volcanoes erupt.

Here is what you could record in the graphic organizer.

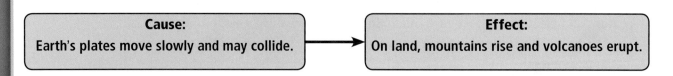

Cause:	Effect:
Earth's plates move slowly and may collide.	On land, mountains rise and volcanoes erupt.

More about Cause and Effect

Events can have more than one cause or effect. For example, suppose a paragraph included a sentence that said "On the ocean floor, deep trenches form." You could then identify two effects of Earth's plates colliding.

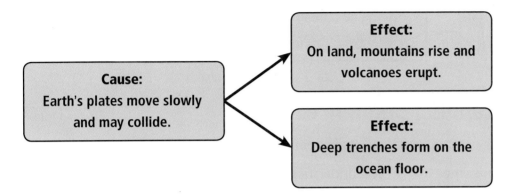

Cause:
Earth's plates move slowly and may collide.

Effect:
On land, mountains rise and volcanoes erupt.

Effect:
Deep trenches form on the ocean floor.

Some paragraphs contain more than one cause and effect. In the paragraph below, one cause and its effect are underlined. Find the second cause and its effect.

> As Earth's plates pull apart on land, valleys with volcanoes develop. Africa's Great Rift Valley was formed by the African and Arabian plates pulling apart. When plates pull apart under the sea, ridges and volcanoes form. New sea floor is formed at the ridges.

Skill Practice

Read the following paragraph. Use the Tips for Identifying Cause and Effect to help you answer the questions.

> When energy is suddenly released in Earth's crust, the ground shakes and an earthquake occurs. The earthquake is a result of plates crushing together, scraping past each other, or bending along jagged boundaries. Because the earth shakes in an earthquake, great damage can occur such as streets splitting open and bridges collapsing.

1. What causes an earthquake to occur?

2. What are some effects of an earthquake?

3. What two signal words or phrases helped you identify the causes and effects in this paragraph?

 **Sequence**

Some lessons in this science book are written to help you understand the order in which things happen. You can use a graphic organizer like this one to show sequence.

1. The first thing that happened	→ **2. The next thing that happened**	→ **3. The last thing that happened**

Tips for Understanding Sequence

- Pay attention to the order in which events happen.

- Remember dates and times to help you understand the sequence.

- Look for signal words such as *first, next, then, last,* and *finally.*

- Sometimes it's helpful to add your own time-order words to help you understand the sequence.

Here is an example.

Time-order words

A substance is buoyant, or will float in a liquid, if its density is less than that of the liquid. Here is a procedure that will show you what it takes for an egg to float in water. First, place an egg in a cup of water. Observe whether or not it floats. Next, remove the egg and stir several spoonfuls of salt into the water. Finally, replace the egg in the water and observe whether or not it floats. By changing the density of the water, you allow its density to become greater than the density of the egg.

You could record this in the graphic organizer.

1. First, place an egg in a cup of water and observe.	→ **2. Next, remove the egg and stir salt into the water.**	→ **3. Finally, replace the egg in the water and observe.**

More About Sequence

Sometimes information is sequenced by dates. For example, models of the atom have changed since the late 1800s. Use the graphic organizer to sequence the order of how the model of an atom has changed over time.

I. Near the end of the 1800s, Thomson's model of an atom was the first to include subatomic particles.	**2.** In the early 1900s, Rutherford's model suggested that the atom was made up mostly of empty space. Bohr's model showed different orbits for electrons.	**3.** Today, the modern model of an atom includes a cloud of electrons around the central positive nucleus.

When time-order words are not given, add your own words to help you understand the sequence. In the paragraph below, one time-order word has been included and underlined. What other time-order words can you add to help you understand the paragraph's sequence?

A person riding a bicycle changes the chemical energy in his or her cells to mechanical energy in order to push the pedals. The energy is transferred from the pedals through the chain to the rear wheel. **<u>Finally</u>**, the kinetic energy of the turning of the wheel is transferred to the whole bicycle.

Skill Practice

Read the following paragraph. Use the Tips for Understanding Sequence to answer the questions.

First, a flashlight is switched on. Then, the chemical energy stored in the battery is changed into electric energy. Next, the circuit is closed. Finally, the electric energy is changed to light energy in the flashlight bulb.

1. What is the first thing that happened in this sequence?

2. About how long did the process take?

3. What signal words helped you identify the sequence in this paragraph?

Draw Conclusions

At the end of each lesson in this science book, you will be asked to draw conclusions. To draw conclusions, use information from the text you are reading and what you already know. Drawing conclusions can help you understand what you read. You can use a graphic organizer like this.

| **What I Read**
List facts from the text. | + | **What I Know**
List related ideas from your own experience. | = | **Conclusion:**
Combine facts from the text with your own experience. |

Tips for Drawing Conclusions

- Ask—*What text information do I need to think about?*

- Ask—*What do I know from my own experience that could help me draw a conclusion?*

- Pay close attention to the information in the text and to your experience to be sure the conclusion is valid, or makes sense.

Here is an example.

> The shore is the area where the ocean and land meet and interact. Waves grind pebbles and rocks against the shore, which can cause erosion. The water pressure from a wave can loosen pebbles and small rocks, which outgoing waves carry into the ocean. Long shore currents move sand, pebbles, and shells along the shore.

Here is what you could record in the graphic organizer.

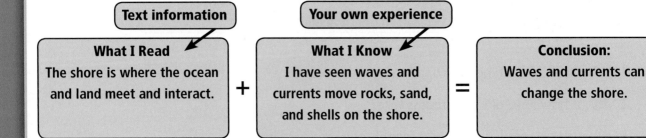

Text information		**Your own experience**		
What I Read The shore is where the ocean and land meet and interact.	+	**What I Know** I have seen waves and currents move rocks, sand, and shells on the shore.	=	**Conclusion:** Waves and currents can change the shore.

More About Drawing Conclusions

Sensible conclusions based on your experience and the facts you read are valid. For example, suppose a paragraph had ended with the sentence "Human activities can also change the shore." You might have come to a different conclusion about what changes the shore.

What I Read The shore is where the ocean and land meet and interact.	**+**	**What I Know** Waves loosen rocks and pebbles. Currents move sand, pebbles, and shells. Structures can be built to prevent erosion.	**=**	**Conclusion:** Waves, currents, and human activities can change the shore.

Sometimes a paragraph might not contain enough information for drawing a valid conclusion. Read the paragraph below. Think of one valid conclusion you could draw. Then think of one invalid conclusion someone might draw from the given information.

> A jetty is a wall-like structure made of rocks that sticks out into the ocean. Jetties are usually built on either side of an opening to a harbor. Jetties catch sand and pebbles that normally flow down the coast with the current. Jetties can change the shore by building up the beach.

Skill Practice

Read the following paragraph. Use the Tips for Drawing Conclusions to answer the questions.

> Most of the movement of water on the ocean's surface is due to waves. A wave is the up-and-down movement of surface water. On a calm day, ocean waves may only be 1.5 meters high or less. However, during a storm, waves can reach heights of 30 meters.

1. What conclusion did you draw about the height of a wave?

2. What information from your personal experience did you use to draw the conclusion?

3. What text information did you use?

☆ Summarize

At the end of every lesson in this science book, you will be asked to summarize. When you summarize, you use your own words to tell what something is about. In the lesson, you will be given ideas for writing your summary. You can also use a graphic organizer like this one to summarize.

Main Idea: Tell about the most important information you have read.	+	Details: Add details that answer important questions Who?, What?, Where?, When?, Why?, and How?	=	Summary: Retell what you have just read, include only the most important details.

Tips for Summarizing

- To write a summary, ask—*What is the most important idea of the paragraph?*

- To include details with your summary, ask—*Who?, What?, When?, Where?, Why?* and *How?*

- Remember to use fewer words than the original has.

- Don't forget to use your own words when you summarize.

Here is an example.

Main Idea

Sound waves are carried by vibrating matter. Most sound waves travel through air, but they may also travel through liquids and even some solids. As the sound waves travel, the energy of the wave decreases. The frequency at which the sound wave moves determines the pitch of the sound. The greater the frequency, the higher the pitch. The strength of a sound wave can also be measured. The more energy a sound has, the louder it is.

Details

Here's what you could record in your graphic organizer.

Main Idea: Sound waves are carried by vibrating matter.	+	Details: Pitch is determined by the frequency at which the sound wave moves. The more energy a sound has, the louder it is.	=	Summary: Sound waves are carried by vibrating matter. Pitch is determined by the frequency at which the sound wave moves. The loudness of a sound is determined by how much energy it has.

More About Summarizing

Sometimes a paragraph includes information that would not be included in a summary. For example, suppose a paragraph included a sentence that said "High musical notes have high pitch and high frequency, and low musical notes have low pitch and low frequency." The graphic organizer would remain the same, because that detail is not important to understanding the paragraph's main idea.

Sometimes the main idea of a paragraph is not in the first sentence. In the following paragraph, two important details are underlined. What is the main idea?

> Air, water, clear glass, and clear plastic are substances which objects can clearly be seen through. Substances that light can travel through are transparent. Substances that are transparent are used to make things like windows and eyeglasses. Some substances are transparent only to certain colors of light. They are described as clear since you can see objects through them, but they have a color.

Skill Practice

Read the following paragraph. Use the Tips for Summarizing to answer the questions.

> Light can be absorbed, reflected, or refracted. Sometimes light waves are absorbed when they strike an object. Most objects absorb some colors of light. Other colors of light bounce off objects, or are reflected. These are the colors we see. The change in speed of light causes it to bend. This bending of light waves is called refraction.

1. If a friend asked you what this paragraph was about, what information would you include? What would you leave out?

2. What is the main idea of the paragraph?

3. What two details would you include in a summary?

Using Tables, Charts, and Graphs

As you do investigations in science, you collect, organize, display, and interpret data. Tables, charts, and graphs are good ways to organize and display data so that others can understand and interpret your data.

The tables, charts, and graphs in this Handbook will help you read and understand data. You can also use the information to choose the best ways to display data so that you can use it to draw conclusions and make predictions.

Reading a Table

A bird-watching group is studying the wingspans of different birds. The members want to find out the birds with the greatest wingspans. The table shows the data the members collected.

Largest Wingspans	
Type of Bird	**Wingspan (in feet)**
Albatross	12
Trumpeter Swan	11
California Condor	10
Marabou Stork	10

Title ← (Largest Wingspans)
Headings ← (Type of Bird / Wingspan)
Data ← (California Condor 10)

How to Read a Table

1. **Read the title** to find out what the table is about.

2. **Read the headings** to find out what information is given.

3. **Study the data.** Look for patterns.

4. **Draw conclusions.** If you display the data in a graph, you might be able to see patterns easily.

By studying the table, you can see the birds with the greatest wingspans. However, suppose the group wants to look for patterns in the data. They might choose to display the data in a different way, such as in a bar graph.

Reading a Bar Graph

The data in this bar graph is the same as in the table. A bar graph can be used to compare the data about different events or groups.

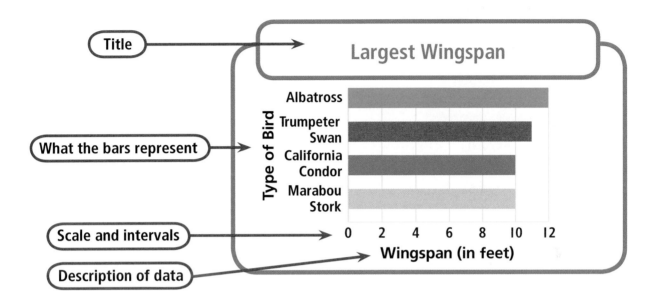

Title

What the bars represent

Scale and intervals

Description of data

Largest Wingspan

How to Read a Bar Graph

1. **Look** at the graph to determine what kind of graph it is.

2. **Read** the graph. Use the labels to guide you.

3. **Analyze** the data. Study the bars to compare the measurements. Look for patterns.

4. **Draw conclusions.** Ask yourself questions, like the ones in the Skills Practice.

Skills Practice

1. Which two birds have the same wingspan?

2. How much greater is the wingspan of an albatross than the wingspan of a California condor?

3. A red-tailed hawk has a wingspan of 4 feet. Which type of bird has a wingspan that is three times that of the hawk?

4. **Predict** A fifth-grade student saw a bird that had a wingspan that was about the same as her height. Could the bird have been an albatross?

5. Was the bar graph a good choice for displaying this data? Explain your answer.

Reading a Line Graph

A scientist collected this data about how the amount of ice in the Nordic Sea area of the Arctic Ocean has changed over the years.

Nordic Sea Area Ice

Year	Number of Square Kilometers (in millions)
1860	2.8
1880	2.7
1900	2.2
1920	2.4
1940	2.0
1960	1.8
1980	1.5
2000	1.6

Here is the same data displayed in a line graph. A line graph is used to show changes over time.

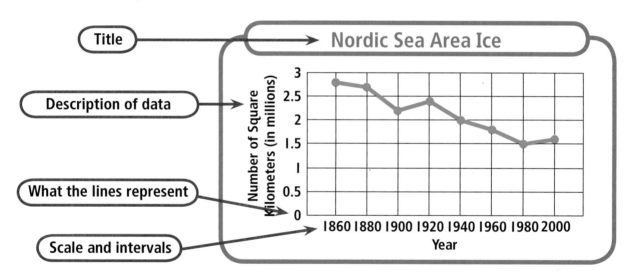

How to Read a Line Graph

1. **Look** at the graph to determine what kind of graph it is.

2. **Read** the graph. Use the labels to guide you.

3. **Analyze** the data. Study the points along the lines. Look for patterns.

4. **Draw conclusions.** Ask yourself questions, like the ones in the Skills Practice to help you draw conclusions.

Skills Practice

1. By how much did the ice in the Nordic Sea area change from 1940 to 1980?

2. **Predict** Will there be more or less than 2.5 million square kilometers of ice in the Nordic Sea area in 2020?

3. Was the line graph a good choice for displaying this data? Explain why.

Reading a Circle Graph

A fifth-grade class is studying U.S. energy sources. They want to know which energy sources are used in the U.S. They classified the different sources by making a table. Here is the data they gathered.

U.S. Energy Sources

Source of Energy	Amount Used
Petroleum	0.38
Natural Gas	0.24
Coal	0.22
Hydroelectric and Nuclear Power	0.12
Other	0.04

The circle graph shows the same data as the table. A circle graph can be used to show data as a whole made up of different parts.

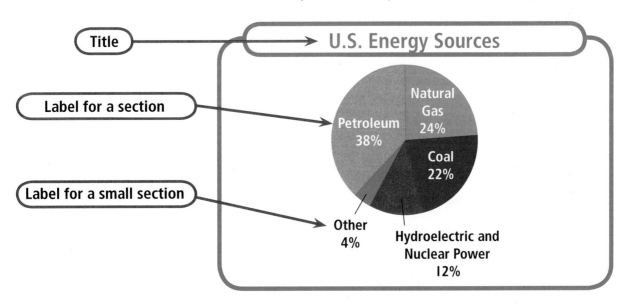

How to Read a Circle Graph

1. **Look** at the title of the graph to learn what kind of information is shown.

2. **Read** the graph. Look at the label of each section to find out what information is shown.

3. **Analyze** the data. Compare the sizes of the sections to determine how they are related.

4. **Draw conclusions.** Ask yourself questions, like the ones in the Skills Practice.

Skills Practice

1. Which source of energy is used most often?

2. **Predict** If wind, geothermal, and solar energy make up some of the other energy sources, will they be a greater or lesser part of U.S. energy sources in the future?

3. Was the circle graph a good choice for displaying this data? Explain why.

Using Metric Measurements

A measurement is a number that represents a comparison of something being measured to a unit of measurement. Scientists use many different tools to measure objects and substances as they work. Scientists almost always use the metric system for their measurements.

Measuring Length and Capacity

When you measure length, you find the distance between two points. The distance may be in a straight line, along a curved path, or around a circle. The table shows the metric units of **length** and how they are related.

Equivalent Measures

1 centimeter (cm) = 10 millimeters (mm)
1 decimeter (dm) = 10 centimeters (cm)
1 meter (m) = 1000 millimeters
1 meter = 10 decimeters
1 kilometer (km) = 1000 meters

You can use these comparisons to help you understand the size of each metric unit of length.

A **millimeter (mm)** is about the thickness of a dime.	A **centimeter (cm)** is about the width of your index finger.	A **decimeter (dm)** is about the width of an adult's hand.	A **meter (m)** is about the width of a door.
			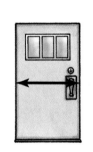

Sometimes you may need to change units of length. The following diagram shows how to multiply and divide to change to larger and smaller units.

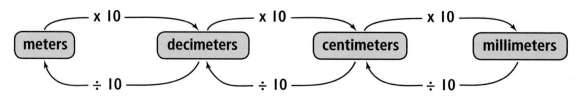

The photos below show the metric units of **capacity** and common comparisons. The metric units of volume are the milliliter (mL) and the liter (L). You can use multiplication to change liters to milliliters. You can use division to change milliliters to liters.

A **milliliter (mL)** is the amount of liquid that can fill part of a dropper.

1 mL

A **liter (L)** is the amount of liquid that can fill a plastic bottle.

1 L

1 L = 1000 mL

To change *larger* units to *smaller* units, you need more of the *smaller units*. So, **multiply** by 10, 100, or 1000. To change *smaller* units to *larger* units, you need *fewer of the larger units*. So, **divide** by 10, 100, or 1000.

500 dm = ____ cm

Think: There are 10 cm in 1 dm.

500 dm = 500 x 10 = 5000

So, 500 dm = 5000 cm.

4000 mL = _____ L

Think: There are 1000 mL in 1 L.

4000 ÷ 1,000 = 4

So, 4000 mL = 4 L.

Skills Practice

Complete. Tell whether you multiply or divide by 10, 100, or 1000.

1. 7 m = _____ cm

2. 4 m = _____ dm

3. 800 _____ = 8 m

4. 9000 mm = _____ m

5. 9 L = _____ mL

6. 6000 mL = _____ L

7. 3000 mL = _____ L

8. 8 _____ = 8000 mL

Measuring Mass

Matter is what all objects are made of. Mass is the amount of matter that is in an object. The metric units of mass are the gram (g) and the kilogram (kg).

You can use these comparisons to help you understand the masses of some everyday objects.

A paper clip is about **1 gram (g)**.

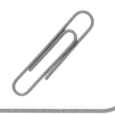

A slice of wheat bread is about **20 grams**.

A box of 12 crayons is about **100 grams**.

A large wedge of cheese is **1 kilogram (kg)**.

You can use multiplication to change kilograms to grams.

You can use division to change grams to kilograms.

2 kg = ____ g	4000 g = ____ kg
Think: There are 1000 g in 1 kg.	Think: There are 1000 g in 1 kg.
2 kg = 2 x 1000 = 2000 g	4,000 ÷ 1000 = 4
So, 2 kg = 2000 g.	So, 4000 g = 4 kg.

Skills Practice

Complete. Tell whether you multiply or divide by 1000.

1. 4000 g = _____ kg

2. 3000 g = _____ kg

3. 7 kg = _____ g

4. 8 _____ = 8000 g

Measurement Systems

SI Measures (Metric)

Temperature

Ice melts at 0 degrees Celsius (°C).
Water freezes at 0°C.
Water boils at 100°C.

Length and Distance

1000 meters (m) = 1 kilometer (km)
100 centimeters (cm) = 1 m
10 millimeters (mm) = 1 cm

Force

1 newton (N) = 1 kilogram x
    1 meter/second/second (kg-m/s^2)

Volume

1 cubic meter (m^3) = 1 m x 1 m x 1 m
1 cubic centimeter (cm^3) =
    1 cm x 1 cm x 1 cm
1 liter (L) = 1000 millimeters (mL)
1 cm^3 = 1 mL

Area

1 square kilometer (km^2) =
    1 km x 1 km
1 hectare = 10,000 m^2

Mass

1000 grams (g) = 1 kilogram (kg)
1000 milligrams (mg) = 1 g

Rates (Metric and Customary)

km/hr = kilometers per hour
m/s = meters per second
mph = miles per hour

Customary Measures

Volume of Fluids

2 c = 1 pint (pt)
2 pt = 1 quart (qt)
4 qt = 1 gallon (gal)

Temperature

Ice melts at 32 degrees
    Fahrenheit (°F).
Water freezes at 32°F.
Water boils at 212°F.

Length and Distance

12 inches (in.) = 1 foot (ft)
3 ft = 1 yard (yd)
5,280 ft = 1 mile (mi)

Weight

16 ounces (oz) = 1 pound (lb)
2,000 pounds = 1 ton (T)

Safety in Science

Doing investigations in science can be fun, but you need to be sure you do them safely. Here are some rules to follow.

1. **Think ahead.** Study the steps of the investigation so you know what to expect. If you have any questions, ask your teacher. Be sure you understand any caution statements or safety reminders.

2. **Be neat.** Keep your work area clean. If you have long hair, pull it back so it doesn't get in the way. Roll or push up long sleeves to keep them away from your activity.

3. **Oops!** If you should spill or break something, or get cut, tell your teacher right away.

4. **Watch your eyes.** Wear safety goggles anytime you are directed to do so. If you get anything in your eyes, tell your teacher right away.

5. **Yuck!** Never eat or drink anything during a science activity.

6. **Don't get shocked.** Be especially careful if an electric appliance is used. Be sure that electric cords are in a safe place where you can't trip over them. Don't ever pull a plug out of an outlet by pulling on the cord.

7. **Keep it clean.** Always clean up when you have finished. Put everything away and wipe your work area. Wash your hands.

Visit the Multimedia Science Glossary to see illustrations of these words and to hear them pronounced. www.hspscience.com

Glossary

As you read your science book, you will notice that new or unfamiliar terms have been respelled to help you pronounce them while you are reading. Those respellings are called *phonetic respellings*. In this Glossary you will see the same kind of respellings.

In phonetic respellings, syllables are separated by a bullet (•). Small, uppercase letters show stressed syllables.

The boldfaced letters in the examples in the Pronunciation Key below show how certain letters and combinations of letters are pronounced in the respellings.

The page number (in parentheses) at the end of a definition tells you where to find the term, defined in context, in your book. Depending on the context in which it is used, a term may have more than one definition.

Pronunciation Key

Sound	As in	Phonetic Respelling	Sound	As in	Phonetic Respelling
a	b**a**t	(BAT)	oh	**o**ver	(OH•ver)
ah	l**o**ck	(LAHK)	oo	p**oo**l	(POOL)
air	r**a**re	(RAIR)	ow	**ou**t	(OWT)
ar	**ar**gue	(AR•gyoo)	oy	f**oi**l	(FOYL)
aw	l**aw**	(LAW)	s	**c**ell	(SEL)
ay	f**a**ce	(FAYS)		**s**it	(SIT)
ch	**ch**apel	(CHAP•uhl)	sh	**sh**eep	(SHEEP)
e	t**e**st	(TEST)	th	**th**at	(THAT)
	m**e**tric	(MEH•trik)		**th**in	(THIN)
ee	**ea**t	(EET)	u	p**u**ll	(PUL)
	f**ee**t	(FEET)	uh	med**a**l	(MED•uhl)
	sk**i**	(SKEE)		tal**e**nt	(TAL•uhnt)
er	pap**er**	(PAY•per)		penc**i**l	(PEN•suhl)
	f**er**n	(FERN)		**o**ni**o**n	(UHN•yuhn)
eye	**i**dea	(eye•DEE•uh)		play**fu**l	(PLAY•fuhl)
i	b**i**t	(BIT)		d**u**ll	(DUHL)
ing	go**ing**	(GOH•ing)	y	**y**es	(YES)
k	**c**ard	(KARD)		r**i**pe	(RYP)
	kite	(KYT)	z	bag**s**	(BAGZ)
ngk	ba**nk**	(BANGK)	zh	trea**s**ure	(TREZH•er)

A

acid rain [AS•id RAYN] A mixture that falls to Earth of rain and acids from air pollution **(144)**

adaptation [ad•uhp•TAY•shuhn] A trait or characteristic that helps an organism survive **(129)**

axis [AK•sis] An imaginary line that passes through Earth's center and its North and South Poles **(32)**

B

balance [BAL•uhns] A tool that measures the amount of matter in an object (the object's mass) **(7)**

C

carnivore [KAHR•nuh•vawr] An animal that eats other animals; also called a second-level consumer **(110)**

chemical energy [KEM•ih•kuhl EN•er•jee] Energy that can be released by a chemical reaction **(208)**

chlorophyll [KLAWR•uh•fihl] A green pigment that allows a plant to absorb the sun's light energy **(104)**

climate zone [KLY•muht ZOHN] A region in which yearly patterns of temperature, rainfall, and the amount of sunlight are similar throughout **(160)**

community [kuh•MYOO•nuh•tee] A group of populations that live together **(128)**

competition [kahm•puh•TISH•uhn] A kind of contest among populations or individuals with the same niche **(129)**

concave lens [kahn•KAYV LENZ] A lens that is thicker at the edges than it is at the center **(288)**

conduction [kuhn•DUK•shuhn] The transfer of heat from one object directly to another **(218)**

conductor [kuhn•DUK•ter] A material that carries electricity well **(252)**

conservation [kahn•ser•VAY•shuhn] The preserving, protecting, or saving of natural resources **(77, 146, 225)**

constellation [kahn•stuh•LAY•shuhn] A pattern of stars named after a mythological or religious figure, an object, or an animal **(49)**

consumer [kuhn•SOOM•er] An organism that eats plants, other animals, or both **(106)**

convection [kuhn•VEK•shuhn] The transfer of heat through the movement of a gas or a liquid **(218)**

convex lens [kahn•VEKS LENZ] A lens that is thicker at the center than it is at the edges **(288)**

crater [KRAYT•er] A bowl-shaped, low area on the surface of a planet or moon **(40)**

current electricity [KER•uhnt ee•lek•TRIS•ih•tee] A kind of kinetic energy that flows as an electric current **(250)**

D

decomposer [dee•kuhm•POHZ•er] A consumer that obtains food energy by breaking down the remains of dead plants and animals **(111)**

E

eclipse [ih•KLIPS] An event that occurs when one object in space passes through the shadow of another object in space **(44)**

ecosystem [EE•koh•sis•tuhm] A community of organisms and the environment in which they live **(110)**

electric circuit [ee•LEK•trik SER•kit] The path an electric current follows **(256)**

electric current [ee•LEK•trik KER•uhnt] The flow of electrons **(250)**

electric energy [ee•LEK•trik EN•er•jee] Energy that comes from an electric current **(210)**

electricity [ee•lek•TRIS•ih•tee] A form of energy produced by moving electrons **(241)**

electromagnet [ee•lek•troh•MAG•nit] A magnet made by coiling a wire around a piece of iron and running electric current through the wire **(242)**

energy [EN•er•jee] The ability to cause changes in matter **(198)**

energy pyramid [EN•er•jee PIR•uh•mid] A diagram that shows how much food energy is passed from each level in a food chain to the next **(115)**

energy transfer [EN•er•jee TRANS•fer] Movement of energy from one place or object to another **(202)**

equator [ee•KWAYT•er] An imaginary line around Earth equally distant from the North and South Poles **(34)**

estuary [ES•tyoo•air•ee] A place where a freshwater river empties into an ocean **(176)**

experiment [ek•SPEHR•uh•muhnt] A procedure carried out under controlled conditions to test a hypothesis **(15)**

extinction [ek•STINGK•shuhn] The death of all the organisms of a species **(140)**

F

food chain [FOOD CHAYN] The transfer of food energy between organisms in an ecosystem **(111)**

food web [FOOD WEB] A diagram that shows the relationships between different food chains in an ecosystem **(112)**

fossil [FAHS•uhl] The remains or traces of past life, found in sedimentary rock **(224)**

frequency [FREE•kwuhn•see] The number of vibrations per second **(274)**

G

galaxy [GAL•uhk•see] A grouping of gas, dust, and many stars, plus any objects that orbit those stars **(54)**

H

habitat [HAB•i•tat] An area where an organism can find everything it needs to survive **(145)**

heat [HEET] The transfer of thermal energy between objects with different temperatures **(216)**

herbivore [HER•buh•vawr] An animal that eats only producers **(110)**

I

inquiry [IN•kwer•ee] An organized way to gather information and answer questions **(12)**

insulator [IN•suh•layt•er] A material that does not conduct electricity well **(252)**

intertidal zone [in•ter•TYD•uhl ZOHN] The area at the ocean's edge where waves lap the shore and the tides rise and fall **(172)**

investigation [in•ves•tuh•GAY•shuhn] A procedure carried out to gather data about an object or event **(12)**

K

kinetic energy [kih•NET•ik EN•er•jee] The energy of motion **(200)**

L

light [LYT] Radiation that we can see **(206)**

M

mechanical energy [muh•KAN•ih•kuhl EN•er•jee] The combination of all the kinetic and potential energy that something has **(208)**

microscope [MY•kruh•skohp] A tool that makes small objects appear larger **(4)**

moon [MOON] Any natural body that revolves around a planet **(40)**

moon phase [MOON FAYZ] One of the shapes the moon seems to have as it orbits Earth **(43)**

N

near-shore zone [neer•SHAWR ZOHN] The area of the ocean with calm water that extends from the intertidal zone out to waters that are about 180 m (about 600 ft) deep **(173)**

nonrenewable resource [nahn•rih•NOO•uh•buhl REE•sawrs] A resource that once used, cannot be replaced in a reasonable amount of time **(69, 225)**

O

opaque [oh•PAYK] Not allowing light to pass through **(286)**

open-ocean zone [oh•puhn•OH•shuhn ZOHN] The area of the ocean that is very deep and not close to land **(173)**

orbit [AWR•bit] The path one body takes in space as it revolves around another body **(34)**

parallel circuit [PAIR•uh•lel SER•kit] An electric circuit that has more than one path for the current to follow **(258)**

photosynthesis [foht•oh•SIHN•thuh•sis] The process in which plants make food by using water from the soil, carbon dioxide from the air, and energy from sunlight **(104)**

pitch [PICH] How high or low a sound is **(274)**

planet [PLAN•it] A large body that revolves around a star **(51)**

pollution [puh•LOO•shuhn] Any change to the natural environment that can harm living organisms and damage an ecosystem **(70, 144, 228)**

population [pahp•yuh•LAY•shuhn] A group of organisms of one kind that live in one location **(128)**

potential energy [poh•TEN•shuhl EN•er•jee] The energy an object has because of its condition or position **(200)**

predator [PRED•uh•ter] An animal that kills and eats other animals **(132)**

prey [PRAY] An animal that is eaten by a predator **(132)**

producer [pruh•DOOS•er] A living thing, such as a plant, that makes its own food **(106)**

radiation [ray•dee•AY•shuhn] The transfer of energy by means of waves that move through matter and space **(219)**

reclamation [rek•luh•MAY•shuhn] The process of cleaning and restoring a damaged ecosystem **(148)**

reflection [rih•FLEK•shuhn] The bouncing of heat or light off an object **(219, 286)**

refraction [rih•FRAK•shuhn] The bending of light as it moves from one material to another **(44, 287)**

renewable resource [rih•NOO•uh•buhl REE•sawrs] A resource that can be replaced within a reasonable amount of time **(68, 226)**

resource [REE•sawrs] Any material that can be used to satisfy a need **(225)**

revolve [rih•VAHLV] To travel in a closed path around something **(34)**

rotate [ROH•tayt] To spin on an axis **(32)**

scientific method [sy•uhn•TIF•ik METH•uhd] A series of steps that scientists use when performing an experiment **(20)**

series circuit [SIR•eez SER•kit] An electric circuit in which the current has only one path to follow **(257)**

solar energy [SOH•ler EN•er•jee] Energy that comes from the sun **(206)**

solar system [SOH•ler SIS•tuhm] A star and all the planets and other objects that revolve around it **(48)**

star [STAR] A huge ball of very hot gases in space **(48)**

static electricity [STAT•ik ee•lek•TRIS•uh•tee] The buildup of charges on an object **(248)**

succession [suhk•SESH•uhn] A gradual change in the kinds of organisms living in an ecosystem **(136)**

sun [SUHN] The star at the center of our solar system **(32)**

symbiosis [sim•by•OH•sis] A relationship between different kinds of organisms **(130)**

system [SIS•tuhm] A group of separate elements that work together to accomplish something **(217)**

translucent [tranz•LOO•suhnt] Allowing only some light to pass through **(287)**

transparent [tranz•PAR•uhnt] Allowing light to pass through **(287)**

transpiration [tran•spuh•RAY•shuhn] The loss of water from a leaf through the stomata **(103)**

universe [YOO•nuh•vers] Everything that exists, including such things as stars, planets, gas, dust, and energy **(54)**

vibration [vy•BRAY•shuhn] A back-and-forth movement of matter **(272)**

volume [VAHL•yoom] The loudness of a sound **(273)**

Index

VISION Jaguars see better at night than during the day.

MOVEMENT If possible, jaguars live near water. They are different from most cats—they LIKE to swim!

CAMOUFLAGE Most jaguars have brownish-yellow fur.

YOUNG Jaguar cubs weigh about two pounds, less than most human babies, when they are born. Their eyes are shut to protect them from sunlight.

Some jaguars have black rosettes and black fur.

COLOR